"We've reached a tipping point. Our planet and our society are at risk. Business has a historic opportunity and a responsibility to lead the world down a more just, rich, and sustainable path—one that creates more value for companies, communities, and countries. But where should executives begin? Winston's *The Big Pivot* offers a radical new direction for business that also represents the most practical path forward. Hand this book to your nearest change agent to get started. This book is a must-read for anyone interested in the future of business and our world."

—Paul Polman, CEO, Unilever

"Andrew Winston's *The Big Pivot* is the blinking red warning light on the dashboard for every CEO responsible for keeping an enterprise running in a world besieged by unprecedented environmental and social challenges and constraints. By focusing on what's most important—the long-term survival and prosperity of the customer—he lays out a road map for a major shift in consciousness and purpose for the private sector. In compelling, earnest language, he describes the 'new normal' of business, giving business leaders a way to formulate a game plan for long-term success by capitalizing on opportunities in the face of the ultimate disruptive change."

—David Crane, President and CEO, NRG Energy

"In *The Big Pivot*, Andrew Winston has identified issues for business that require more than just a minor change of behavior—these big challenges demand an urgent 'pivot' by business for our own survival. NGOs and government have urged change, but Winston knows from his work with big corporates that if business leaders change incentives and demand engagement throughout their value chains, pivots will happen. I hope CEOs and other business leaders step up and read this book and then own the drive for much better outcomes for their companies and the world."

—Lauralee Martin, CEO, HCP

"Andrew Winston offers a unique perspective in the ocean of writers who focus on sustainability. Winston completely understands what drives environmental issues, but he also understands what can *solve* environmental issues—a focus on how companies can drive growth and innovation through sustainability. Winston's practical approach to the largest issues of our generation makes his a voice that's respected by the world's leaders in politics, NGOs, and business."

—David Steiner, CEO, Waste Management

"*The Big Pivot* is Winston's most important and impactful work to date—better even than *Green to Gold*. It's a wake-up call for you, your boss, and whoever sits in the corner office. Winston gives us a uniquely useful take on strategy in a volatile world. *The Big Pivot* offers business a much-needed plan of action and links the actual impacts of climate change and other planet-scale pressures to business's bottom line. Capitalism is about to change for the better."

**—L. Hunter Lovins, founder and President,
Natural Capital Solutions; coauthor, *The Way Out***

"Andrew Winston's *The Big Pivot* provides thought-provoking perspectives into some of the biggest issues facing companies around the world. Increasingly, business leaders are realizing that 'business as usual' will not be enough to address the world's challenges. Winston issues a call to action in a time of radical change and competing priorities."

—Thomas J. Falk, Chairman and CEO, Kimberly-Clark

"A resounding call to action for business to embrace the risks of climate change, resource constraints, and radical transparency and turn them into strategic growth opportunities ... a must-read road map for business success in the twenty-first century."

**—Jeff Seabright, Vice President,
Environment & Water Resources, Coca-Cola**

"Andrew Winston zeroes in on the important issues we need to address in this century, while providing a guide to realistic tools and strategies that companies can use to tackle them. *The Big Pivot* distills many of the complexities and challenges in the business community and beyond, and it provides a thoughtful and informative analysis for all readers."

**—Jochen Zeitz, cofounder and Cochairman, The B Team;
former CEO, PUMA**

"Andrew Winston is a radical pragmatist. For anyone despairing that we can't move beyond incrementalism, here is an antidote. In *The Big Pivot*, Winston shows with guts and gusto how companies can address a hotter, scarcer, and more open world—and thrive."

—Malini Mehra, founder, Centre for Social Markets (India)

"*The Big Pivot* is a must-read for environmental and business professionals alike. Winston makes a compelling and logical case for why companies and leaders have a tremendous opportunity to drive transformative changes. *The Big Pivot* shows that the perception that radical equals risky is false. Non-action, more than action, is where the real risk lies. A compelling and fascinating read."

—Rob Bernard, Chief Environmental Strategist, Microsoft

"Winston powerfully articulates more than just the mega-trends impacting the dynamics of the new world order for business; he also provides an instructive guide to how business can not only survive but thrive in this new reality. *The Big Pivot* offers an invaluable blueprint for building a resilient company in the rapidly changing context of a planet in peril."

—John Replogle, President and CEO, Seventh Generation

"Once we burned heretics at the stake, but as we move further into the Big Pivot we must find, empower, and replicate the heretical innovators, entrepreneurs, investors, and policy makers now blazing trails to a more sustainable future. Andrew Winston serves as a modern Dante, guiding us through a seismically convulsed landscape of risk and opportunity."

—John Elkington, cofounder, Environmental Data Services, SustainAbility, and Volans; coauthor,
The Power of Unreasonable People*; and author, *The Zeronauts

"All businesses today need smart sustainability strategies that make both economic and environmental sense. Those who make the 'pivot'—to incorporate natural resources into their bottom line—will thrive in a rapidly changing world. *The Big Pivot* shows the way."

—Mark Tercek, President and CEO, The Nature Conservancy; author, *Nature's Fortune*

"In the coming years, the fate of the planet and all species, including humans, will be decided. The threats are real, and all our global organizations—companies, governments, and nonprofits—will need to collaborate in new ways to solve the world's largest challenges. Andrew Winston's *The Big Pivot* is the right book for these challenging times, providing business and public-sector leaders a radical, yet practical, new plan for how business will need to operate."

—Peter Seligmann, Chairman and CEO, Conservation International

"The science is clear: man-made climate change represents a serious threat to our collective well-being, and we're running out of time to take action. *The Big Pivot* shows what climate change and other human-caused pressures such as resource constraints mean for business—and what companies can do about it."

—**Michael E. Mann, Distinguished Professor of Meteorology,
Penn State University; author,
*The Hockey Stick and the Climate Wars***

"In *The Big Pivot*, Andrew Winston makes the choice stark: large corporates can embrace the greatest wealth creation opportunity of our time, or go the way of companies whose business models were destroyed by previous rounds of innovation—in this case resource-efficiency innovation."

—**Jigar Shah, founder, SunEdison; author,
*Creating Climate Wealth***

"The world of corporate sustainability is fast-moving, subtle, and correspondingly hard to interpret. Andrew Winston is the archetypal 'insider-outsider'—with huge knowledge of the inner workings of many of the key companies in the vanguard of corporate sustainability today, combined with a robust independence and analytical flair. That's what makes *The Big Pivot* such a timely and fascinating read."

—**Jonathon Porritt, founder, Forum for the Future; author,
*The World We Made***

"Our times call for a massive elevation of consciousness around societal imperatives—and we must leverage the power of capitalism to that end. Andrew Winston takes a pragmatic approach in calling for dramatic business-model evolution to drive progress. In particular, to 'collaborate radically' we need much greater transparency and aligned incentive structures across the capital markets. Private-sector leadership has the capacity to make this Big Pivot. Now it needs the will."

—**Erika Karp, CEO, Cornerstone Capital**

"In *The Big Pivot*, Andrew Winston has beautifully captured the changing nature of our world. More important, his highly readable book shows the way forward for businesses that want to take advantage of and profit from new opportunities—and build twenty-first century solutions."

—**Aron Cramer, President and CEO, BSR**

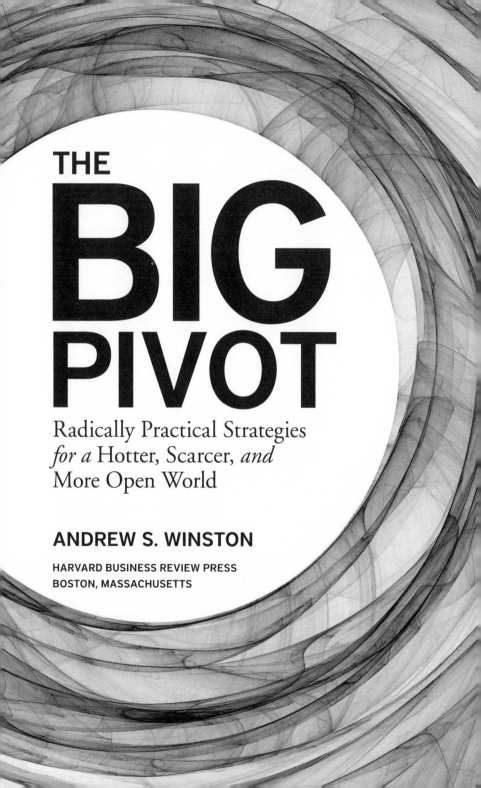

THE BIG PIVOT

Radically Practical Strategies *for a* Hotter, Scarcer, *and* More Open World

ANDREW S. WINSTON

HARVARD BUSINESS REVIEW PRESS
BOSTON, MASSACHUSETTS

Copyright 2014 Andrew S. Winston
All rights reserved
Printed in the United States of America

10 9 8 7 6 5 4

No part of this publication may be reproduced, stored in or introduced into
a retrieval system, or transmitted, in any form, or by any means (electronic,
mechanical, photocopying, recording, or otherwise), without the prior
permission of the publisher. Requests for permission should be directed to
permissions@hbsp.harvard.edu, or mailed to Permissions, Harvard Business
School Publishing, 60 Harvard Way, Boston, Massachusetts 02163.

The web addresses referenced in this book were live and correct at the time of the
book's publication but may be subject to change.

Library of Congress Cataloging-in-Publication Data

Winston, Andrew S.
  The big pivot : radically practical strategies for a hotter, scarcer, and more open
world / Andrew S. Winston.
    pages cm
  ISBN 978-1-4221-6781-6
1. Management—Environmental aspects. 2. Organizational change. 3. Sustainable
development. 4. Strategic planning. 5. Business forecasting. I. Title.
  HD30.255.W574 2014
  658.4'083—dc23

                              2013045503

The paper used in this publication meets the requirements of the American
National Standard for Permanence of Paper for Publications and Documents in
Libraries and Archives Z39.48-1992.

The text of this book is printed using vegetable-based ink. The paper used for
the jacket contains 10 percent post-consumer waste, and the paper used for the
text contains 30 percent post-consumer waste.

CONTENTS

Signals from a New World

NEW YORK, NEW YORK. At 9:00 p.m. on October 29, 2012, an explosion rocked the Lower East Side of Manhattan. An electric substation belonging to New York utility Consolidated Edison (ConEd) had gone up in flames after the rising seas from Hurricane Sandy flooded the building. A large portion of the world's most recognizable skyline went dark for four days, including ConEd's headquarters. In just a few weeks, ConEd lost $2 billion of market cap (one-eighth of the company's value).[1]

ConEd estimated that it would spend $550 million after the storm, only a fraction of the $6 billion (at least) lost by other businesses in the region. New York State would ask for $42 billion in aid to repair housing, infrastructure, and transit systems.[2] The human toll of the superstorm was hard to grasp—nearly 200 people in the United States and Caribbean were killed, and tens of thousands lost their homes.

While no single weather event can be definitively connected to climate change, it's now clear that a hotter planet means more intense heat waves, windier hurricanes, and bigger floods—with ever-increasing economic impacts.[3]

Is your business ready for the coming storm?

PLAINVIEW, TEXAS.   In February 2013, a beef processing plant that had been running for decades shut down, eliminating 2,300 jobs—10 percent of the town's population—and $55 million in payroll. It was one of many ripples from the never-ending drought that the *New York Times* reported "has dried up pastures and increased the costs of hay and feed, forcing some ranchers to sell off their herds to reduce expenses."[4] There just isn't enough water in the region to keep the cattle industry thriving.

The drought gripping Texas has cost the state's businesses billions of dollars, and water availability has become a critical issue for industry. The president of the Texas Association of Business says that "not having an adequate water supply will harm us in terms of bringing jobs to Texas and is doing so now, already ... If we don't address these issues, the message is—don't go to Texas."[5]

Texas is not alone. As most resources—water, cotton, wheat, iron, oil, and many more—get harder to find or more expensive, the cost of doing business everywhere rises.

Is your company prepared for resource crunches?

DHAKA, BANGLADESH.   On April 23, 2013, an apparel factory in the capital city of Bangladesh collapsed, killing more than 1,100 people. This unthinkable tragedy came just six months after a deadly fire raged through the nearby Tazreen Fashions facility, causing more than 100 deaths.[6] The loss is unfathomable, but if we learn nothing from these disasters, then people have died in vain.

Outside of all the ramifications around safety in manufacturing, companies should heed one lesson: any operation, anywhere in your supply chain, no matter how remote, is now your responsibility. The Dhaka factories made clothing for some of the world's best-known brands, names that were *immediately* splashed on front-page articles around the world. There is nothing exclusively local in a deeply connected, transparent world.

Some companies acted fast on these tragedies. Big brands like H&M, Zara, Primark, Tesco, and Abercrombie & Fitch signed on to a plan to help pay for factory safety improvements in Bangladesh. The Walt Disney Company ended apparel production in Bangladesh after the Tazreen tragedy.[7] Walmart, which only found out *after* the fire that Tazreen was a subcontractor to its suppliers, demanded information from all its partners about which firms they contract with. Clearly, better data about who supplies you makes it easier to send higher safety and environmental standards rippling up the chain. Transparency and openness are the new norm.

Are you ready to own everything that's going on in your supply chain?

An old friend of mine, a cardiologist, recently told me something that got me thinking. Even today, with all the information about heart health out there, at least 40 percent of first heart attacks are fatal. Mehmet Oz, the well-known cardiothoracic surgeon with his own TV show, has said that these first attack victims die "because they don't know their risk factors or recognize the warning signs."[8] So while some attacks come with no warning, for most, there were clues—family history or lifestyle choices like smoking and obesity.

With this sobering statistic in mind, I was reading the fitness magazine *Men's Health*, and a regular feature, the "Belly Off" story, caught my eye. This heartwarming tale always focuses on someone losing a lot of weight, usually 100 pounds or more. The profile starts with "The Wake-Up Call," a moment in the man's life that scared him—maybe he couldn't run around with his child, or a doctor told him he would likely die young. These men experienced what I call a "Big-Pivot" moment. At these critical junctures, the signs are clear, we know we need to change our lives substantially—quit smoking, eat a lot less, exercise much more—and the stakes are life and death.

Nobody can avoid all risks, but the earlier we act on the signals we get, the better. Waiting until *after* a heart attack to change your personal health strategy is tremendously risky—what if you don't survive?

When the pivot call comes, it can seem daunting, but it's also an amazing opportunity. Eating better, exercising, meditating—whatever path to health you choose—makes your life better and more enjoyable in both the short and the long run.

The same is true for our businesses, our economies, our society, and our species. Our Big-Pivot moment has arrived. We're receiving plenty of wake-up calls to improve how we operate and make our businesses more profitable and longer lasting. The signals are loud and clear ... and getting more frequent.

Can you hear them?

A Fast-Changing World of Risk and Opportunity

We live in an extreme world now. Our natural resources are under unprecedented pressure as a billion more people enter the global middle class, demanding more of everything. Radical transparency is opening up operations and supply chains to public scrutiny. And most tangibly, extreme weather is breaking records all over the planet, affecting millions of people and costing the private sector dearly.

In 2011, historic floods in Thailand greatly disrupted supply chains for hard drives and cars around the world. In January 2013, extreme temperatures forced Australia's meteorologists to add two new colors to weather maps to handle temperatures now ranging up to 129 degrees Fahrenheit (54 degrees Celsius).[9] And in November 2013, after the devastation wrought in the Philippines by Typhoon Haiyan—the most powerful storm ever recorded, with gusts over 200 miles per hour—some climatologists suggested adding a "Category 6" to the top end of the storm scale.[10] The frequency of these extreme weather events is increasing: as New York's governor Andrew Cuomo said after Hurricane Sandy, "We've had two 100-year storms in three years."[11]

More people are sensing this extremity in their everyday lives and acknowledging that the world is changing profoundly. Last year, Dan Akerson, then the CEO of GM, talked about his company's past climate-change denial, saying "it's kind of hard to refute it … and it's pretty hard not to be convinced that something is going on in the world."[12] Akerson acted on this new conviction and signed GM onto a proclimate policy advocacy group, joining a growing list of committed companies like Autodesk, eBay, Intel, Levi Strauss, Nestlé, Nike, Starbucks, Swiss Re, Timberland, and Unilever.

For those who have not yet felt such a change of heart, they may become more convinced by what they feel in their wallets. At the macroeconomic level, natural disasters cost the United States over $100 billion in 2012 alone.[13] As CNN reported recently, "nearly one third of the world's economic output will come from countries facing 'high' to 'extreme' risks from the impacts of climate change within 12 years." That's $44 trillion of global economy at risk by 2025.[14]

These macro global numbers are sobering, but it's businesses and individuals that are feeling the economic pressures from a hotter world with fewer, more expensive resources. The price of cotton rose 300 percent over one recent 18-month period.[15] Food prices have skyrocketed globally, creating a new hunger crisis and deeply impacting both economies and corporate bottom lines.

Coca-Cola took an $800 million hit to earnings from rising corn prices (besides water, liquid corn is the main ingredient in soda). Morningstar analysts calculated that feeding chickens would cost Tyson Foods $700 million more per year, an amount roughly equal to the meat producer's annual net income.[16] It's not a rounding error; it's the difference between profit and loss.

No country, city, or business can ignore this new reality of extreme weather and expensive resources. Political leaders and CEOs who avoid acknowledging and dealing proactively with it are looking increasingly foolish and irresponsible. And they're not acting in the best interests of their citizens or shareholders.

The vast challenges of this fundamentally changed world can be broken down into three mega challenges that we now must face: (1) climate change, (2) resource constraints and rising commodity prices, and (3) technology-driven demands for more transparency. These three mega forces are what I'm calling "hotter, scarcer, and more open." Consider the first two forces as nonnegotiable system conditions, which we have to manage for our own survival and prosperity. The third pressure, a profound new level of openness, is more like an enforcer or multiplier, which allows everyone to see (and judge) how companies and countries are handling the first two.

The three mega challenges working in concert are dramatically changing "business as usual" and even what we'd consider "life as usual." Because they're growing stronger every day, executives must quickly figure out how to navigate these pressures.

The fundamental biophysical, technological, and economic realities hitting us create deeply dangerous pitfalls for all organizations, but also vast canyons of opportunity for those who understand and skillfully ride these shifts. Each mega challenge comes with a built-in complementary mega opportunity: (1) the fight against climate change is one driver of the rise of the clean economy (currently about a $250 billion-per-year global investment), (2) resource constraints are happening because of the rise of a new middle class demanding a higher standard of living and more products and services, and (3) connectedness and transparency are also tools of open innovation, driving new ideas and creativity.[17]

Unfortunately, today's organizations are not up to the task of managing and profiting from shifts this large. Even putting aside nature's extremes, the business world has been struggling to manage constant, disruptive change. The big threats to business that students learn about in business school are still going strong: new entrants with disruptive business models, increasingly complex supply chains, growing requirements from fickle customers, and new demands from millennial workers who want meaningful work. As John Kotter, a renowned professor from Harvard Business School, wrote recently, "We can't keep up with the pace of change, let alone get ahead of it. The stakes—financial, social, environmental, and political—are rising. The hierarchical structures and organizational processes we have used for decades to run and improve our enterprises are no longer up to the task of winning in this faster-moving world."[18]

Whether you take a purely fiscal view of these challenges or look through a human-focused lens, one thing is clear: we've passed the economic tipping point. A weakening of the pillars of our planetary infrastructure—a stable climate, clean air and water, healthy biodiversity, and abundant resources—is costing business real money. It's not some futuristic scenario and model to debate, but reality now, and it threatens our ability to sustain an expanding global economy.

We need a new approach to prepare for, avoid, manage, and even profit from the challenges we're facing. We need to build organizations that help bring about the necessary changes in our economic system, but from within. These new companies will be more resilient, robust, and able to thrive in fast-changing times. They will be what Nassim Taleb, an author and an expert on uncertainty calls "antifragile."[19] But to get there, companies must shift how they operate in fundamental ways, starting with a deep change in perspective.

The Big Pivot

We can't pretend there are two sides to every issue. Of course, details of how the mega challenges will play out are hazy, but they are happening, full stop. If you don't believe—or you're not at least willing to consider—that climate change and resource constraints are very serious problems, then this may not be the book for you ... just yet. If you don't see that these challenges also create enormous opportunities as we try to figure out how to support what will be 9 billion people, all getting richer and freer and demanding more of everything, then you may not be ready for these ideas today.

This book is for those who know (or are starting to sense) that the pressures we face are so large and intertwined, and the time growing so short, that addressing them aggressively represents the only logical path forward for humanity and for every government, community, business, and individual.

In short, if you believe that these pressures are real, then what has until now been called green business, or sustainability, cannot be a side department or a niche conversation in commerce. Instead, we must *pivot*—sometimes painfully, always purposefully—so that solving the world's biggest challenges profitably becomes the core pursuit of business.

We're now testing the limits of all the natural systems that support our economy and society. Thus, we need to establish a new paradigm for how companies operate. This book is an attempt to answer a fundamental question: If this hotter, scarcer, more transparent, and unpredictable world is the new normal, then how must companies act to ensure a prosperous future for all, including themselves?

Asking whether it makes business sense to tackle the mega challenges is no longer the relevant question. Instead, we must ask ourselves some new core questions, such as, "What do we need to do to manage our businesses effectively in light of these challenges?" Then, and only then, do we figure out how to profit massively from the journey. Profits will still drive much of corporate action—an unprofitable model won't survive—but ultimately it's ludicrous to prioritize *short-term* profit at the cost of our very survival.

We need a major shift in perspective to see that we can deal with the challenges profitably. It's a both-and argument, not the usual false either-or hurdle that's placed in front of advocates for change. Organizations can no longer afford to address massive issues like energy, climate, water, and global development and poverty only when every initiative on the table meets some predetermined, somewhat arbitrary hurdle rate. We have to flip these priorities on their head.

That's the Big Pivot ... and it's nonnegotiable.

Big-Pivot strategy represents a major shift in consciousness for the private sector, but it's not entirely radical. In fact, this kind of thinking is highly conservative, with a major dose of self-interest. We need to conserve the planet's capacity to support us for our own good.

So consider this second core question: If we start from an assumption that we must solve massive challenges to ensure our survival, and then we work back from there to find profitable models, what would a company look like? (This is, critically, distinct from how we operate now, where we start with profit maximization first and then get to environmental and social issues when we decide it's "affordable.")

The companies of the near-future will do many things differently to bring about, operate successfully within, and profit from a new reality. Successful leaders are already starting to pursue a new agenda and set of principles, including the following:

- **Fighting the short-term focus that distracts business from creating value.** Leaders need a much deeper concept than just earnings (which is one particular, warped and narrow view of business success). Executives will worry a great deal more about customers and communities than about stock analysts. Unilever, for example, no longer provides quarterly guidance to Wall Street, greatly reducing its time spent "talking up" the stock and, instead, freeing up management attention to focus on products and customers.

- **Basing company goals on science and the targets we all must hit.** Organizations must set big goals—like a drastic reduction in carbon emissions globally (perhaps by using only renewable energy) or operating within local water-availability limits—based on what science is telling us.

Companies can no longer simply follow a bottom-up exercise to discover what they think they *can* do. Ford is just one example of a company setting its product development goals on the basis of global climate science.

- **Systematically asking heretical questions.** Executives and employees at all levels need to challenge everything, from processes to the way we innovate (openly, not in private) to business models to capitalism itself. A few leaders, such as home improvement retailer Kingfisher in the United Kingdom, are exploring whether they can, through their operations, improve the environment, going beyond the goal of just zero impact and making their enterprises regenerative.

- **Helping to craft and promote governmental policies.** Smart, proactive regulations can really move the needle on the mega issues and level the playing field. Instead of fighting all regulations, companies like Nike and Starbucks are calling on government to pass aggressive carbon legislation.

- **Collaborating with unexpected partners.** Companies must take a more strategic view on how different stakeholders can help make them successful, including seeing employees, customers, and maybe even the fiercest competitors as partners and cocreators. If Coca-Cola and PepsiCo can share the burden of finding new, lower-emitting technologies for keeping drinks cold, anyone can work together.

- **Using new tools to put numbers on benefits that are hard to value.** Putting a number on intangibles—those things that create value but we don't measure well—can help companies make smarter investment decisions. Companies ranging from Johnson & Johnson and IKEA to Diversey and 3M are finding ways to modify their return on investment (ROI) calculations to drive investments in efficiency and renewable energy. And estimating the value that nature provides a business—as Puma and Dow have done—can help companies better understand, for example, our dependency on clean water or on having an atmosphere to dump carbon into. These exercises will help companies prepare for the day when these so-called externalities quickly become internal costs (or benefits).

- **Setting out to build resilient and regenerative (not just profitable) businesses.** A resilient organization can handle deep change and is decoupled from resource use and reliance on the physical capacity of the world. Nestlé and Unilever, among others, are attempting to grow while holding their environmental impacts flat—and they're succeeding.

At its core, the Big Pivot mind-set is about prioritizing environmental and social challenges and opportunities and treating them as central to business success or failure, not as philanthropy or niche issues. This means funding and supporting these initiatives like the high priorities they are.

The mind-set also means understanding not just value chains, but systems, and looking to nature for successful business and operational models (usually ones that are circular, where resources are valued highly and don't go to waste). A food company, for example, will need to consider how what many are calling the "nexus" of food, energy, water, and security interact in each growing region and what those connections mean for the business.

None of these principles or approaches is necessarily easy, but they are required for success and thus will certainly be more profitable than doing nothing. At a macropractical level, on a planet that's under more stress than it can take, no business can profit. Or as a tech executive put it to me memorably, "Nobody will care what operating system they have if they can't eat."

This is an important point to remember and one that often gets lost in a discussion about tackling big environmental and social challenges: none of the core strategies or principles of the Big Pivot are really about "saving the planet." Our Earth will be fine with or without us. As comedian George Carlin once said, "The planet isn't going anywhere. *We* are! ... The planet'll shake us off like a bad case of fleas."[20]

No, this is about humans—all 7 billion of us and counting—and our ability to survive and thrive.

What's in It for You?

Of course, survival itself is a good payback. But more seriously, if we can redefine what good management and strategy look like in a hotter, scarcer, more open world, we will clearly reduce some large-scale risks to our businesses and society (*Scientific American* recently reported that floods alone could cost the world's cities $1 trillion annually by 2050).[21]

And there's another significant upside. The case for meeting these massive changes head-on has a hard-nosed, number-crunching, good-for-business logic behind it. It's not pie-in-the-sky or naive; it's the most realistic solution.

Creating a healthier, cleaner, more stable, and more equitable and just world—with business using its enormous resources and skills to lead the charge—will drive the global economy forward.

In fact, some brave leaders among the large public companies of the world are already well on their way, and we'll visit many of them in this book. They're realizing that this pursuit represents a multi-trillion-dollar opportunity to reconceive how we design, manufacture, and deliver buildings, transportation, energy, and much more.

In the words of billionaire entrepreneur Sir Richard Branson, tackling climate change is "one of the greatest wealth-generating opportunities of our generation."[22] How can this be? It's important to remember that the problems we face, no matter how large, are just constraints on a system. And constraints propel innovation, new thinking, and new business models, which make a lot of money for the fast movers.

My goal then is to establish what companies need to do, not just to survive in a world with so many new challenges and constraints, but to thrive. How will we as a society create a system that provides for those 9 billion people, in ways that use drastically less stuff, produce no carbon, preserve water for everyone's use, and result in no waste or toxicity, all while paying people fairly for their work?

The private sector can and will provide many of the answers. The companies (or communities, cities, or countries) likely to come out on top by making the Big Pivot will be more flexible, resilient, and better able to weather whatever storms the economy and planet throw at us.

Map of the Book

Let me be clear up front. This book is meant to be short, not comprehensive. I fully realize that each one of the 10 core strategies I'm proposing could fill a book. My goal, however, is to provide something appropriate to the urgency of the task at hand—something that gives managers a game plan and a set of priorities for strategizing and operating differently in a fundamentally changed world.

Part 1 begins with four chapters that set the stage with an overview of the mega challenges (hotter, scarcer, more open) and a quick look at both the hurdles in our way and the new mind-set we'll need to conquer them. This section of the book describes what we're facing and starts to paint a picture of how business will need to operate.

Part 2 dives into the ten radically practical strategies, broken into a few pivot categories that comprise the Big Pivot (figure I-1). I start with the *Vision Pivot*, the chapters that help companies

FIGURE I-1

The Big Pivot strategies

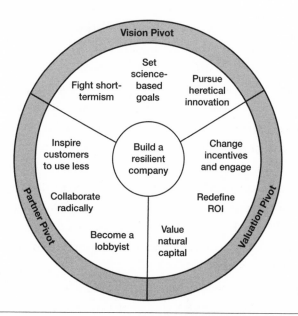

take a longer, broader view, establishing core operating principles through three key strategies: chapter 5, "Fight Short-Termism," offers options for battling the relentless pressure for immediate performance coming from Wall Street and other investors. Chapter 6, "Set Big, Science-Based Goals," makes the case that for the largest challenges, reality dictates that we work outside in from the problem we must solve, not bottom up from what we think we can easily do. Chapter 7, "Pursue Heretical Innovation," explores the kinds of questions we need to ask to move beyond incremental change.

The next three chapters, part of the *Valuation Pivot*, get more tactical, looking closely at what we value in business. Chapter 8, "Change the Incentives," looks at culture and the different ways we motivate employees and executives. In chapter 9, "Redefine ROI to Make Better Strategic Decisions," I describe how one of our core management tools is broken and applied unequally, and I ask the question, "What's the ROI of a Super Bowl ad?" Chapter 10, "Put a Number on the Value of Natural Capital," explores how companies can value what nature provides.

Then I turn to the *Partner Pivot*, focusing on changing the way companies deal with three big external stakeholders. Chapter 11, "Become a Lobbyist," recognizes the impossibility of solving our mega challenges without changing some of the government's rules of the game and asks companies to stop obstructing or get off the sidelines. In chapter 12, "Collaborate Radically," I describe how companies can work with everyone in their value chain, and even their fiercest competitors. Chapter 13, "Inspire Customers to Care and to Use Less," treads carefully on sacred "more is better" grounds by exploring how companies can profit from asking customers to actually buy less.

The final two chapters round up the *Big Pivot*. In chapter 14, "Build a Resilient, Antifragile Company," I explore the tenth, overarching strategy. A result of the other nine strategies, it also requires a set of distinct actions in its own right. The chapter offers some key principles from the emerging study of resilience and describes how some systems can come back stronger after being knocked down. In the conclusion, "Envisioning a Big-Pivot World," I attempt to paint a picture of what companies and the world will look like after we make the Big Pivot.

There is truly no time to lose, so let's get started.

PART I

Today's Mega Challenges

Imagine this scenario. You're in a large ship that has hit something big, and the boat is in trouble. It's filling with a significant amount of water, which needs to be bailed. The captain and the ship's engineer think they can keep the vessel afloat, but only with some serious effort by everyone on board. Wouldn't all the passengers pivot immediately from whatever they were doing to start bailing water?

But perhaps it would have been better to pivot earlier and change the focus of this boat (or organization), or at least its leaders, toward spotting obstacles and avoiding the problem entirely. Or go back further: we could have designed the ship with a double hull or with much better radar. Or maybe we would want to rethink the entire trip and fly or conduct a teleconference instead.

In the mid-1980s, Intel faced a similarly profound moment of decision, when its business looked like it would be taking on water soon. The early warning signs of a deep market shift were there. Intel was being outcompeted by Japanese firms, and its profits were plummeting. The question the leaders faced was this: should Intel keep competing in the memory business it had been so successful with, or should it move into semiconductors?

CEO Andy Grove and founder Gordon Moore heard the wake-up call, asked themselves what a new CEO coming into the company would do, and realized they needed to pivot. Recognizing that it was a life-or-death situation for the company, they made a brutal shift in their business model.[1] There were layoffs and early financial losses, but Intel began a remarkable run in the microprocessor business by first acknowledging some hard truths.

Like Intel in the 1980s, we need to face some tough realities today about the global human experiment. We have enough information now to hear the wake-up call and address these truths. A Big Pivot is necessary, and it will make us healthier and more profitable. So let's start by listening to the three loudest wake-up calls.

CHAPTER ONE

Hotter (and Cleaner)

Doing Business in a More Extreme, Unstable World

When Hurricane Sandy raged toward the Eastern Seaboard of the United States, the eye of the storm bore down on New Jersey. But with its record 900-mile breadth, Sandy wreaked havoc from West Virginia to Maine. The oceans rose up to cover downtown New York City and rendered major chunks of the Jersey Shore uninhabitable.

As the scope of the devastation became clearer, another reality came into sharper focus. Along with cars and trees and homes, the storm swept away some of the continuing public resistance to the facts of climate change. *BusinessWeek* blared on its cover, "It's Global Warming, Stupid." *Time* magazine journalist Michael Grunwald, noting that climate change had long been treated like a niche, secondary issue that only environmentalists would care about, cleanly summed up the absurdity: "Sandy was a blunt reminder that the technical term for people affected by climate change is *people*. It's an environmental issue, a security issue and, yes, an economic issue."[1]

Within a week of the storm, New York City Mayor Bloomberg, Governor Cuomo, and many other leaders had decided that the connection between climate change and extreme weather was getting clearer. We must change how we operate, they all warned, to prepare for a climate-change-riddled present that we had all hoped was still years away.

Global warming, global weirding, climate change, climate disruption, climate crisis—whatever we call it, it amounts to the same thing. The greenhouse gases (GHG) that have kept the planet warm enough for us to evolve and develop our society are now building up dangerously high. This warming is overwhelmingly due to humanity's burning of fossil fuels and its use of the atmosphere as a carbon dumping ground. Skeptics point out that the planet has warmed up before, but as climate expert Ken Caldeira described it in *Scientific American*, "humanity is altering the climate 5,000 times faster than the pace of the most rapid natural warming episode in our planet's past."[2]

Climate bands—regions with differing average temperatures—are shifting by about twenty meters per day: By the latter decades of this century, the weather in Illinois will feel a lot like Texas does today, with summer months spent mostly above 90 or 100 degrees Fahrenheit.[3] The pace of change is a big problem. As Caldeira says dryly, "Squirrels may be able to keep up with this rate, but oak trees and earthworms have difficulty moving that fast."[4] And to put a human face on this reality, a family can move if it has the means, a business can move sometimes, but a city—or entire swaths of productive farmland—can't just pick up and go.

But even with warning signs hitting us over the head, we have trouble acting on a problem like this. It would be easy just to say it's denial, but it's not so simple: we have deep-seated reasons for avoiding the topic.

The Psychology of Climate Change

If we wanted to create a problem to test our species' ability to take on tough challenges, climate change would be close to ideal. It's slow-moving (until recently), complex, and seemingly remote in distance and time. In addition, tackling climate change requires proactive action (we're better at reacting), and unlike air or water pollution, climate change is invisible. But hardest of all, the responsibility for climate change and its effects are spread out over 7 billion of us, and taking action on it can feel like a sacrifice, which—let's be honest—we don't like very much.

Climate change plays to all our psychological strengths and foibles, most of which served us pretty well for the first ten thousand years of society. But they're failing us now. Anthony Leiserowitz, director of the Yale Project on Climate Change Communication, sums it up well: "You almost couldn't design a problem that is a worse fit with our underlying psychology."[5]

Climate can also seem easy to write off because the warming numbers don't sound scary. A couple degrees warmer may sound pleasant, but we're not really talking about going from 75 to 77 degrees Fahrenheit on a nice spring day. As many others have pointed out, the right metaphor is a fever. Take your core body temperature up one degree, and you don't feel so great. Five degrees, and you're sick as a dog. Ten degrees, and you're dead.

Think also about how urgent your doctor's actions would become as your fever rises. At some point, lowering your body temperature becomes the only thing that matters. Similarly, for society and business, addressing climate change is rapidly becoming an "at all costs" issue, with every other goal secondary. Understanding this reality is the core of the Big Pivot.

Think of climate change as the final exam for humanity. The core question, for all the credit, is this: Can we come together to solve a problem that hits so many of our psychological barriers, when the solutions involve effort, some investment, and disruption to many of our traditional ways of doing business?

If we have any hope of passing the test, we must trust the scientific community when it tells us how big the problem is and how fast we have to move. Of course, scientists are sometimes wrong. Unfortunately, climate scientists *have* been wrong repeatedly ... but usually they err on the conservative side. How often have we all seen headlines that say something like, "The Arctic is melting even faster than experts thought."

But experts are getting bolder and blunter as the situation gets more serious. Hundreds of the world's best scientists have signed a joint statement telling us that our very survival is at stake. Titled "Maintaining Humanity's Life Support Systems in the 21st Century," the consensus document says bluntly, "It is extremely likely that Earth's life-support systems, critical for human prosperity and existence, will be irretrievably damaged" by what we humans are doing to natural systems. And they called for "concrete, immediate actions."[6]

This view is hard to accept because it sounds so extreme, the consequences are frightening, and a reasonable response would be to make fundamental changes in how we live and do business. Companies today require a clear profit motive for all initiatives, and execs don't enjoy the idea that some actions might be both expensive and required. But a big part of making the Big Pivot is taking a hard look at what "expensive" means and truly considering all the short- and long-term value that the strategies in this book can create. Yes, there can be trade-offs as we invest in making our businesses more resilient for the long haul, but a great deal of what we need to do is actually profitable in the short run (energy efficiency, for example).

Before getting to value-creating tactics, however, we need to understand the scale of the challenge, or what we could call "the math of it all."

The Math and Physics of Climate Change

While we are an intuitive species and our psychology creates some challenges, we also respect hard numbers, particularly in business. And climate math is getting clearer every day. In a wonky but popular essay in *Rolling Stone* magazine, climate activist Bill McKibben—leveraging some very important analysis from the NGO Carbon Tracker—laid out three fundamental climate numbers that we should all heed:

1. The world's scientists say that the increase in global temperature from pre-industrial times must not exceed *2 degrees Celsius* (3.6 degrees Fahrenheit) if we're to avoid the worst of climate change.

2. The world can only emit an additional *565 gigatons* (that is, 565 billion tons) of carbon dioxide (CO_2) to keep global warming below this 2-degree limit.

3. Unfortunately, the fossil fuel industry has *2,795 gigatons* of carbon dioxide equivalent in reserve, or five times the "safe" amount to emit.[7]

The first two numbers will guide regulations and the goals that countries and companies set for a long time (for example, 141 countries, including all of the largest ones, have signed the Copenhagen Accord, a nonbinding agreement to hold the line at 2 degrees). But what do these numbers really mean? How fast do we have to change? To answer these tough questions, we can turn to two of the world's best number crunchers, McKinsey and PricewaterhouseCoopers (PwC).

McKinsey's Global Institute reconciled what it called two global objectives, "stabilizing atmospheric greenhouse gases (GHGs) and maintaining economic growth." First, the institute assumed significant growth in China, India, Africa, and many other places. Then it looked at how much carbon the world needs to drive the global economy. Every ton of carbon dioxide we emit—when we combust coal or natural gas to turn the lights on or when we burn oil to get around—creates economic value. McKinsey calculates that the world currently reaps $740 of GDP for every ton of CO_2 produced.

To meet the 2-degree hard target for warming, McKinsey says, the amount of GDP that we wring out of every ton of CO_2, called *carbon productivity*, must rise. And it must go up fast—tenfold by 2050, which is quicker than productivity has ever risen for any input into our economy.[8] On top of this sobering news, a PwC report added that time was our enemy, with the 2-degree warming target looking increasingly out of reach. PwC recommended a significant increase in the pace of change.[9] (See the sidebar "The Most Important Number in the World?" for more on these numbers.)

Of course, all of these calculations are based on overwhelming evidence from thousands of studies published in peer-reviewed journals—and 98 percent of climate scientists agree with all the major findings. Climate change data is assembled from scientists around the world and then summarized by the Intergovernmental Panel on Climate Change (IPCC). In its latest report, which came out in segments in 2013 and 2014, the IPCC stated clearly that it was "extremely likely" that human activity was causing the current unprecedented rate of climate change.[10] That's how scientists say, "we know this."

But of course, this doesn't mean that every detail is locked down—the IPCC numbers are based on complex models of the entire, massively complicated global climate system. While the science is very clear that we humans are behind the dangerous changes to the climate, there remains uncertainty around how it will all play out. For example, there's still ambiguity about the exact magnitude of temperature change that will result from specific additional quantities of greenhouse gases emitted. Or how emissions and temperature changes will affect specific kinds of weather—from droughts to floods to hurricanes.

Even the numbers that are more solid, such as the global carbon budget that McKibben writes about, are shifting somewhat (partly because he wrote his article in 2012 and, as of this writing, the IPCC has released some of the numbers from its 2014 report). Broadly speaking, though, to have at least a two-thirds chance of staying below the 2-degree warming barrier (I'd prefer more certainty, but that's the probability band the IPCC has proposed), the budget for how many gigatons of CO_2 we can still put into the atmosphere by 2050 is at most 565 and perhaps much lower. Most updates to these numbers show that the time left to confront these problems is quickly getting shorter. The PwC numbers in this book reflect the latest, reduced budgets.[11]

Another short-hand number that may be easier to grasp than all of these gigaton calculations is something the IPCC has for years strongly advocated, and the new numbers don't change that. In short, we must reduce carbon emissions by at least 80 percent by 2050. And in business terms, while 565 gigatons is kind of meaningless, an 80 percent cut is a comprehensible target.

Now let's quickly address McKibben's third number, the estimate of global fossil fuel reserves measured in gigatons of CO_2.

The Most Important Number in the World?

PricewaterhouseCoopers has reported that to hold warming to 2 degrees Celsius, we need to pursue one simple, powerful goal: reduce global carbon intensity—the amount of carbon emitted for every dollar of GDP—by 6 percent every year until 2100, about nine times faster than the present rate of improvement. This 6-percent-per-year target may be the most important metric of our collective well-being.

The International Energy Agency (IEA), in its *World Energy Outlook 2012*, reached a similar conclusion about the problem with those assets: "No more than one-third of proven reserves of fossil fuels can be consumed prior to 2050 if the world is to achieve the 2°C goal, unless carbon capture and storage (CCS) technology is widely deployed."[12] That's a very big "unless," since CCS at scale is still mostly on the drawing board.

So whether it's McKibben's five-to-one ratio or the IEA's three-to-one ratio, the energy sector, along with the petro-dictatorships controlling national reserves, have more than enough carbon to threaten civilization. We have a serious political and economic challenge, since the fossil fuel reserves are already on the oil giants' books and baked into their market caps. These oil companies and the oil-based dictator-ships around the world are expecting many trillions in prof-its over the coming decades (John Fullerton from the Capital Institute estimates that these excess, "unburnable" reserves are worth at least $20 trillion).[13] If we don't burn the fuel, analysts at HSBC bank calculate, 60 percent of the asset value of major oil companies goes away. So how much would you spend to defend trillions in assets and profits?

Despite these discouraging numbers and the lack of incentives for action on the part of the fossil fuel industry, there are three big reasons for optimism around action on carbon (outside the fossil fuel sector). First, it's incredibly profitable to pursue science-based reduction targets. A study by the World Wildlife Fund and CDP (the Carbon Disclosure Project)—a study based largely on McKinsey data—calculates that pursuing the annual reductions we need in carbon would, over a decade, produce a net present value of $780 billion for US companies.[14] That's the gold we leave on the table if we *don't* go that fast.

Second, many of the largest companies have set goals on the necessary scale, and some have hit giant reduction targets already. For example, the North American division of Diageo, the $17 billion spirits company, cut its emissions by nearly 80 percent in five years (more on this story later).

And third, a large and growing group of companies recognize that climate change is a serious business concern and are beginning to make the Big Pivot on this most important issue. Of the companies that answer the CDP's annual questionnaire—a large majority of the world's biggest organizations—over three-quarters say they integrate climate change into business strategy (up from 10 percent in 2010). Eighty percent identify physical risks to their business from climate change, and 37 percent see these risks as "immediate."[15]

Better yet, companies are discovering that the attack on carbon emissions is profitable. CDP's 2013 study is clear on this issue: "79 percent of US companies responding to CDP report higher ROI on emission reductions investments than on the average business investment."[16]

Climate is not a hidden issue anymore. And business is quickly figuring out that a shift of this magnitude creates large-scale opportunities.

The Growth of the Clean Economy

According to the bank HSBC, by 2020, the climate economy—technologies and services that improve efficiency, produce renewable energy, and generally tackle climate change—will top $2.2 trillion annually. It's likely a low estimate. We're talking about deep changes to multi-trillion-dollar sectors: transportation, energy, construction and buildings, and, to some extent, water.

This greener economy will create lots of jobs. A study by the International Labour Organization estimates that five million people already work in renewable energy and that a greener economy will create a net gain of tens of millions of jobs over the next generation. Many countries are going after this vast, job-creating prize aggressively, investing enormous sums in new efficiency technologies, water infrastructure, the "smart grid," renewable energy, high-speed rail, and much more.

A shift of this scale is hard to encapsulate quickly. But like the proverbial blind men describing an elephant, we get glimpses. Here are a few data points on money being spent:

- Total global investment on clean tech has reached $250 billion annually, a scale that's similar to the mobile technology build-out in the 1990s and 2000s.

- Saudi Arabia, with 19 percent of the world's oil reserves, is investing $109 billion … in solar power.

- South Korea committed about $135 billion, or 2 percent of its GDP, to environmental industries and renewable energy.

- China is investing $372 billion in energy conservation and pollution control.

- Japan has made building a $600 billion–plus green energy market a central target of the country's growth strategy.[17]

And here are a few more examples of what all this investment is accomplishing:

- On a sunny day in May 2012, Germany produced more than 50 percent of its electricity needs from solar alone.

- One winter evening in 2013, Denmark's offshore wind farms made more than 100 percent of what the country needed that night.

- In 2012, half the new electrical capacity put on the grid in the United States came from renewables (it was over 70 percent in the European Union).

- Wind power has passed nuclear as China's third-largest energy source.[18]

From an admittedly small base, renewables are growing very fast (solar grew 900 percent from 2007 to 2012) and gaining country-level scale.[19] Countries are experimenting with a range of policies to make this all happen, from feed-in tariffs that made not-so-sunny Germany the world's largest buyer of solar, to a carbon tax in Australia and carbon trading in the European Union, parts of China, regions of North America, and South Korea.

Who knows who will win when all of this investment tops trillions and sectors shift dramatically? Consider what the mobile technology build-out did for the world. The collected knowledge of humanity is now available at nearly anyone's fingertips, and we can reach out and connect with any of 6 billion cell phone subscribers. But that's hindsight. Early in the development of innovative technologies, it's hard to say what the benefits will be. When computers were new, for example, they seemed kind of niche. In 1943, Thomas Watson, the chairman of IBM, declared, "I think there is a world market for maybe five computers." Twenty-four years later, Ken Olson, president of Digital Equipment Corporation, was still stuck in the short view: "There is no reason anyone would want a computer in their home."[20]

It's easy to laugh now, but even those with foresight would have been hard-pressed to predict how the IT revolution played out. Who knew that FedEx would be king of data? Delivering packages didn't seem like a technology business, but it is. World-changing ideas rarely fan out the way you'd expect.

How different will the world look after the clean tech build-out? It's nearly impossible to predict. But we know that there will be surprising winners who leverage clean energy, water, and material technologies in new ways. And we can say with near certainty that the investment and innovation that's coming will make our lives better.

This is the powerful upside of a hotter, but cleaner world.

CHAPTER TWO

Scarcer (and Richer)

Resources Are Getting More Expensive

Nearly 50 percent of the world's pigs live in China. For some reason, this little factoid keeps me up at night.

The pigs are just one indication of how China's relentless growth and climb up the wealth ladder are creating extraordinary demand for the world's resources. It's hard to get your head around a country with 1.4 billion people, where an economic slowdown means "only" 7 or 8 percent growth.

New Demand for Everything

The numbers on China (and India) are staggering. The pig statistic and many others are part of a compelling, and fun, analysis from investor Jeremy Grantham, founder of GMO, a firm with $100 billion of assets under management. Grantham, an expert in commodities, has painted a simple picture of China's growing and relentless draw on global resources. China's economy represents about 10 percent of global GDP, he points out. So we might expect the country to demand about 10 percent of all resources.

But China now consumes 25 percent of the world's soybeans, more than 40 percent of the steel and aluminum, and over half the cement.[1]

China is keenly aware of its own resource needs. The country has been looking to cut deals around the world, snapping up resources and companies, from coal and power in Australia to oil in Brazil and Nigeria. China is now Africa's largest trading partner. And in late 2013, China's biggest pork producer bought Smithfield Foods, the US-based meat giant. Apparently, the Chinese needed even more pigs.[2]

It's not just China. Hundreds of millions of people in India, Brazil, Africa, and elsewhere are now standing in line, waiting to enter the global middle class within a generation if—and this is a big if—there's enough stuff. All of this demand is a core driver of a new reality: resources are getting scarcer and therefore more expensive.

The Upside: The World Gets Richer

The middle class in China is already approaching half a *billion* people. The Chinese consumer has arrived. On November 11, 2013, during China's version of the online shopping spree known as "Cyber Monday" in the United States, Chinese online retailers moved nearly $6 billion in merchandise. The revenues set a global single-day sales record (and doubled the US mark).[3] As countries get richer, citizens want more of everything—cars, food, buildings, clothing, insurance, banking, vacations, and much more. This astonishing rise from poverty creates both an amazing opportunity for businesses to satisfy new demands, and an unprecedented draw on shared resources. To meet the call, we will need to make the Big Pivot to new ways of operating.

The Supply Challenge

Resources and *commodities* are somewhat cold, detached words for the things that support our lives and underpin our economies. Everything that we eat or use to keep us warm, clothe us, move us around—all the crops, metals, and energy—came from Earth. This basic biophysical reality goes unnoticed most of the time until prices rise enough or an accident highlights the dangers of extracting these materials from the ground.

It's only getting harder to find and extract traditional resources. We don't dig a mile under the surface of the Gulf of Mexico for oil or develop new technologies to unlock natural gas from bedrock miles underground just for the fun of it. The easy dirty energy is gone.

For business, the idea that resources are tight and expensive is the clearest, least debatable "burning platform" for change. You can't deny actual prices. Companies that are the most directly reliant on food, for example, are facing rising input prices; as a result, many millions of people are now dealing with terrifying food insecurity.

The key question for business is whether higher prices are here to stay. All evidence and statistics point to a resounding yes. For the best research on long-term commodity prices, I turn again to Jeremy Grantham, who tells a two-part story. First, commodity prices, on average, declined for the entire twentieth century, with huge volatility around world wars. And second, since the early 2000s, prices have trended up dramatically.

The analysis, which comes from McKinsey, shows that in the first ten years of this millennium, we wiped out all the productivity gains and price decline of the previous century. In real terms, prices are now literally higher than ever (see figure 2-1).[4]

FIGURE 2-1

McKinsey commodity price index

Index: 100 = years 1999–2001

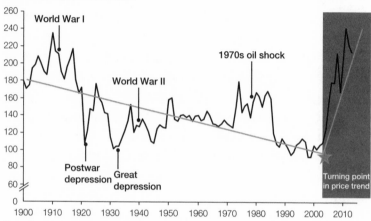

Note: Based on arithmetic average of four commodity sub-indexes: food, nonfood agricultural items, metals, and energy.

Source: McKinsey Global Institute

But here's where Grantham's analysis gets really interesting. He posed a basic statistical question: Does the relatively recent rise in prices represent normal volatility around the relentless decline of the previous century, or has the slope fundamentally changed? His team ran the numbers on dozens of individual commodities. By their calculations, iron, for example, "has a 1 in 2.2 million chance that it is still on its original declining price trend."[5] Or to simplify the statistics, that means it isn't.

Iron was the most extreme example, but for most major commodities, the odds ran from 1 in 50, to 1 in 50,000. In short, the cost of inputs into our economy and society is now, on average, sloping upward. But do business leaders understand this reality? Yes and no.

A study by PwC showed that CEOs are becoming increasingly concerned about energy and resource risks. Over half of the executives surveyed now say that these issues have "overtaken consumer spending and behavior as one of the top three threats to growth prospects."[6] So executives are feeling the price pressures, but concern can wane if they think it's a short-term problem. Anecdotally, I find that the new normal, a *rising* slope for input prices rather than a long-term decline, is somewhat lost on many execs. After witnessing a doubling of the price of the core input into his business, one top exec at a major consumer products company said something like this: "When the prices go up, we take a hit on earnings, but when they come down, we do better."

This perspective reflects a poor understanding of reality. Commodity prices, while volatile, are now fundamentally heading higher. Think about what that upward slope means in everyday terms. When prices come down—and they will, because they're volatile—they'll come down to a generally higher spot than the last time they decreased. And when they go up again, they'll go even higher than the last peak. This change in resource price patterns is a true paradigm shift, and it's a driver of the Big Pivot that most companies are not ready for. The imperative to reduce material use is rising. The only practical path for countries and companies that want to keep functioning profitably, or at all, is radical efficiency.

Grantham summarized it well in a quarterly report to investors: "The world is using up its natural resources at an alarming rate, and this has caused a permanent shift in their value. We all need to adjust our behavior to this new environment. It would help if we did it quickly."[7]

There will be many who claim that Chicken Little cries about resources have come and gone before, stemming back to Thomas Malthus in the late 1700s. The doubters point out that technology has always saved us. We are getting better at finding and extracting resources from extremely inhospitable places, they say (even though the easy stuff is gone). Malthus was wrong, goes the argument, because he couldn't foresee the explosion of fossil fuels, which would propel the world forward for over 150 years. On some level, I agree. We absolutely *can* avoid some of our current resource crunch with another energy explosion, but this time in renewable energy.

But putting renewables aside for the moment, it should be clear that the math of compound growth in anything is impossible in a finite world. We can rely on renewables for energy, but we can't create metals or food or water out of thin air.

Water in particular presents a number of unique challenges.

Water, Water, Everywhere ...

Water is life. We need it for drinking, growing our food, health, recreation, and nearly every other aspect of life. Water connects the mega forces—it shows us what hotter and scarcer really mean. And because climate change is affecting water so profoundly, we need to understand some important details about this resource.

First, some topline data from the US Geological Survey. Even though water covers two-thirds of the planet's surface, a sphere just 860 miles in diameter would hold *all* of Earth's water. Only 2.5 percent of the total is freshwater, but most of that small portion is locked up in ice or in the ground. So a ball just 35 miles in diameter would hold all the water we can access in freshwater lakes and rivers. This amount is everything that, as the USGS says, "serves most of life's needs."[8]

It isn't much for 7 billion of us (and counting) to share.

Climate change is shifting water patterns everywhere, making some areas wetter, but many areas much drier. Water availability has become a crucial limiting factor in human development, population growth, and business operations. The resource is obviously critical to companies in agriculture or those with water-based products—companies like Coca-Cola, Pepsi, Nestlé Waters, and SABMiller. These companies have been aggressively addressing what is now a make-or-break issue. In some regions, their license to operate depends on how they manage water. Most notably, in the Kerala region of India, Coca-Cola's water use once threatened its ability to do business in this big and growing market.

But water is also pivotal for commercial and industrial development, from the millions of gallons needed to hydraulically fracture ("frack") natural gas to the amount needed in construction, electronics, and pharma, just to name a few. Even if your business doesn't seem too reliant on water, check your value chain. Someone you depend on needs it badly. Add in the infrastructure providers and municipal systems that make up the actual business of water, and you get a resource issue affecting trillions of dollars in market value.

The availability of water, or lack thereof, can support or threaten the economy, and the situation is not getting better. Today, about 20 percent of the world's economy is produced in areas facing severe water scarcity. By 2050, projections show, 45 percent of global GDP (about $63 trillion) will be at risk.[9]

But all of that said, water is not like other commodities. Many have called it the next oil or the new carbon, but the shorthand doesn't fit. As I've written with my colleague Will Sarni, a water expert and consultant, water is very different from carbon. It is inherently local and is thus not transferable (with carbon, reducing emissions anywhere has equal value). In addition, water is chronically underpriced relative to its real value, in part because it's seen as a human right. Finally, it's necessary for our very existence.[10]

Besides climate change, how we manage water for our collective use will be the largest challenge of this century. But unfortunately, water is not a stand-alone issue. As we're quickly figuring out, the world is not only finite, but it's also complicated and interconnected.

The Nexus: Food, Energy, Water ... and the Tortilla Riots

Shell Oil has produced numerous reports and websites on what it calls the "stress nexus" that stems from a basic projection from the United Nations: "By 2030 the world's growing population and increased prosperity will push up global demand for water by 30 percent, energy by 40 percent, and food by 50 percent."[11] It's a hot topic among the many companies feeling resource constraints. The idea of the nexus may sound touchy-feely—a "we're all in this together" merging of issues—but it has significant ramifications for how society and businesses function. The challenge is not just how we increase production that much, but the interconnectedness of the resources.

Figure 2-2 provides a few basic statistics on how connected the nexus elements really are. We need a large amount of water to produce energy, we use tons of energy to treat and heat water, much of our food goes to produce biofuel energy, and so on. Complicating and darkening the picture further, many of these resources are just lost: we Americans waste 58 percent of our energy and the world throws out about one-third of its food (worth $750 billion).[12]

The connections can ripple around the world in surprising ways. In 2007, more than 75,000 people took to the streets in Mexico to protest high prices for tortillas, a critical staple for

FIGURE 2-2

The food-energy-water nexus

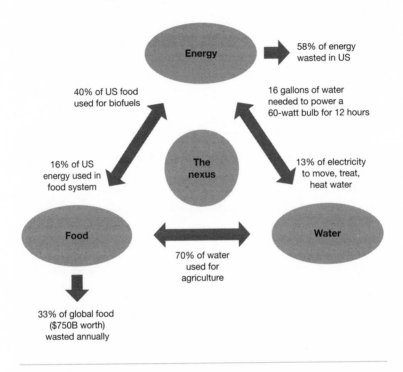

millions of families. The chain of events leading up to a sudden 400 percent increase in corn prices is described clearly in the book *Resilience* as follows:

1. Hurricane Katrina shut down 95 percent of oil production in the Gulf of Mexico for months.

2. Gasoline prices surged.

3. Ethanol, as an alternative to oil, began to look much cheaper by comparison.

4. Ethanol investment surged.

5. Demand for inedible corn for ethanol rose, undercutting production of food corn.

Thus a storm and the subsequent push for more ethanol in the United States drove some Mexicans to near starvation.[13]

Ecological Footprint and Overshoot

So, you might ask, if we're facing such a resource crunch, why does there seem to be plenty of stuff (for those who can afford it)? The shelves of Costco are well stocked, after all. The answer comes in part from the idea of overshoot. One international nongovernmental organization (NGO), the Global Footprint Network, is the epicenter of work on calculating our collective *ecological footprint* (which the network defines as "a measure of how much biologically productive land and sea area an individual, population, or activity requires to produce all the resources it consumes and to absorb its waste"). In short, the Global Footprint Network tells us that we need 1.5 Earths to support our current consumption—we overshoot our capacity every year by roughly 50 percent.[14]

But there remains a disconnect with our seeming abundance, and it stems from a core problem that we can put in simple business terms—the serious difference between assets and income. We have a store of assets (trees, metals, fertilizer, fish, and so on), some of which are replenished every year—that's the new interest deposited in our global natural endowment account. But we're spending down our savings faster than it's being replaced (using about 1.5 times our interest). If you start with a large enough endowment and then treat assets like income, you can hide a fundamental problem for a long time.

Leaders around the world are waking up to the risks stemming from water, energy, and resource constraints. In the World Economic Forum's Global Risks 2013 report, the respondents named rising greenhouse gas emissions and water supply crises as two of the four most likely risks to the global economy. In terms of the risks that would create the largest impacts if they came to pass, the respondents rated water supply second only to "major systemic financial failure." And in an earlier study, WEF's 2012 Global Agenda, "scarcity of resources" came in fourth among top global trends.[15]

"We're Going to Need a Bigger Boat"

When I contemplate the resource crunch, I'm reminded of Police Chief Brody in the classic movie *Jaws*, when he memorably realized that the boat they had wasn't going to be big enough to fight the beast.

We're facing rapid growth in demand and a major squeeze on supply for nearly everything, and it mostly stems from continued increases in population and wealth. Some smart people have calmly pronounced that the world may only be able to support a couple billion people. But how exactly would we go from 9 billion down to 2 billion? A lottery wouldn't work—it's not likely that 7 billion people will voluntarily check out. Perhaps the shortages would provoke a brutish, Hobbesian war for resources. But this little nuclear-powered battle could cause us to overshoot the two billion population "goal" by just a bit and hit zero instead.

Mad Max–type visions aside, we need to think realistically and become a lot more optimistic. We *can* deal with these resource pressures. But first we probably need to assume that population projections are fairly accurate and that we just have to deal with the reality of more mouths to feed. So given the rise in demand and wealth around the world, which is creating an unparalleled resource squeeze, and all the interconnections of the food-energy-water nexus, what's the radically practical conclusion?

First, companies and countries that don't get much leaner are going to face some serious challenges to their viability as they are outcompeted. Second, we must innovate our way to solutions, creating massive new wealth along the way.

Innovation in technologies will be critical, but we must also question the strategic choices we make—and the values reflected in those choices—and explore models for shared or collaborative consumption. Deep changes in both technologies and belief systems will create some losers, such as material- and energy-intensive companies that can't make the transition. But it will also spawn some big winners. The organizations that help customers use less and reduce their impacts will do well.

To make this kind of pivot and support billions of people with a good quality of life, we need radical innovations in resource efficiency (particularly energy and water) and in material science. We also need heretical innovation in how business operates—creating processes that recapture valuable materials from products at the end of their useful lives—and toward business models that help reduce consumption.

Heretical innovation is our bigger boat.

CHAPTER THREE

More Open (and Smarter)

There's Nowhere to Hide

During the 15th hole of the second round of the 2013 Masters golf tournament, Tiger Woods hit his third shot into the water. He then took his "drop," placing the ball near where he had entered the hazard, and continued playing, just three shots out of the lead. What happened next was a first for professional sports.

A knowledgeable fan, a part-time golf tournament official, was watching on TV. He noted that Woods had broken an obscure rule on how you drop the ball and texted in his concerns. Officials penalized the world's most famous athlete two strokes, placing him just out of contention (he finished in fourth). Some commentators believe the call actually kept Woods from being disqualified altogether.[1]

All of our opinions seem to matter now—or at least we think they do. Sharing and collaboration are good. But there are some downsides, as Woods discovered. If one fan can affect the outcome of a globally televised sport, think about what thousands could do with the megaphone that technology gives them.

Everyone's a Critic

A few passionate customers using platforms like Change.org can gather many others to challenge companies about how they operate. Over 120,000 people have signed a petition asking Dunkin' Donuts to eliminate Styrofoam cups. When the environmentally themed movie *The Lorax* came out, a fourth-grade class started a petition to Universal Studios asking the company to discuss environmental issues on the movie's website. Universal changed the site in a few days.

Some kids were also unhappy with Crayola because they couldn't recycle the company's markers. A 2012 petition through Change.org carried quotes from kids like nine-year-old Zachary, who said, "I love your markers, but I'd like to tell you it's polluting. So can I please send some back? I love your product, but hate pollution." These stories are small wake-up calls for companies.[2]

Over the next year, Crayola did create a new program, Colorcycle, to collect markers from schools and to turn the waste plastic into liquid fuels. But shouldn't companies identify environmental and social issues that could diminish their brand and sales *before* a fourth-grader does?

Of course there's often a fine line between customer input and customer wrath, and companies need to be careful if they actually seek out opinions. In 2006, General Motors tried a "fun" experiment, one of the first attempts at user-generated or crowdsourced advertising. GM asked the public to create customized commercials for the Chevy Tahoe—ads that the company hoped would then go viral. Thousands of submissions poured in, but to say that many were highly critical would be an understatement.

"Like this snowy wilderness?" asked one homemade commercial. "Better get your fill of it now. Then say hello to global warming. Chevy Tahoe."

Another submission offered this advice: "$70 to fill up the tank, which will last less than 400 miles. Chevy Tahoe."[3]

This could not have been what Chevy brand execs were hoping for. Companies are much better prepared today, I hope. But in an open, everybody's-opinion-gets-heard world, you never know what someone might do to your brand.

Nothing Is Local

If you go to YouTube and start to type "FedEx" into the search box, one of the first auto-fill suggestions reads "FedEx Guy Throwing My Computer Monitor." The video, viewed more than 9 million times, shows a delivery person dropping a box containing fragile electronics over a seven-foot-high security fence.

FedEx is arguably one of America's best business success stories, a tale of an entrepreneur creating a world-class juggernaut that helped create an entirely new sector. The company ranked tenth on *Fortune's* World's Most Admired Companies list for 2013. And FedEx is considered a leader in many dimensions, from innovation (it made IT a strategic advantage long before most companies knew how to boot up) to financial, environmental, and social performance. So it must be frustrating for executives to see the company's reputation partly hinging on the behavior of a single employee.

FedEx is not alone by any stretch. In recent years, many companies have found out that an embarrassing video can go viral quickly. Welcome to the new transparent world, where anything that happens anywhere can shape the global brand. We're living in a post–WikiLeaks/Bradley Manning, post–Edward Snowden world. We now know that the US National Security Agency

(NSA) has been collecting a great deal of data on the Internet and phone use of its citizens.

Anything can get out now, and nothing is local anymore.

You can't completely avoid having an employee do something stupid, but you can get proactive, tracking and sharing information with customers and other stakeholders long before something potentially damaging to the brand can be revealed.

In one of the best examples of preemptive sharing, apparel leader Patagonia launched the Footprint Chronicles, a web-based tool that the company says uses "transparency about our supply chain to help us reduce our adverse social and environmental impacts." The site lets users click and zoom in on a map of all the textile mills and factories Patagonia uses, and then trace particular products back through the chain, showing their total energy, water, and waste impacts.

Big companies are gathering more info on their supply chains as well. After the 2012 and 2013 factory tragedies in Bangladesh, American companies were reluctant to sign on to multiparty agreements to improve conditions for workers (there were concerns about legal liability). But Walmart did take one fascinating step, contracting with a small start-up called Labor Voices, which has a shockingly simple way to find out more about employees' lives and working conditions: talk to them on the phone.

It may sound silly, but consider that there are more than a billion cell phones in China and 100 million in Bangladesh— a vast majority of adults have one. Labor Voices gives workers a number to call where they can answer automated surveys about the conditions where they work. The company also conducts interviews with workers and creates anonymous reports, by factory, on working conditions, pay, worker recruitment tactics, and many other issues. Walmart hired this little, transparency-driven company to contact and collect information from workers at the nearly 300 factories in Bangladesh that subcontract to the world's largest retailer.[4]

In this way, Walmart gains transparency and insight into its supply chain, improving its odds of avoiding massive and expensive disruptions (and even deadly situations like fires and factory collapses). Walmart is smart to try and find out what's going on upstream before a damaging story surfaces on its own.

Consider what happened to Apple in early 2012. The story broke globally about horrible working conditions at factories, run by Chinese giant Foxconn, that were assembling iPads and iPhones. Apple found out the hard way that what happens in China does not stay in China. We now have deeper insight into life on the assembly line, ironically enabled by the kind of camera-in-your-pocket technologies that these workers assemble. The truth will come out. Increasingly, employees, customers, and consumers will use information about how things are produced to make critical decisions about which companies they work for and which products they buy.

Deal Breaker

A large hotel chain shared with me a list of questions it received from big corporate customers—the ones that book hundreds of hotel rooms for events. "Do you measure carbon emissions? How much energy do you use and how much is renewable? Do you use environmentally-friendly cleaning products? Do you have a waste reduction program?" and so on. But my favorite was the simple demand "Please provide documentation."

Every company is facing more of these kinds of questions every day. A few years ago, IBM started requiring its major suppliers (28,000 of them) to track core environmental data like energy use, greenhouse gas emissions, and waste. IBM's suppliers would also have to share the data publicly. But the most interesting aspect of the new demands was that suppliers would be required to ask *their* subcontractors to do all the same things. IBM execs called this approach "cascading" demands. So not only was IBM forcing openness, it was sending a large ripple of transparency up the supply chain.[5]

Radical transparency is here to stay. Every company that wants to remain competitive needs to answer tough questions, especially the ones coming from business customers (or even the customer's customers in the case of IBM's supply chain). Many companies talk about how their environmental or social performance is often a tiebreaker in sales: the company and products with a better backstory, supported by good data, land more contracts.

But there's something more subtle going on than just breaking ties. Consider the most famous and successful green product ever, the Toyota Prius. At one point during a high point in its popularity, when there were very few competing hybrids, more than half of the people shopping for a Prius were only looking at the Prius—no other models of car entered their decision set.[6] Environmental and social issues are becoming a deal breaker in more situations, especially business-to-business. If you don't meet the rising standards your customers set, you won't be in the running at all.

This new, open world is not optional. We'll all be sharing more information about our operations, whether we like it or not. Many companies are understandably nervous about giving out what could be competitive or proprietary information, or they're worried about being unable to answer customer questions. But there are clearly upsides to this movement.

Companies can use openness to engage in a real dialogue with customers and other stakeholders, using the tools of open innovation to gather new ideas, create new products and services, and solve big problems. Radical transparency also creates a compelling rationale for greatly improving your performance. To stay competitive in an open world, you'll be making better products, ones that are low-carbon, low-water, low-waste, and nontoxic. They will be made by people who are working in safe conditions and making a living wage. And all of this will apply to your whole supply chain.

As a few watchers of the unstoppable transparency train of radical openness—including digital guru Don Tapscott and Dara O'Rourke, the founder of GoodGuide—have said, "If we're all going to get naked, we better get buff!"[7]

Big, Heavy Data

Consider these statistics:

- Every minute, we swarm the Internet with 550 new websites; 82,000 wireless app downloads; and 2.2 million Facebook likes and comments.

- Half of 18- to 34-year-olds check Facebook the first thing when they wake up; 28 percent before getting out of bed.

- Every hour, we upload 6,000 hours of video to YouTube (and watch more than one trillion of these videos each year).

- Every day, we tweet 400 million times.

- Every month, the average American teenager sends 4,000 texts.[8]

All of these statistics became obsolete while you read them.

Individuals—not to mention governments (or the NSA) and businesses—are collecting terabytes and zettabytes of data on every aspect of our digital lives. And our physical lives now too: people are buying Nike Fuel bands, Fitbits, and other trackers to measure the steps they take, the calories they burn, and the hours they sleep. All of this data is just what we generate in our own personal lives.

Contributing to the information avalanche is the relatively new practice of gathering data on our physical world as well—from city traffic flows to building systems that track temperatures and energy use, to water system flows and quality, to food tracking systems. Consider just the data we collect from building and home energy meters, which once generated just 12 data points per year (a meter reader would come by monthly). But in North America, utilities have installed more than 60 million smart meters, each of which can collect 35,000 data points per year (one every 15 minutes).[9]

All of this new data is part of the "convergence of physical and digital infrastructure," IBM exec Wayne Balta says, "and it's creating a vast new 'natural resource' to mine." Throw in the 3 billion e-mails sent every day and all the business data collected, and you get some gargantuan numbers. Balta talks about the 2.5 quintillion bytes of data people create every day.[10] How much is that? I have no earthly idea, but it's apparently a ton.

So we can use all this information to make our world leaner, greener, and more prosperous, right? Well, yes, but there are a couple important hurdles. First, one little-known challenge stands in the way of this seemingly unstoppable growth in data, and it brings us back to the "scarcer" part of our story. It turns out that it takes serious physical infrastructure, and a lot of energy, to store all of this information. The cloud isn't so light after all.

The Internet of Things

It's not enough that we're sharing so much personal data. Now our appliances can talk to each other as well. A study by AT&T and the Carbon War Room estimates that machine-to-machine technology (or M2M) could cut global carbon emissions 19 percent and save trillions of dollars.[11] Our home and business equipment will apparently talk to the grid, powering up and down at the most efficient and cheapest times of day. M2M will optimize routes for planes, trucks, cars, and trains; make buildings more efficient; and reduce food waste—all without humans getting their digital hands dirty.

Tech giant HP has been sounding some alarm bells about the scale of this growth. In a series of ads it ran in the *Washington Post*, HP shared some amazing statistics. The fifth-largest country in electricity use, HP says, isn't a country at all—it's the cloud (it falls behind China, the United States, Russia, and India, but sits ahead of Japan, Germany, and Canada). Every two days, HP calculates, the world creates more data than it did from the dawn of history up until 2003. The company calculates that we'll need 10 new power plants to support this growth in data within just three years. HP's ads about these numbers summarized the problem clearly: "It's unsustainable. In every sense of the word."[12]

Clearly HP isn't advocating that we pack up and stop collecting data. No, the ads were part of a push for its new product line, Moonshot, a data center system that uses dramatically less energy. The tech sector will be racing to provide new energy-saving ways to support our data habit. It's all part of the clean economy we're building.

So assuming we figure out the back-end issues and can keep building these data storehouses using less carbon energy, there remains one burning question about Big Data: What do we do with it? Can all those the newly minted "data scientists" out there, using the latest analytical tools, leverage the information to help solve our mega challenges? Can we dramatically reduce energy, water, food, and material waste? Can we make our buildings and transportation and energy systems much more efficient?

The big tech companies seem to think so. Many are positioning themselves as the saviors of analysis, riding in to figure out all of this data for us in the service of solving big problems. Making decisions based "on analytics, not just instinct," as IBM's Balta says, is certainly part of IBM's mission. The ability to use data to make businesses, cities, and the whole world more efficient and productive is at the heart of the company's Smarter Planet brand positioning.

Caution: Data-Driven versus Data-Guided

Companies are using data in new ways every day to get leaner, to understand their operations and customers better, and to drive innovation. This big data will help us find new solutions. But we need to be guided by data, not controlled by it. As we gather more information, we might find spurious correlations that don't tell us much. We can analyze a product's impacts up and down the value chain in increasingly detailed ways, but there is a declining marginal benefit. We need to operate in directionally correct ways and find the hot spots of risk and opportunity in our value chains.[13]

Little Data

On top of the vast amount of information we're collecting about the big things in our world like buildings and infrastructure, we're also collecting more information at the product level, much of it previously unavailable. And we have new tools for getting that data into the hands of business customers and even consumers. GoodGuide is a company that collects information on 200,000 products and scores each item on three dimensions: health, safety, and environment. It adds a layer of assessment and judgment to raw data about ingredients, life-cycle impacts, and the environmental and social performance of the corporations behind the products. GoodGuide allows its millions of website visitors and iPhone app users to compare products in real time, either online or in the store (shoppers can use their phones to scan the product bar code).

Some companies are trying to get ahead of the new transparency demands. Seventh Generation lists all of its ingredients on every product label. SC Johnson, the large, privately held maker of Windex and Glade, launched www.whatsinsidescjohnson.com so that retailers and consumers can explore all its products' ingredients.

We can zoom in now to nearly any level of detail we want. We're slicing and dicing the Big Data into bite-sized chunks with real-time availability. Think of it as "Little Data." And when little data at the product and service level is available, and buyers are empowered with the information they need, it affects sales.

But what would happen if consumers felt so empowered by all the new information and connectivity that an open world enables that they stopped, well, consuming as much?

Let's Share: Collaborative Consumption

The information technology and data revolutions have helped create a new form of commerce. We're witnessing the beginning of collaborative consumption, a fancy phrase for sharing (so maybe it's really a very old form of commerce).

Car sharing is the best-known example of the trend, and Zipcar is the best-known player. Its 760,000 members can go online, find a Zipcar nearby, unlock it with their own key card, and use the vehicle on an hourly basis. The company owns the car, insures it, and cleans it periodically.

The sharing bug is infecting many sectors. Airbnb, a site where you can rent out a room in your home, now has more than 250,000 beds listed in 192 countries, which makes it one of the largest "hotel" chains in the world.[14] A recent entrant to the sharing economy, Yerdle, is like eBay, but with free stuff. You post a possession that you're ready to part with, and friends in your Facebook network can request the item. They just pay for shipping (which Yerdle takes a piece of).

The environmental benefits of these new sharing models could be sizable. Not building another car or hotel, or finding another use for something you're ready to throw out, can dramatically reduce the draw on resources for that product or service. For each shared Zipcar, the members sell (or don't buy) 20 cars. Zipcar users also drive 80 percent fewer miles than car owners do.[15]

Sharing is a threat to business-as-usual. Yerdle cofounder Andy Ruben, the former sustainability lead at Walmart, admits that collaborative consumption is deeply disruptive to normal business models. Large-scale sharing should, for example, reduce overall demand for clothes. But, Ruben says, companies that make the more sustainable, longest-lasting products, like Patagonia or Nike, could command a larger share of a shrinking consumption

Crowd-Funding *Veronica Mars*

People are sharing more than products; they're sharing missions. Sites like Kiva.org and Kickstarter enable us to donate to causes we care about or to chip in to launch a new business or product. Instead of shopping ideas to venture capitalists or other funders, innovators can appeal directly to the public. For example, more than ninety thousand fans of the cult TV hit *Veronica Mars* pitched in on Kickstarter to fund a movie featuring the defunct show's characters. The producer reached his $2 million goal in just eleven hours (and made $5.7 million total). Movie funding and entertainment will never be the same.[16]

pie. In a scarcer world, people will gravitate to products that will last longer and can be passed on to friends and family for another use.[17]

The next generation of consumers and employees is growing up in a very different world, with complete openness and sharing. They don't expect secrets to last long, no matter how sensitive (WikiLeaks, anyone?). And everything is their business.

But on the upside, if everyone is involved, then you can pick the brains of millions of people at once.

Open Green Innovation

In the eighteenth century, sailors could figure out their position on the open sea only on the north-south axis (latitude). Outside of dead reckoning, they had no way to figure out how far east or west they were (longitude). It made trips to the New World even more dangerous. In 1714, the British government offered a prize of up to £20,000 (£4 million in today's money) to anyone who could come up with a practical way to determine longitude.[18]

Centuries later, in 1927, Charles Lindbergh won the $25,000 Orteig Prize for his record-breaking solo flight across the Atlantic Ocean. In 2004, the X Prize Foundation awarded $10 million to the first private enterprise that successfully launched (twice) a reusable, manned craft into space.

Clearly, innovation has long been open. Ideas can come from anywhere—and they do.

The idea of asking the world for solutions to a problem has regained a tremendous head of steam in recent years, particularly in the business world. The movie streaming company Netflix offered a $1 million prize to anyone who could improve its movie recommendation algorithm. The contest was one of the first examples of what this new, data-rich, transparent, IT-enabled world can accomplish. Netflix opened up a portion of its data on customer likes and dislikes to the world. The winning team of seven engineers and statisticians hailed from four countries, worked together remotely, and met for the first time in person at the awards ceremony.

More than a decade ago, P&G created one of the first large-scale open-innovation processes. The company asked for any good product ideas, offering in return some royalties and the leverage of its prodigious marketing and product rollout machine. Outsiders brought to P&G a range of ideas for brand extensions for the Swiffer floor-cleaning device, the Crest SpinBrush, and a line of Olay skin care products.[19]

Other companies have used open tools to engage a large number of people, particularly their employees, in conversations. IBM started innovation "jams" using online discussion tools in 2001. The third attempt in 2008 involved 150,000 employees and generated ideas for new businesses, including a "big green" initiative, the precursor to the company's global Smarter Planet campaign.[20]

The open-innovation toolkit can be very useful for tackling mega challenges. We're at the beginning of a powerful trend, with companies mostly dabbling. Heineken offered $10,000 for the best idea to improve the environmental performance of packaging. Both of my favorite entrants—which, unfortunately, didn't win—came from one guy. He proposed (1) a honeycomb-shaped can, which would pack much tighter into trucks, saving lots of fuel, and (2) a "tap truck," a rolling giant keg with basically zero packaging. Just imagine driving that rig up to a frat house.

Other companies, from GE to Lufthansa to Unilever, have been experimenting with prizes, jams, and open calls for help on mega challenges. The open-innovation revolution will be a critical tool in the pivot. We can now engage employees, customers, and just about anyone to collaborate and solve complicated problems in profitable ways. The more brains we bring to the table, the smarter we are.

So in the end, I'm a techno-optimist about the rising tide of transparency, connection, sharing, and open innovation. This mega force should help us work through the challenges we face in a hotter, scarcer world.

But before we jump into the 10 key strategies that will help us pivot, let's look at some key principles and some systemic hurdles standing in our way.

CHAPTER FOUR

A New Mind-Set

Principles and Hurdles

The stark picture outlined in the preceding chapters should motivate us to get moving. But before acting, we need a new mind-set that aligns with this hotter, scarcer, more open world. Making the Big Pivot will require companies and executives to leave behind old, preconceived notions about how business deals with social and environmental challenges.

This Is Not Philanthropy

First, we need to stop asking the increasingly surreal question "What's the business case?" The word *sustainability* means, by definition, the ability to keep doing what you're doing. So why must we justify investing in initiatives that allow us to continue operating? Or in strategies that drive innovation and create lower-risk, resilient enterprises?

The easy and most typical answers are that (1) everything in business must prove itself worthy in terms of ROI and (2) all ideas compete for capital. The first answer is partly a myth: of course any business strategy or tactic needs to prove it can create value, but we make plenty of big decisions in business without perfect (or any) information on payback. For example, investments in marketing, R&D, or entry into new geographies are often made with little expectation of knowing what the exact financial return will be (I'll dig deeper into this idea in chapter 9).

The second answer is more compelling and a real issue. Companies do not have infinite financial or human resources to focus on every issue. Yet ironically, our economic theories assume that the world as a whole does have limitless physical resources. Clearly that can't be true.

Slowly, the reality of what sustainability truly means is creeping into the strategies of leading companies, and they're moving away from the stale business case debate. In late 2013, at one of Walmart's large sustainability "milestone meetings," the EVP of public affairs, Dan Bartlett, declared clearly, "We can put to rest that old debate about whether sustainability and business go hand in hand … [W]e can demonstrate with real metrics that it's good business."[1]

So I'm making one key assumption in this book to save time: we don't need to review in depth the basic idea that green can be very good for business. (If you're still skeptical, please see appendix A, where I summarize the basic business case for green strategy. Or stop here for now and read the full story in my earlier book *Green to Gold*.)

But it's vital that we dispel one damaging and related notion—that green business is not about business at all but about "saving the planet," as if that were some separate entity from us. In fact, "planet" is a vague word for what's really a vast storehouse, providing a stable climate, food, minerals, clean air and water, and every other resource we need to live. These are not nice-to-haves—they're the world's asset base, which our economy and society rest on. And this leads us to a logical question. As the late, great entrepreneur Ray Anderson liked to ask, "What's the business case for ending life on earth?!"[2]

Big-Pivot strategies and initiatives create business value as well as environmental and social value. This is not about citizenship or corporate social responsibility (CSR) or just about "doing the right thing."

Or to put it even more simply: This is not philanthropy.

Of course there's a moral dimension to many environmental and social issues, such as fixing supply chains so that production is nontoxic and nobody dies making a T-shirt. But the kinds of strategies we're talking about—managing scarce resources, reducing the risks of relying on fossil fuels, building organizations that are resilient to extreme weather and climate change, creating safe work spaces, leveraging open technologies to access new ideas from all stakeholders—can create tremendous value.

The companies that don't make the pivot to manage these issues well will find their margins, market position, and overall enterprise

---

Signs of the Pivot: Alcoa

Alcoa's CEO Klaus Kleinfeld has said, "Sustainability is not a catalog of processes, nor merely a philosophy at Alcoa. Rather, it is part of everything we do." The company's sustainability report states clearly, "At Alcoa, sustainability is defined as using our values to build financial success, environmental excellence, and social responsibility in partnership with all stakeholders in order to deliver net long-term benefits to our shareholders, employees, customers, suppliers, and the communities in which we operate."[3] Does that sound like philanthropy?

value eroding over time. And at the macro level, we either tackle these challenges or threaten our ability to function and prosper. So there's a tautology here: acting in a way that ensures a future, well, ensures a future. That's a pretty good business case.

But to get there, we need a new set of operating guidelines and principles.

The Big Pivot Principles

Albert Einstein wisely noted, "We can't solve problems by using the same kind of thinking we used when we created them."[4] What does our thinking need to look like to solve today's mega challenges? What principles should guide our businesses?

To answer that question, I considered a range of issues for which business leaders have a typical perspective. Three ways of thinking about these issues are shown in table 4-1: (1) the *traditional* views from the heyday of business in the twentieth century, which a solid majority of Western executives still likely hold; (2) a *clean and green* movement, the more evolved perspectives of a growing number of companies that are largely in line with the green-to-gold philosophy; and (3) the *Big-Pivot* principles, with which we can—and must—sustain the success of our businesses, economy, and species.

Consider an example of how business leaders might evolve their views on what the operational focus of the business should be.

Traditional		Clean and green		Big Pivot
"Four walls"	→	Value chain	→	Systems

For most of the history of business, the focus and responsibility of the organization has been on what is directly controlled, within the proverbial "four walls." In the clean and green world, an

TABLE 4-1

Three ways of approaching various business issues

Corporate view on:	Traditional	Clean and green	Big Pivot
Operations			
Operational focus	"Four walls"	Value chain	Systems
Operational model	Linear	Curved (partly circular)	Circular
Impact, footprint	Necessary, unmeasured	Reduced	Zero to regenerative
Value chain metrics, data	Impossible	Lacking, wanting	Required, hot spots, data-guided
Employees	Lifetime contract	At-will, but engaging	Partners, cocreators
Regulations	Hostile	Defensive	Leveraging, guiding
Clean innovation	Unexplored	Incremental, eco-efficient	Open, disruptive, heretical
Green goals	Superficial	Bottom-up	Science-based
Sustainability organization	Silo-ed	Matrixed	Integrated
Sustainability goal	Public relations (if at all)	Cost & risk-cutting	Relevance, flourishing
Philosophy, outlook			
Risk, continuity	"We're insured"	Measured, prepared	Resilient to "antifragile"
Externalities	Externalized	Recognized	Internalized
Nature	Exploitive	Wary, respectful	Biomimetic
External stakeholders	Ambivalent	Cataloging, appeasing	Open, collaborative, inclusive
Competition	War	Truce, co-opetition	Pre-competitive
Value creation	Short-term earnings	Short-term earnings	Short- and long-term shared value
Contribution to society	Jobs, economic	Jobs, economic, but cleaner	Solving mega challenges
Growth, consumption	Sign of progress	Necessary, managed	Redefined, decoupled
Mega challenges	Unaware, dismissive	Dawning, confident	Fully activated, humble

evolution from the earlier mode, companies start to think about the whole value chain and may help reduce supplier and customer impacts. But in the next step, the Big-Pivot view, companies look beyond even their own value chain to understand systems—the food system as a whole for the agriculture business, for example, or a regional system of water use.

In table 4-1, I lay out a range of issues and suggest principles for the three worldviews. I won't describe every line in detail here, but I want to touch on three overarching principles that underpin a new, Big Pivot mind-set and that run throughout the book: decoupling, regeneration (zero and beyond), and circularity.

Decoupling (Redefining "Growth")

In terms of growth, we have two major physics-based problems. *First, there isn't enough stuff* of the easy-to-get-to and low-cost variety to support the expected improvement in material well-being (the billion or so people entering the middle class in the next generation). This is, again, the essence of the "scarcer" mega challenge. Leading companies are realizing that to continue growing, which Wall Street and their own interests demand, they need to do so without increasing the use of energy, water, and other materials. A few organizations have effectively decoupled growth from inputs.

Figure 4-1 presents data on Nestlé's operations. Over a decade, the food giant increased production by 53 percent, but *cut* all major inputs—waste by nearly half, on-site energy use by 6 percent, and water withdrawals by 29 percent.[5] These changes are more than impressive; they are required given the scale of our climate and resource challenges—if we want to continue to improve the standard of living for all, we must do so without stressing our natural asset base any further.

FIGURE 4-1

Nestlé decoupling data

Nestlé environmental performance indicators indexed (2002 = 100)

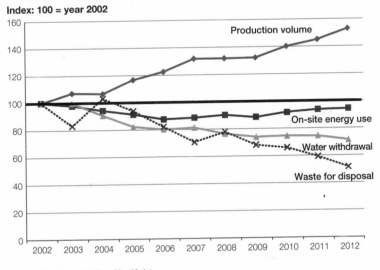

Index: 100 = year 2002

Source: Graph created from Nestlé data.

Decoupling is gaining traction. Unilever, led by CEO Paul Polman—who was, not coincidentally, formerly Nestlé's CFO—has set a big goal of doubling revenue while seeking to "halve the environmental footprint of the making and use of our products," all by the year 2020.[6] When Walmart recently announced aggressive new renewable energy and efficiency goals, CEO Mike Duke said, "We'll further separate the link between our growth and our GHG emissions."[7]

Decoupling business growth from material use is the first crucial step. But we have a second, bigger challenge: *all growth has to be reexamined.* It's hard not to be persuaded by the basic logic. Even though renewables can give us some serious latitude for growth in energy use—by decoupling a good thing (energy) from a bad thing (carbon)—that's just one input. The basic math of growth just does not work indefinitely, or even for much longer.[8]

The current mode of operating—the pursuit of consistent and compounding growth—is frankly incompatible with physical reality. At current global GDP growth rates (5 to 6 percent), the world economy would grow from $70 trillion today to $1 quadrillion (nominal) in 49 years. If the largest companies, the $450 billion–plus Walmart and Exxon, set double-digit growth goals—a common-enough demand from Wall Street—they would each have to achieve $4 trillion in sales in 23 years … and reach $50 trillion in sales in 50 years.

Expecting profit growth to continue past the short term sets us up for serious problems as we overshoot our planet's capacity to support us. It's just math. We'll need to redefine what success looks like in our economy and particularly for large companies. Growth as a goal in and of itself needs to give way to *prosperity*, a much healthier, more mathematically feasible idea. Instead of increasing profits indefinitely, companies could improve the quality of their products and services, the experience of their customers, the health of their communities, and the lives of their employees.

The companies that pursue an expanded view of success will succeed in the traditional sense. They will outperform their competitors and may grow by taking market share. But they won't do so for very long. To continue growing, they'll need to reduce their use of physical resources to zero, or even less.

Regeneration (Zero and Beyond)

Zero is the new black. The goal of "zero waste to landfill" has moved quickly from being a green pipe dream to becoming the norm in business. Nearly 50 of P&G's 140 manufacturing sites are waste-free. GM now has more than 100 plants with no waste going to landfill, turning an expense into a multi-billion-dollar profit center. DuPont's construction materials business went from 81 million pounds of waste to zero in three years. The leftovers from all these companies, the small amounts that can't be recycled, are also going to good use—Waste Management (WM) now creates enough energy from its waste-to-energy plants to power more than a million homes.[9]

Zero is popping up outside of waste. Tough mandates from retailers have eliminated chemicals like phthalates and BPA from plastics on their shelves and have demonstrated zero tolerance for some toxics. Walmart and P&G set aspirational goals of 100 percent renewable energy, which is basically zero carbon (when the energy is generated). HP Labs is working to create a data center "that consumes net-zero energy over its entire life cycle—from resource extraction and manufacturing to operation and end of life."[10]

Shooting for zero clearly drives innovation. John Elkington, the man behind the idea of the triple bottom line, more recently wrote *Zeronauts*, a book about "a new breed of innovator, determined to drive problems such as carbon, waste, toxics, and poverty to zero."[11]

But some are even asking if zero goes far enough. Green architect Bill McDonough and his thought partner, Michael Braungart, suggest we rethink waste, going beyond their own book *Cradle to Cradle* (a term coined in the 1970s by architect Walter Stahel), and seek to "upcycle" everything, making things *more* valuable after their use.

Companies truly making the Big Pivot consider zero as the *starting* point and then create restorative products and enterprises. Imagine buildings that make the air around them healthier (Alcoa produces building panels that clean smog). Or houses that produce more energy than they need and contribute to the grid.

The "Preconditional"

We need many basic planetary functions to support a working economy and pursue a decent quality of life. Jonathan Porritt, cofounder of the Forum for the Future in England, described the challenge this way: "If we can't secure our own biophysical survival, then it is game over for every other noble aspiration or venal self-interest that we may entertain ... [A]ll else is conditional upon learning to live sustainably within the Earth's systems and limits. Not only is the pursuit of biophysical sustainability nonnegotiable; it's preconditional."[12]

This word *preconditional* is startling in its brutal simplicity. The message is clear: if we don't protect our natural capital, those assets on the balance sheet of the world, we'll go bankrupt and we'll stop functioning.

Or shoes you can bury when you're done with them and they'll biodegrade, releasing seeds that grow into trees. Or farmland that is managed so that it sucks a massive amount of carbon out of the air. These things exist now.

Circularity

One key way to get to zero impacts is to close every loop we can. Our current system throws out a lot of valuable stuff. Consulting giant McKinsey calculated that a "circular economy," one that reuses dramatically more products, components, and "precious material," would be worth up to $630 billion per year in the European Union economy.[13] Globally, the value of circularity is in the trillions.

By avoiding the mining, harvesting, and processing of raw resources, the use of recycled materials translates into radically reduced impacts and big savings. A number of industries, particularly aluminum, steel, cement, plastics, and paper, are well aware of these economics—recycled steel, for example, saves from 40 to 75 percent of the energy required to make virgin steel.

One sector, apparel, is diving into this arena with both feet. Patagonia, probably the first clothing company to take back products for recycling, is launching circular products like a new flip-flop that can be recycled back into more flip-flops. Puma has produced a collection of "cradle-to-cradle-certified" footwear, apparel, and accessories, including the Puma Track Jacket made from 98 percent recycled polyester from used bottles.[14] As part of its Shwop campaign to collect old clothes, British retailer Marks & Spencer sells a coat made from recycled, collected fibers. North Face has its own similar initiative, called Clothes the Loop. And Nike, never one to be outdone, recently created a concept store in Shanghai made entirely of trash (including reused materials from more than 5,000 aluminum cans, 2,000 water bottles, and 50,000 CDs and DVDs).[15]

These efforts are all a good start, but a true circular economy will require many new technologies, some forethought in design, and challenges to environmental sacred cows, such as what we mean by "green" and whether "natural" is always preferable. For example, life-cycle studies often show that the lowest-impact option for apparel is polyester, not organic cotton.

All three principles—decoupling, regeneration, and circularity—are increasingly part of the current management toolkit, not part of a distant future. Rupert Stadler, the chairman of the board of automaker giant Audi, says it well: "The circular economy and the decoupling of growth and impact isn't a future trend—it's our current reality."[16]

Decoupling, regeneration, and circularity combine to tell a simple story: in the natural world, nothing goes to waste. The last two principles in particular are arguably the core operating principles of nature. Our planet is a closed system, with the pivotal exception of solar energy (and the occasional meteor that wipes out dinosaurs or scares commuting Russians). What dies or decomposes is eaten or used by something else.

With principles honed over 5 billion years, the natural world is the ultimate efficiency machine, and we would be wise to learn from it. Our mechanical and people-focused systems can mimic these fundamental precepts while adding our own ingenuity to the mix. We can give the system a modern, human twist. The idea of emulating nature in business, made famous by biologist Janine Benyus, who coined the term *biomimicry*, can feel squishy. But it has a hard logic to it. Nature plays a harsh game of survivor, brutally winnowing out the weakest ideas from trillions of experiments. It's the best-funded, longest-lasting lab in history.

In his book *Antifragile*, Nassim Taleb expresses intense respect for what nature has produced. The longer things last, he says, the more they've demonstrated resilience and strength. As he says, "my deference to Mother Nature is entirely statistical and risk-management-based."[17] In other words, it would defy logic not to learn from nature's best practices.

These three foundational principles are at the core of a Big-Pivot world. The implications of thinking and operating by these principles are profound, and they lead directly to the other system conditions laid out in the Big-Pivot column of table 4-1. They also provide a roadmap to the strategies we'll need. Turning the principles—really, the preconditions for a sustainable world—into reality will require many radically practical strategies. Among these are longer-term thinking about value, the use of science-based goals, and the pursuit of heretical innovation (the elements of the *Vision Pivot*). We must also learn to value and internalize externalities, guide policy and regulations for competitive or communal advantage, and form collaborative and precompetitive partnerships that create shared value. Finally, we need to focus on building into our systems resilience, not just reducing risk. All these strategies are the focus of part 2 of this book.

Before moving on, I have two additional thoughts on how we'll successfully make what is ultimately a deep transformation in how business operates. First, my work, and much of this book, examines the fundamental underpinnings of our economy and society—the biophysical capacity of the planet to support us. But obviously, there is no society, and no saving of society, without people. We need to be *inclusive* and seek insight and help from people of all backgrounds, because everyone has a stake in our collective future. Moreover, the solutions we come up with will be most effective and most creative if we draw on everyone's perspective and contributions.[18]

Second, with mega challenges creating business-threatening risks and enormous opportunities, this pursuit of sustainability, or whatever we choose to call it, needs to be *well funded and integrated*. In most companies, the executive responsible for thinking about mega challenges and crafting a response is respected—frequently coming from a serious line operating job and often moving on to another senior position—but rarely given the resources he or she needs. Telling an executive to use influence and a matrix organization to make change happen is a cop-out.

For every one of these executives lucky enough to have a boss like Paul Polman at Unilever or Muhtar Kent at Coca-Cola (Kent has declared that *he* is the chief sustainability officer), there are a hundred more at companies without that level of CEO support. The budgets set aside for managing environmental and social risks and opportunities are small and seem to be on the chopping block at any sign of economic distress. Now imagine the same being said for your chief marketing, financial, procurement, or manufacturing officer. Absurd, right?

In a Big-Pivot world, we're going to build companies and economies that borrow the best from nature. We'll then add our own ingenuity, reduce our footprint down to zero (or even restore resources), and decouple growth in material well-being from physical inputs. And the systems we'll build will focus on the long term and will be science-based and data-guided, heretical, collaborative, resilient, inclusive, and well-funded.

It sounds beautiful, but getting there won't be easy and there may be a few hurdles along the way.

The Macro and Micro Problems

To put the barriers blocking the pivot into context, let's examine capitalism, the global victor in centuries of economic experimentation, in a clear, practical light. By its very nature, capitalism can present big hurdles to a sustainable world, but it may also offer the best hope if we use it right.

Capitalism's Strengths—and Flaws

Winston Churchill famously said, "Democracy is the worst form of government except all those other forms that have been tried." Similarly, capitalism is the best economic system we've hit upon—and it's arguably much better than "the worst except for all the others." No other system has come close to its efficiency in matching solutions to needs, capital to ideas, and people to work that needs doing.

But losing critical perspective on capitalism and assuming it has no imperfections is dangerous. Capitalism is a complex set of equations that solve for a range of outcomes, but it does not inherently optimize conditions for our survival. We could easily utilize this powerful, brutally efficient system to speed up our demise—and that's exactly the problem. Corporations, using markets and capitalism to their ultimate ends, will drain *shared* resources such as fisheries, clean water, or a stable climate with ruthless precision.

Drawing from some key thinkers who have come before me, and from my own work, I see a few macro-level thematic problems with the current capitalist system:[19]

- A monumental failure to value what economists call *externalities*, those inputs into the economy (natural capital) and outputs or impacts from that economy (pollution, climate change, and so on) that fall outside the normal workings of the market

- A systematic bias against the future, with discount rates that make benefits in the longer term worthless (or as asset manager Jeremy Grantham put it memorably, the use of discount rates means that "your grandchildren have no value")

- An unshakable belief in unfettered markets and Adam Smith's "invisible hand" to solve any problem

- The use of flawed metrics, especially GDP, which take stock of some of the wrong things (e.g., negative outcomes like disease and oil spills *increase* GDP) and fail to measure prosperity

- An unthinking drive toward "maximizing" growth itself, rather than optimizing for value and well-being, plus a complete lack of recognition of the impossibility of continued exponential growth

- The historic and growing gap between the rich and poor

- The systematic alienation of segments of society and voices in the global discourse (although technology is now connecting us all, giving the disenfranchised a megaphone)

- An inability to deal with large, systemic, and long-term threats to society and economies

To call all of these issues flaws may not be accurate. As Hunter Lovins, a longtime thinker about our economic system, told me, "the real issue is that we are practicing *bad* capitalism." In *Natural Capitalism*, Lovins and her coauthors created and then debunked a devastating list of the "fantasies" inherent in an economist's definition of a free market. The illusions include perfect information; the widespread pursuit of maximum personal utility; and the absence of monopolies, subsidies, barriers, friction, or any other distortions in how markets would optimally operate.[20]

But we can address all of these problems. Putting a number on the things we don't currently value, for example, is a core tactic that will close many gaps. With the right valuations, such as a price on carbon, markets can do their magic.

And magic is often the right word. We generally accept capitalism as the economic victor for good reason. The system has tremendous strengths. None of the books or theories I draw on—and most certainly not this one—are anticapitalist or anticorporate screeds. I'm not against markets, making money, or even making a lot of money.

But we can't prioritize short-term profit maximization and an idealized version of markets over ensuring our prosperity and survival. If we don't make solving the challenges of climate change and resource scarcity the core pursuit of business and society, we won't be maximizing value, or even profits, at all—we'll be ensuring a great deal of pain, scarcity, and human and financial loss.

The challenges to capitalism correspond closely with other questions the private sector is facing today. Business is at a historic low point in popularity. Strategy guru Gary Hamel put it this way in the foreword to Umair Haque's book, *The New Capitalist Manifesto*: "I may be an ardent supporter of capitalism—but I also understand that while individuals have inalienable, God-given rights, corporations do not ... Executives need to understand that today they face the same hard choices that confront every teenager—drive responsibly or lose your license."[21]

Luckily, the next wave of corporate leaders is very much ready to question how the system works and perhaps to fix its battered reputation. When Harvard Business School professor Rebecca Henderson launched a new class, Reimagining Capitalism, she thought the elective would attract a normal number of students, perhaps in the dozens. But during the latest term, 400 students—nearly half the graduating class—wanted in.[22]

The Big Pivot is, to a large extent, about rethinking how capitalism and companies operate and how we can leverage them to create a more prosperous world for all.

The Four Big Hurdles Blocking the Big Pivot

While the macro-level concerns are compelling, I'm more focused on how it plays out at the microeconomic level. In other words, what is standing in the way of corporations making the Big Pivot, and what are the possible solutions? Table 4-2 summarizes those corporate-level hurdles and the key strategies for leaping over them (and lists the chapters that address these ideas). For each issue, companies need to solve a unique set of challenges. Let's

TABLE 4-2

Big Pivot hurdles and solutions

Hurdle	Solutions (corporate level)	Chapter
Scale (and interconnectedness)	• Data and feedbacks (circular)	3, 4
	• Radical efficiency (big goals)	6
	• Resilience planning	14
	• New technologies, products, services	7, 13
Time frames (short-termism)	• Incentives	5, 8
	• Big, science-based goals	6
Valuation (what's not measured)	• Internal policy	9
	○ Modified investment tools (ROI)	
	○ New valuation tools	
	• Valuing externalities	10
	• Influencing policy (external)	11
Silos	• Systems and value-chain thinking	All
	• Transparency, dialogue	3, 12
	• Open innovation	7, 12
	• Partnership	12

now look at the four main barriers that most companies and organizations face.

Scale and Interconnectedness

This point may seem obvious, but the planet-scale challenges we face are so huge, they are often hard to grasp. And they're deeply intertwined in complicated ways. The food-energy-water "nexus" that I discussed in chapter 2 makes it clear that we're all connected. The scale alone can cause your brain to shut down. As we try to comprehend the math of climate change, we wonder, "What's a gigaton of carbon, let alone 565 of them?"

The size of any solution needs to match the scale of the challenge. So only through *radical efficiency*—say, 80 to 100 percent improvements—will we bring some problems down to a manageable scale. We'll need good data and other feedback mechanisms to track our progress. The innovation in technologies, products, and services must be disruptive and heretical. Finally, given the level of uncertainty, the prudent and logical path is to build resilient companies and systems that can handle whatever the world throws at us.

Short-Termism

John Bogle, the legendary investor and founder of Vanguard, opens his foreword to the fascinating book *Saving Capitalism from Short-Termism* this way: "I am profoundly concerned about the overbearing focus of our financial markets on short-term movements in stock prices, at the expense of the traditional focus on the long-term creation of intrinsic corporate value."[23]

And it's not just Wall Street. If there's anyone more concerned about stock price than investors, it's the executives at public companies with lots of stock options. When you're focused only on the next few months, it's hard to invest for the long haul in anything—products, ideas, people, new markets—let alone more controversial topics such as climate change and resource constraints. To make the Big Pivot, we need to think beyond the easy wins (reductions in energy, water, and waste) and make some big bets for the long haul.

A relentless focus on the short term is standing firmly in our way. And so this hurdle and some of its solutions will be the focus of chapter 5, the first radically practical strategy to drive the pivot.

Valuation Gaps (What Is Not Measured)

In business, we invest time, money, and resources according to estimates of the value we'll reap. In many cases, benefits that are hard to value are, in a painful shorthand logic, assumed to have *no* worth. Some of the things we don't value are described right-fully as externalities, but many others are real benefits or risks that may deeply impact the value of the enterprise, albeit indirectly—we just don't put a number on them. These intangibles include brand value, a license to operate, customer loyalty, and the ability to attract and retain the best people.

Short-termism and valuation problems combine to form the core blockade to the Big Pivot. To get around them, we'll need new incentives so that people do what's right for the long haul. We'll need science-based goals that recognize and work within physical realities, and we'll need to modify our tools for making investments, such as ROI. And since companies cannot easily put a value on some things, like the societal impact of carbon pollution, without some risk of competitive disadvantage, they will need to wade into policy and lobbying in new ways.

Silos

All of the Big-Pivot principles and solutions add up to one thing: a holistic, systems view of the world. We're all connected, like it or not, so we'd better act as if it were true. Climate change; resource constraints; the link between food, energy, and water; the new openness—all of these are perfect examples of systems with deep and complex interconnections. But we're not set up to deal with them.

Ever since the process-efficiency days of Henry Ford and Frederick Taylor a century ago, we've focused on linear efficiency. We may not have as many assembly lines anymore, and we do love our matrix organizational structures, but big enterprises still deal with issues mainly in step-by-step fashion. People specialize.

Linear isn't bad—it gets stuff done. But we're facing issues that require not just logic, but also empathy and understanding about the ripple effects of our actions. We need to work across normal boundaries and move to systems-based thinking.[24] We must draw on open innovation and leverage transparency. In doing so, we'll create different kinds of partnerships that will both challenge how we think about competition and blur the lines between supplier, employees, and customers. The tools for breaking down corporate and societal silos are emerging and evolving, but we also need to break down some of the barriers in our own minds.

The Final Hurdle: Us

Many aspects of how we view the world can get in the way of change.[25] Most of these psychological issues fall outside the scope of this book, but we need to keep some barriers in mind as we explore the radically practical strategies of the Big Pivot.

First, we all use similar processes to interpret the world, such as the *confirmation bias*, the tendency to seek only information that supports our current views. Or the tendency to think that events for which we have a clear example (e.g., 9/11 and other acts of terrorism) are more likely than the things we can't picture easily (like climate change).[26] We also have what some social scientists have reported on as a "finite pool of worry," which leads to the classic urgent-versus-important dilemma.[27]

We evolved to recognize threats that are visible, credible, short-term, and right in front of our face, so for many problems, it's out of sight, out of mind. A problem like climate change, which is basically slow-moving, remote, invisible, and the responsibility of billions of people, is hard for us to grasp. And our trouble with numbers that are moving exponentially, such as population or resource use, drives some wishful thinking about how long our consumption can continue to grow (trust me, it's not indefinitely).[28]

Finally, we all bring our own values and personal connections to the table. It's nearly impossible to predict what's going to cause executives or political leaders to reassess how they've looked at the world. Often, the personal pivot happens after a conversation with a child or grandchild shifts a person's view and values subtly or profoundly.

Playing on all of these leanings, we also have to deal with purposeful misinformation. To be blunt, there's been a concerted effort for years, funded mainly by fossil fuel interests, to undermine climate science. And the media seems content to present every issue as if there are two equal sides.

In total, the list of hurdles can seem daunting. But hurdles create real opportunities. Martin Senn, CEO of Zurich Insurance Group, points out that "the world is more complex, and risks are more interconnected; but a complex world is an opportunity, if you can deal with its complexity."[29]

So if we understand the challenges and then quickly outline the most logical strategies for changing how we operate—and this is, at heart, the purpose of this book—then we can change course in time and profit from it. We can build a much more prosperous and much safer world.

The number of people concerned about the future and starting to pivot is growing into an army. Many people are working across several disciplines to hack through these hurdles and apply new principles. So even with the hurdles in our way, I'm optimistic.

With that all in mind, let's now dive into the radically practical strategies that enable the Big Pivot.

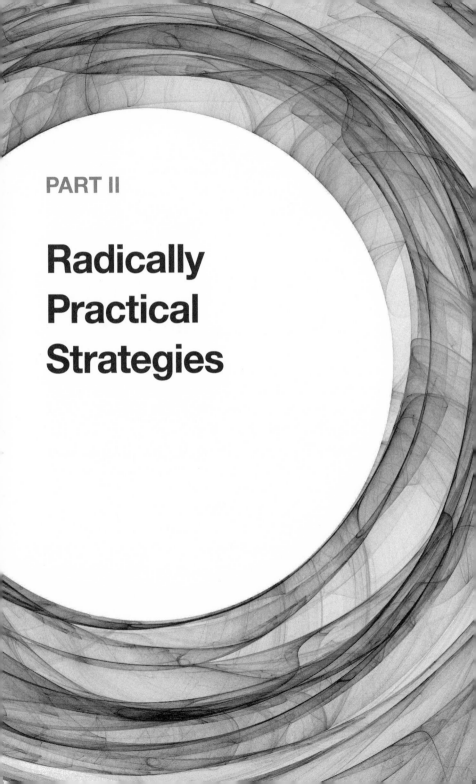

PART II

Radically
Practical
Strategies

The late, great entrepreneur Ray Anderson often talked about his famous "spear in the chest" conversion. His story is about how he read *The Ecology of Commerce* by Paul Hawken and instantly saw the world differently. It was this profound, personal pivot in perspective that set Anderson's life in a new direction. He pointed the company he founded, Interface Flooring, toward "mount sustainability" with the most aggressive green corporate goals in the world, years ahead of nearly everyone else. Today, the company is still climbing the mountain, on its way to becoming a zero-impact, or even regenerative, enterprise.

Which Is the Circle, and Which Is the Square?

A few years ago, I saw Anderson give a speech. During the Q&A portion of his presentation, Anderson said something fascinating that captures the spirit of the Big Pivot. A young man stood up and said, "Mr. Anderson, I'm in business school. How do I know whether my professors really 'get' sustainability?"

Anderson replied simply, "Draw a circle with a square inside it. Ask your professors which one is the environment and which one is business." (See figure P2-1.)

We grow up, in life and in business, taking an awful lot of our world for granted. We treat environmental issues as a niche area of business operations. But in reality, we are the niche. Every human endeavor, all our hopes and dreams, our very lives and

FIGURE P2-1

The square and the circle

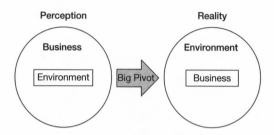

Source: Andrew Winston interpretation of Ray Anderson comments.

existence depend on our one planet. This is not hippie earth-love philosophy; it's just reality.

I've spent years trying to understand this deep truth, train myself not to ignore it, and grapple with its repercussions for business. When you truly internalize Anderson's simple lesson, you've started to pivot.

But knowing something and acting on it are very different things. We need a toolkit to act on this new understanding. So we now turn to the 10 radically practical strategies that will help your company make the Big Pivot. But before getting started, a reminder: this book is intended to provide a road map, not an encyclopedia. It's a strategic guide, so the descriptions that follow are not meant to offer comprehensive or industry-specific plans for implementation. But each chapter will describe why these strategies are necessary, how they create value for those leaders who are already employing them, and how to get started down the path.

While meant to be succinct, the total effect of these 10 strategies should be anything but minimal. These ideas can drive a profound shift in how business is done. They are a practical response to the mega challenges we face, but many of these strategies will seem radical to most executives. As radical as flipping one's view on which is the circle and which is the square.

The Big Pivot Strategies

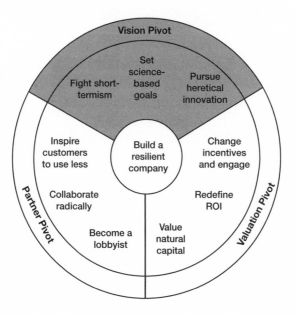

Vision Pivot

Set science-based goals

Fight short-termism

Pursue heretical innovation

Inspire customers to use less

Build a resilient company

Change incentives and engage

Collaborate radically

Redefine ROI

Partner Pivot

Become a lobbyist

Value natural capital

Valuation Pivot

CHAPTER FIVE

Fight Short-Termism

In a tough, but fair analysis of consumer products giant Procter & Gamble, *Fortune* magazine cataloged the challenges that then-CEO Bob McDonald was facing in early 2013—lost market share, reputational decline, and a general sense that, in the words of the chief marketing officer, "the organizational structure may not be right for today."

After laying out a compelling case for change at P&G, journalist Jennifer Reingold asked, "Will the CEO be willing to undertake real organizational transformation, which can depress short-term profits, at the very moment that Wall Street is clamoring for better earnings?"[1]

When I read Reingold's query, I thought that the whole article—actually, the whole magazine—should focus on what the question says about business today. If CEOs or boards cannot overhaul their organizations or make other investments because they might damage the current quarter's earnings, then how can these companies ever grow or innovate?

Imagine this scenario: It's nearing the end of the quarter, and on your desk sits a project that you know will make money—it has a guaranteed positive net present value (NPV)—but it would reduce your earnings this quarter. Do you invest?

In a study that posed this question to 400 CFOs, a majority said they would not do it. In addition, 80 percent of the execs would decrease spending on R&D, advertising, and general maintenance.[2] So what happens if you cut back on these things to prop up short-term earnings *every* quarter? Logically, you don't invest in projects with good paybacks and you underspend on initiatives that build longer-term value. Your earnings targets in future quarters actually get harder to hit.

While this study highlighted the short-termism plaguing corporations, it's not useful to just say, "Think longer term." As Kimberly-Clark CEO Tom Falk told me, "Great teams do both—they have a big vision, but they also get there by hitting short-term milestones."[3] So we need to manage for short-term value, which generates resources for larger investments, and simultaneously create long-term value. This is easier said than done, but the pendulum has swung way too far toward the short end.

Let's briefly turn from business to discuss personal well-being. Don't people have to balance the short and long run to create a happy life? In the very short run, the maximization of happiness would be eating as many french fries as you'd like and sitting on the couch watching Netflix. The long-term view would get you to the gym and eating a well-balanced meal. And it would have you investing your time in longer-term projects that are very fulfilling over time, but pretty hard in the short run (like getting a graduate degree or raising children). Your happiness, health, and survival are at stake if you don't balance short- and long-term thinking in your life. The same life-and-death stakes are at play for business.

What's at Stake?

A great deal rides on our ability to fight the obsession with quarterly or yearly results. In *The Clash of Cultures: Investment vs. Speculation*, John Bogle, founder of Vanguard, makes a clear connection between investor time horizons and how companies operate:

> Today's dominance of a culture based on short-term speculation instead of long-term investment has major implications that go far beyond the narrow confines of our financial sector. It distorts our markets and the way our businesses are run. If market participants demand short-term results and predictable earnings in an inevitably unpredictable world, corporations respond accordingly. When they do, there is heavy pressure to reduce the workforce, to cut corners, to rethink expenditures on research and development ... to "make the numbers" ... When a corporation's focus on meeting Wall Street's expectations takes precedence over providing products and services that meet the ever-more-demanding needs of today's customers, that corporation is unlikely to serve our society as it should. Yet that corporation's service to its customers and the broader society is the ultimate goal of free-market capitalism.[4]

How can an organization possibly make the Big Pivot—that is, focus on mega challenges first and work back to find the most profitable path to get there—if it has no leeway to think about the longer term? We can't tackle global issues like climate change and resource constraints without releasing the bonds of short-term thinking. The core of the challenge is the relationship between companies and their investors, be it public shareholders, private-equity owners, or even the various relatives who own pieces of a family-run business.

Focusing for now on the public shareholders—or what many are now rightly calling share*owners*—it's important to distinguish between a few groups: (1) the sell-side analysts on Wall Street, and (2) institutional investors, which are made up of both buy-side guys (big funds like Blackrock and Fidelity) and asset owners (pensions, retirement funds, endowments).

The sell-side shareholders are all about the quarter. The others are theoretically concerned with the long term. But as one CEO told me, "long term for the buy side is, like, 18 months," so they don't ask about resource constraints or climate change, either. The asset owners, in contrast, do appear to care more about the mega challenges and how their investments will hold up in a volatile world.

For example, the Association of British Insurers, which holds 20 percent of the UK stock market, has been studying the effects of short-termism closely. And institutional investors representing more than $87 trillion in assets are backing the CDP (Carbon Disclosure Project), giving added weight to the questions CDP sends out to the world's largest companies asking how they're handling climate issues.

For this chapter, I'm mainly focused on the more short-term buyers, the analysts, and the traders, all of whom are creating a market that has changed beyond recognition.

The Market Is a Casino

Today's stock market is not your grandfather's trading pit. One oft-repeated statistic is that stocks are held an average of 11 seconds. This turns out to be an urban legend, partly driven by the rapid rise of high-speed trading, which Bogle pegs at 50 percent or more of total market volume.

The exact numbers on this are hard to obtain, but it's clear that shareholders are not holding stocks for very long. Unilever's CEO Paul Polman estimates that "the average holding of a Unilever share in 1960 was 12 years; 15 years ago it was about five years, now it is less than a year. Our stock is not an exception." In *Saving Capitalism from Short-Termism*, Alfred Rappaport reports similar numbers. Professionally managed funds, he says, hold stocks for about a year, an enormous drop from the average seven-year holding period of 60 years ago. Even those numbers hide the effect of high-speed trading on the markets—sudden movements in stock prices are much more likely today.[5]

But then again, nearly everything is quicker now. The average CEO tenure in the world's largest companies has dropped from eight years to six.[6] Given their shorter tenures and the rise of fast, casino-like trading, some executives might logically try to match their strategies to the time-frame expectations of the market. That's unfortunate, since the CEO should be looking out for the enterprise and the employees, not just investors with short horizons.

Obviously we have an incentives problem here. Since most stock options have short-term vesting periods, CEOs are basically paid to keep the stock price up today. But can they hope to do that consistently in a market that has less and less logic to it?

Is the Market Rational?

Executives often tell me that they don't talk to investors about longer-term green initiatives because "their stock will take a hit." But if the market is rational, shouldn't that hit be very short-lived?

Two Key Issues

Most business leaders would agree that executives are supposed to create value. But is there agreement on what that means? Even if they took a long-term view, which piece of the financial equation are executives supposed to maximize, earnings or cash flow (or something else)? And whose value are they maximizing, shareholders or a larger group of stakeholders?

1. Shareholders versus Stakeholders

Many of us in the sustainability game have lamented that shareholders are placed above all other stakeholders, and we have pointed to this problem as the source of many of our ills. But Alfred Rappaport's *Saving Capitalism from Short-Termism* challenged my views. He makes the case that shareholder value isn't really the problem; it's short-termism and the definition of value. Rappaport describes maximizing shareholder value as "focusing on cash flow, not earnings; it means managing for the long term, not the short term; and, importantly, it means that managers must take risk into account. Instead, many managers seem obsessed with Wall Street's quarterly earnings expectations game and the short-term share price, thereby compromising long-term shareholder value."[7]

In other words, if your stock dips solely because you talk about strategic, longer-term investments that *may* affect short-term results, shouldn't value investors of the Warren Buffet type sweep in and bid the stock back up?

On the other hand, what if the market is irrational? Stock prices can bounce around for much weirder reasons than an investment decision. When someone hacked the Twitter account of the Associated Press and falsely reported a terrorist attack on the White

If you're creating value for the long term, Rappaport suggests, then you must take into account stakeholder needs. If you don't please customers, employees, communities, and so on—and you don't invest to do so—then you will destroy value over time. Basically, if your time frames are adjusted appropriately, shareholder value *is* stakeholder value.

2. Earnings versus Cash Flow

Considering the many ways we can measure corporate performance, it's odd that we've become obsessed with net income or earnings, since earnings may be the easiest number to mess with. Many companies— General Electric most notably—will "smooth" their earnings using a range of (legal) tactics, including timing restructuring charges and write-offs carefully, planning product releases to hit at the right time, and adjusting the level of cash reserves.

The legal accounting methods available to businesses are, to put it charitably, screwy. Wall Street likes steadiness, which is completely unrealistic in a volatile world. More importantly, earnings may be a poor indication of the real value of the company. The stock price should reflect an expectation of how much cash the company can generate over time—that is, discounted cash flows. Reality often diverges from theory, but the stock price should revert to a value grounded in something real or it's irrational.

House, the market lost $136 billion in seconds. Or consider the "flash crash" of 2010, when the market lost 9 percent and gained it back in minutes, all triggered by one large trade and then tons of high-frequency trading.[8]

And if the market is irrational, then why are we allowing it to set the direction for our businesses? Why would we make strategic decisions on the basis of what, in total, may be the demands of a raving lunatic?

A Giant Distraction

Investing legend John Bogle has said many times, "counterintuitive as it may seem, the stock market is a giant distraction to the business of investing."[9] His point is that the flurry of activity—only heightened by today's 24-7 coverage of markets—is unrelated to the business of accumulating assets and seeking good returns. It's economics, he says, not expectations or emotions that matter.

If the stock market is a distraction to investors, imagine how distracting it is to executives trying to run a business! Short-term investors can stand in the way of leaders making hard choices. A few years ago, *Fortune* covered the changes sweeping through an old industry, waste hauling. Waste Management's CEO Dave Steiner was trying to fundamentally change the company in response to deep market shifts. As corporate customers set and reached the goal of zero waste to landfill, the core hauling business was at risk. So, Steiner decided, Waste Management (WM) would increasingly shift its focus, making money from recycling, waste-to-energy plants, and other services such as helping customers actually *reduce* waste.

The plan was innovative, smart, and forward-thinking, and it reduced risk to the business. But analysts weren't too happy. One commented that WM didn't want to be a trash company anymore, but an "environmental services shop ... We worry they will get distracted. Steiner's got too much on his plate."[10]

It's ironic. Bogle says the stock market is a distraction, but this analyst basically says that managing threats to your business is the distraction. That assessment completely misses the fact that the zero-waste goals sweeping the business world aren't a mild hindrance for WM. No, they threaten the company at an existential level. The top line for pure-play waste haulers is going to zero. So WM had to change, and whether or not analysts disliked the story was irrelevant.

When I asked one *Fortune* 500 CEO (who wanted to remain anonymous) about the pressure from Wall Street, he said bluntly, "I don't know any CEO that would want to run a company the way analysts would want us to." It's not just about strategic issues—analysts are often unhappy with results that fall short of arbitrary growth-rate targets. A few years ago, Exxon Mobil netted $10.3 billion—in one quarter. But as the *New York Times* reported, "analysts were not impressed." Apple saw its share price plummet *after* one of the most profitable quarters in corporate history, mostly because Wall Street, again, wasn't wowed.[11] This insanity, a reality in our short-term, analyst-focused world, is pushing companies away from doing the right things, including anything truly innovative, for their businesses.

A Drag on Investment and Innovation

If the stock market is a distraction, what is it distracting us from? The evidence that the short-term pressure from Wall Street is hurting investment in innovation is starting to amass. In 2013, a report in the *Journal of Financial Economics* determined that "firms covered by a larger number of analysts generate fewer patents and patents with lower impact." So by this important measure of innovation, the more analysts watching a company, the worse the company performed. The report also concluded that the pressure to meet short-term goals was "impeding firms' investment in long-term innovative projects."[12]

When you're obsessed with your immediate numbers, you don't invest to build out capabilities and strengths for the longer term. In business, short-termism generally means playing it safe. Nearly every company I work with says it's a "fast follower." But always waiting, never leading, is a recipe for middle-of-the pack performance. First-mover advantage is not a sure thing, but on a philosophical level, how can you be a leader if you don't lead?

Analyst pressure is hard on innovators. Consider Google X, the search giant's semi-secret lab. It's one of the few corporate-run pure research centers spending money on heretical ideas and dreams. When asked about the investment in R&D, one stock analyst told a reporter that investors "don't love it, but they tolerate it because [Google's] core search business is firing away." So you have to have ridiculously high free cash flow before analysts "allow" you to invest in new ideas? In the same article, the analysts were meant to be comforted by the fact that "[Google CEO] Page has tried to appease analysts by saying that crazy projects are a tiny proportion of Google's work."[13] Think about how wrong this is—"crazy projects" are exactly what created Google and made it so successful.

In a profile of Apple, arguably the greatest corporate innovator of the twenty-first century, *Fortune* magazine described how far the company goes to avoid focusing on traditional financial measures: "It's a radical example of Apple's different course: most companies view the P&L as the ultimate proof of a manager's accountability; Apple turns that dictum on its head by labeling P&L a distraction only the finance chief needs to consider."[14]

To make the Big Pivot, we'll want to free up managers to think differently, as Apple and Google do. Tackling mega challenges can create value in the short run, but we will also want to make bets for the future. Heretical innovation that changes a product into a service or that drastically reduces material use and energy requires some leaps of faith and some funding.

Changing business models, or finding new ones to exploit, often means taking a short-term financial hit—but that's just called investment. And it's far better to initiate the change and profit from it than sit back and watch it erode your business.

HOW TO EXECUTE: THREE PATHS

The best way to lengthen your time horizons is to change the incentives, especially at the top. We'll look at this topic more closely in chapter 10. Here we'll focus on three paths to unhooking business from Wall Street's grasp or at least changing the conversation.

Again, I'm using "Wall Street" as a catch-all term for the mindset of short-term earnings obsession. Even private companies are working under many of the same misperceptions and demands—and many *want* to become public companies someday. In short, you can either walk away from Wall Street, talk to investors in a different way, or change the legal structure of the company to allow for maximizing value for all stakeholders, not just the shareholders.

Path 1. Walk Away: Let a Thousand Polmans Bloom

In 2009, right after Paul Polman was named Unilever's CEO, he told Wall Street that he would not be speaking to analysts so frequently anymore. Quarterly guidance was going to stop. I've heard Polman say, half-jokingly, that he made the move just a couple weeks into his tenure because he figured the board couldn't fire him that quickly. Since then, Polman has become a tireless advocate for longer-term thinking, telling the media, his CEO peers at the World Economic Forum (WEF), and almost anyone else who will listen why he has chosen this route.

"Unilever has been around for 100-plus years," Polman has said. "We want to be around for several hundred more … If you buy into this long-term value-creation model, which is equitable, which is shared, which is sustainable, then come and invest with us … If you don't buy into this, I respect you as a human being, but don't put your money in our company."[15]

Polman clearly has distaste for the "three-month rat race," as he calls it, and for some investor segments. He talked about hedge funds at the WEF meeting in Davos, Switzerland: "They would sell their grandmother if they could make money. They are not there in the long-term interests of the company … [H]edge funds undoubtedly have a role to play … but they might not have a role to play with companies like ours."[16]

Polman has probably freed up some time for himself and his company. One CEO I know had 200 meetings with the investment community in one year. Call that 30 days of effort—days spent selling the stock, not products. Days not spent building the bench of leaders, creating breakthrough strategies, or engaging with customers. Doing the real business of the company, focusing on consumers and solving real problems for them, Polman says, will ultimately reward the shareholder.

When Polman talks about what this all means operationally within the company, it should be music to the ears of value investors. "I want people to focus on cash flow," he says, "a much longer-term measure than short-term profit, which doesn't take cost of capital [or] capital investment into account." Day-to-day choices are different, he says: "It allowed us to have our people do the right things. We don't manipulate, now, the advertising spent by quarter or other things."[17]

So far the results have been good. As of this writing, the company's stock performance has matched or beaten the FTSE 100 index and key competitors since mid-2009. Revenues, profit, and cash from operations are up 29, 32, and 18 percent, respectively (through fiscal 2012). The company is generating an extra billion euros in cash annually, and revenues crossed the 50 billion euros mark for the first time.

Polman's approach suggests an unexpected question: if we want to get truly radical, should companies go private? Imagine the freedom of not having to talk to analysts at all. Perhaps, in some weird twist of fate, the companies owned by private-equity firms— which have the reputation of maximizing profit above all—have *more* degrees of freedom. At some point, the largest companies can't meet constant growth goals to make public investors happy anyway, so maybe these firms should get off the treadmill entirely.

Path 2. Talk to Wall Street: Tell Investors Why It Matters

Unfortunately, almost no companies have followed Polman's brave lead, but it's hard to say why. Maybe it's a combination of inertia, fear, and some legitimate concerns.

I heard the chairman of a large company complain that the CEO was far too focused on short-term cost cutting and should concentrate on innovation. But 20 seconds later, he said the CEO "needs to hit the numbers." When I asked whether his company should stop quarterly guidance to avoid this pressure, he looked at me strangely and said that analysts would build their earnings models anyway. My point was that perhaps we shouldn't care about analysts' short-term models and should focus on value creation instead.

But Wall Street is its own mega force, so most companies will continue to engage. And perhaps we should. As Johnson & Johnson exec Paulette Frank said to me, "It's like engaging suppliers in sustainability. If you want to see change, it may be better not to walk away, but to engage and try to help improve the situation."[18]

Companies should proactively talk to analysts about how making the Big Pivot creates value. Tell them why it matters. There are now a few leading-edge analysts who are listening, like Eva Zlotnicka, sustainability research analyst for UBS. Her job is to help incorporate environmental, social, and governance (ESG) issues into UBS reports and thinking.

Zlotnicka's former boss established at the top the tone that allows Zlotnicka to be a different kind of analyst. Erika Karp, formerly UBS managing director and head of global sector research, recently left to start her own firm. Karp says that "there is no dichotomy between long-term value creation and corporate sustainability," but that there's also a "deficit of long-term incentives and long-term thinking."[19]

Zlotnicka told me that there's a big opportunity for companies to "break the vicious cycle" of silence on these issues and build the discussion into mainstream communications to investors. While quarterly calls may not be conducive to having strategic conversations, there are many other opportunities. "It's meaningful if they use space in a report or website to talk about these issues," she says. It's about "integration, integration, integration" of ESG information into the annual report and all communications.[20]

A few companies are already changing the conversation with Wall Street. Kevin Anton, an exec at aluminum giant Alcoa, says, "We weave a sustainability thread into shareholder and analysts communications because it is embedded into our core business strategy. It's impactful to have our business leaders talk about how we create value for customers by improving energy efficiency in airplanes, cars, and buildings."[21]

Philips, the Dutch health-care and lighting company, talks to analysts about its efforts to make less toxic, more efficient products, even though these initiatives may raise costs at times. The company starts by putting the work in context and in traditional business terms. As North American chairman Greg Sebasky told me, Philips executives first talk about everything the company is doing to drive cost out of operations—from lowering supply chain input costs to running plants more efficiently—so the investors are comfortable that the company is still focused on maximizing value. By couching their work in this way, he says, "analysts wouldn't think twice about us spending more to create sustainable products."[22]

At software giant SAP, Peter Graf, the chief sustainability officer, worked with his investor relations team to develop an "investor outreach program." The purpose was to explain the connections between what Graf calls "nonfinancial performance" and traditional financial metrics. For example, initiatives that reduce carbon emissions, improve worker health, or increase employee engagement, attraction, and retention—critical issues for a software company, where talent is everything—create real value even if it's hard to measure. So SAP is now demonstrating to analysts, as Graf says, "how sustainability drives our ability to innovate and increase margins—two topics in which investors are vitally interested."[23]

Many other companies can make a compelling case for value creation around mega challenges, all in terms that Wall Street understands. Companies can learn from sectors, like pharma, that have found a way to talk about longer-term R&D investments and break them down into shorter-term accomplishments that investors like. Some companies, specifically Jones Lang LaSalle and Walt Disney Company, have ensured that the financial officers can speak the ESG language to investors by structuring the organization so that the CFO *is* the lead sustainability officer—an unusual and forward-looking approach.

It's not always radical for companies to talk about the long term to Wall Street. Amazon.com has made investors wait for steady earnings for 15-plus years—all with the logic of long-term investment, brand-building, and pleasing consumers. Many more firms can follow their lead.

At this point, the vast majority of analysts don't ask executives any questions about how the companies are handling the mega challenges. But Mindy Lubber, director of Ceres, a group working tirelessly to integrate environmental and social issues into capital markets, believes that "in two years, analysts will be asking these questions ... [T]he risks are getting too big to ignore."[24]

So why not start answering before they ask? Get ahead of the Big Pivot now.

Path 3. Redefine the Company: Become a B Corp

There's a fascinating movement afoot to create a new kind of corporation that allows executives to satisfy multiple goals, not just maximizing shareholder value. Much of the credit goes to B Lab, the nonprofit behind the B Corp certification, a rigorous process that gauges your social and environmental performance and requires you to change your corporate charter to reflect a broader mission.

A quick explanation of the landscape and three key terms—B Corp, benefit corporation, and flexible purpose corporation—is in order. *B Corp* is a certification, not a legal structure. Its name purposely distinguishes it from the C corporation (C corp), the dominant corporate form in the United States, and one that legally places shareholder wealth maximization above all else. The community of 850 certified B Corps in 29 countries has helped 20 US states pass *benefit corporation* legislation. The benefit corporation designation requires companies to focus on creating value for multiple stakeholders, not just shareholders. A *flexible purpose corporation* is yet another legal model, available only in California, that requires companies to specify an additional purpose beyond just maximizing profit.

Jay Coen Gilbert, one of B Lab's founders, neatly summarized the general idea: "If we're building a new economy that's more inclusive and durable, we need a new foundation, a new corporate structure ... and the only game in town that expands fiduciary duty is the B Corp. You commit to a higher purpose, you're held accountable, and you give the world more transparency about your performance so people can vote with their feet and dollars."[25]

In essence, the companies that have made the B Corp commitment are in the process of making the Big Pivot. It's a Who's Who of mission-driven companies such as Ben & Jerry's, Sungevity, Etsy, Revolution Foods, Seventh Generation, and Patagonia (which is not only B Corp certified, but is also the largest company to choose legal benefit corporation status).

But the core question is whether we need a separate corporate form to enable companies to tackle the mega challenges as part of their normal profit-making operations. The answer to this question could fill books, and I'll punt by saying yes and no.

Suz Mac Cormac, one of the lawyers who helped draft the legislation in California that created flexible purpose corporations, suggests that a new form may not be necessary. The well-established legal concept of the "business judgment rule," she says, already gives executives tremendous wiggle room to make strategic decisions without being accused of abdicating fiduciary responsibility.[26] This, I realized, is why no CEO gets sued for a bad Super Bowl ad or for investing in R&D that goes nowhere.

But in Delaware, where the most powerful attorneys and judges who influence corporate law work, the state's bar association has said that a new corporate form will be necessary. But necessary for what? Specifically, according to years of legal precedent, a Delaware corporation—which includes half of public companies and two-thirds of the *Fortune* 500—must prioritize shareholders. So if an entity wants to consider anything but shareholder value maximization, it needs the benefit corporation designation—or so say the legal powers that be in Delaware.

No doubt, it's a bit confusing. In theory, tackling the issues posed by the mega challenges will create shareholder value, as long as we define value correctly. So there should be no conflict that requires a legal change.

Nevertheless, both the benefit corporation designation and B Corp certification have some big advantages. They drive broader, longer-term thinking—as Coen Gilbert says, "it's an inoculation to fight the virus of short-termism." Companies that publicly pursue one of these options make an important statement that can help attract and retain talent. All current and potential employees will know that they can bring their values to work with them.

Organizations can also use the designation or certification to drive change up the supply chain and reward and encourage better business practices. The city of San Francisco, for example, gives benefit corporations a leg up in its procurement choices, and Philadelphia offers tax credits to certified B Corps. Finally, going through the B Corp process raises awareness and drives concrete improvement on a range of environmental and social issues. It's a tool to change outcomes, which is the end goal here.

The bottom line is this: to face the world's mega challenges, every company should pivot and become a B Corp, if not literally in name, then in spirit, in thinking, and in action.

Family-Owned and Private Corporations

B Corps and family-run companies have many similarities. For example, Lyell Clarke, CEO of The Clarke Group, recalls a conversation with another CEO of a family-run business about renewable energy. When Lyell pointed out that the payback on renewables could sometimes take more than a few years, the other CEO said, "Yeah, but in six to seven years, it'll pay off and I have no energy costs along the way! I'm still going to be here in seven years—it's my business—where am I going?"[27] It's a great point, but why should a longer-term view apply only to family-run businesses? Shouldn't C-level execs of large, public companies run them as though the firms were going to be around in seven years?

The Purpose of a Company

Kimberly-Clark CEO Tom Falk tells me that when he meets with investors, their "eyes glaze over" when he talks about longer-term initiatives such as the company's investments in alternative fibers like bamboo (which is the company's strategic reaction to the rapid rise of pulp prices). But, he says, "they're only one stakeholder." Falk focuses on two groups, "those with $40 billion invested and who want a return today, and the 58,000 employees counting on me to make the right decisions so they can feed their families and achieve their life goals. Often their needs are in alignment, but sometimes there are trade-offs."[28]

And that's why CEOs get the big bucks.

But one of these stakeholders has gotten more than its fair share of attention already. The trade-off is often not between stakeholders at all, but between our collective short- and long-term interests.

Who declared earnings growth the core pursuit of a company, above all other corporate goals? If you believe the best-selling business books from the last 25 years, companies are *In Search of Excellence* or trying to go from *Good to Great*. Nobody writes a paean to the search for 9 percent earnings-per-share growth.

Imagine for a moment that the proverbial aliens landed on the planet and looked at the financial statements of the largest corporations. Seeing tons of cash and healthy balance sheets, the aliens would declare the firms very successful, whether or not any of the companies had missed an earnings growth target recently. The big, profitable companies have the resources to do everything that executives might consider a priority in the long run—invest in R&D, pay shareholders well, build new businesses and hire people, or create a more sustainable enterprise.

It begs the question: What is the real purpose of a company, to maximize short-term earnings, or something else? A. G. Lafley, the CEO (again) of P&G, recently described his vision of a company's mission: "I believe very deeply the purpose of any business is to create a customer and then try to serve that customer better than anyone else."[29] This idea of focusing on solving a problem for a customer—or on something more than just profit in and of itself—is not radical. It's not new at all, and in fact, it's really old-school.

Robert Wood Johnson wrote Johnson & Johnson's famous Credo in 1943—just before the company went public—as a statement of values that was intended to guide the company's operations. It begins, "We believe our first responsibility is to the doctors, nurses and patients, to mothers and fathers and all others who use our products and services." After medical professionals and parents, he lists customers, then employees, and then communities. The last section reads, "Our final responsibility is to stockholders," who, when the company operates by the principles of the Credo, "should realize a fair return."[30]

In recent years, Johnson & Johnson—arguably one of the first B Corps in spirit—has reported annual net income in the $10 billion range, and $15 billion annually in operating cash flow. During its 70 years as a public company, Johnson & Johnson has been one of the most profitable enterprises in history.

It's not radical to move away from focusing only on the short term or only on shareholders—those obsessions never made any sense to begin with. In 2009, the hardest of hard-nosed CEOs, Jack Welch, told the *Financial Times* that the idea of shareholder value was the "dumbest idea in the world" and that pursuing it as a strategy was "insane." He went on: "Shareholder value is a result, not a strategy ... Your main constituencies are your employees, your customers and your products."[31]

The very best and longest-lasting companies of today and tomorrow will recognize that shareholders are only one group to please. The companies that make the Big Pivot will find themselves focusing on larger issues and a bigger group of stakeholders. And they will be more profitable because of it.

CHAPTER SIX

Set Big, Science-Based Goals

Let's go back to that ship filling up with water. Time is running short, and everyone needs to help bail. But how fast should we work? We could ask people in the boat how much they think they can scoop out in the next hour, and then suggest they stretch a bit. But shouldn't we first calculate how much water we *must* bail to keep afloat, and then divvy up the task? It's the only practical path, right? Anything short of that would be suicide.

Setting bottom-up goals makes some sense, but only if the targets have no larger ramifications or connections to the real world. Think about what happens when a company can only survive if it hits certain goals. Consider chip makers Intel and AMD, for decades trying to reach innovation targets driven by Moore's Law (doubling the number of transistors on a chip every two years) just to keep their products relevant in the marketplace. These two competitors couldn't use a bottom-up approach.

When it comes to the planet's ability to support us, and in particular the carbon reduction we have to achieve, few entities— companies and countries alike—are working backward from what we *have* to do. Instead, most organizations are planning forward from what they *think* they can do. So how fast do we have to bail?

Let's recall the simple, stark math. To hold the planet's warming to 2 degrees Celsius (3.6 degrees Fahrenheit), we must emit no more than 565 billion tons of carbon dioxide globally (and the most recent scenarios suggest far less). According to PwC, we have to bring down the global economy's carbon intensity (how much carbon it takes to generate a dollar of GDP) by an *average* of 6 percent annually until 2100. And since climate change is cumulative, the earlier the better.

Corporate Leaders

A growing number of large companies have set goals in line with what the science is telling us. Let's look at how they've approached the challenge.

Ford Motor Company's Science-Based Goals

Ford has had highly educated people on staff studying atmospheric science since the 1960s. The company knew about the environmental impacts of burning fuels and has had engineers redesigning engines to reduce emissions for decades. The focus used to be on old-school regulated air pollution: mainly sulfur oxides and nitrogen oxides (SO_x and NO_x), ozone, and particulates. But it wasn't a big leap to focus on carbon dioxide. As Ford atmospheric scientist Tim Wallington put it, "it has served us well to have people with in-depth knowledge of climate change and air pollution."[1]

What makes Ford Motor Company different is that they actually listen to these guys. Chairman Bill Ford has long had a keen interest in environmental issues. He made official statements supporting the science of climate change at least as far back as 2001. By 2005, Wallington and other Ford scientists were figuring out what climate change meant for the automaker. With senior executive backing, and science to support their position, Ford was ready to start pivoting.

At the time, the scientific community's best estimate on where to hold the line on carbon dioxide in the atmosphere was 450 parts per million (ppm). Scientists like Jim Hansen have since reduced the recommended "safe" level to 350 ppm, much lower than the 400 we've already reached. But working from the 450 ppm goal, Ford's scientists asked themselves how the company could help the world meet the target. Since use of the company's vehicles represents about 2 percent of global emissions, it wasn't an idle conversation.

The scientists mapped out a "glide path" to climate stabilization for the world, with two parallel tracks, one of which was a plan for the auto industry. The other track was aimed at the energy industry, for the simple reason that if Ford produces more electric cars, it needs a cleaner, lower-carbon electric grid to plug the cars into.

Ford also created a "technology migration plan" to guide its product development and to keep the company on the climate stabilization path. Under this plan, Ford will double fuel efficiency by 2025. It sounds tough, but Wallington puts the challenge in perspective: "If we went back 30 or 40 years and asked how we'd get vehicle air pollutant emissions down by over 99 percent, we would probably have said it was impossible, and yet we've done it."[2]

To meet its goals, Ford is pursuing three core strategies: (1) improving fuel efficiency by making better combustion engines, reducing weight, and improving aerodynamics; (2) exploring low-carbon alternative fuels with oil company partners; and

(3) developing hybrid and electric vehicles. The hard math of climate change forces Ford to map out which mix of the three solutions will help the company achieve its targets, and by when.

Without the science-based goals in place, and their regular product portfolio reviews to track progress, how would the executives know what percentage of Ford's products need to be electric by, say, 2020 or 2040? They wouldn't.

The business logic is incredibly sound. Ford executives believe that all car buyers now want four key product attributes: quality, fuel efficiency (along with low CO_2 emissions), value, and smart design (which underpins safety). Ford CEO Alan Mulally says that customers in different geographies once wanted very different things, but now, "all four of these requirements have coalesced around the world."[3] With fuel economy one of just four harmonized customer demands, leading in this area of innovation will drive sales and keep Ford relevant.

Second, the goals help create more certainty for the organization. As the company gets ahead of market needs and government standards, says Ford exec John Viera, "we can avoid the dizzying worry about what regulations could be and what that would do to our product plans."[4] And in fact, Ford's science-based plan heavily influenced the 2012 fuel efficiency regulations that put the entire

---

Signs of the Pivot: Ford

Consider this statement from Ford's 2009–2010 sustainability report: "By 2050, there will be 9 billion people on Earth, 75 percent of whom will live in urban areas. Putting 9 billion people into private automobiles is neither practical nor desirable."[5] Imagine that—a car company saying it doesn't want everyone in the world to own a car.

US industry on the same general trajectory (of roughly doubling efficiency by 2025). With a seven-year jump on planning for this mandate, guess which company was likely ahead of the competition.

British Telecom's Net Good: Thinking Value Chain

In 2007, BT (British Telecom) pledged to cut its own carbon emissions by 80 percent by 2016 (from a baseline of 1997 levels). The company is well on its way, finding new reductions every year, which is a difficult feat given the continuing massive growth in network volume. The efficiency efforts saved the company £22 million ($33 million) in 2012 alone.[6]

For BT, this quest is not a side issue. The company's goal to be "a responsible and sustainable business leader" is one of just six publicly stated strategic priorities. To support this goal, BT developed a new program called Net Good. The initiative's aim is to help customers reduce their carbon footprints by three times the amount of BT's own "end-to-end" impacts (which run from supplier footprints to customer use). This three-to-one ratio goes beyond radical efficiency to pursue a more restorative model, whereby BT's products reduce the total carbon in the world.

How is this possible? You have to consider the whole value chain. Teleconferencing is a prime example. By helping customers avoid business travel, the equipment saves more energy, in theory, than it uses. That "in theory" is a critical issue. It's hard to measure a reduction in something that might have happened. But for a goal like this, the exact numbers may matter far less than what the bold target does for the organization.

Listen to Kevin Moss, BT's head of Net Good: "This is how we get to our 'three-times' goal … (1) Improve the 'one' part of the ratio by getting better at measuring and reducing our entire footprint, including our products, and then raise the 'three' part of the ratio by (2) selling more of our current carbon-reducing products and (3) developing new carbon-reducing products that change our portfolio mix."[7]

With its unusual goal, the Net Good initiative is as much an innovation strategy as a tactical program: to hit the three-to-one target, the company will need to create even more solutions that help customers reduce their impacts. It's a lot like Ford's glide path and another example of a company starting to make the Big Pivot.

Granted, the strategy of reducing the customers' footprint more than the company's own does not work for every sector. It's particularly appropriate for IT companies (and this idea is a core pitch of IBM's Smarter Planet campaign). But it could work for any product that uses energy or helps customers reduce their foot-print, such as advanced building materials, new lighting systems, and water efficiency technologies.

For BT, it's a win-win proposition. By slashing its own energy use, the company is saving money and building a more flexible, resilient enterprise. And by establishing big goals to help custom-ers do the same, BT is setting itself up for innovation, growth, and competitive advantage.

Other Corporate Leaders

Ford and BT are not the only ones playing this deep, science-based radical efficiency game. Interface was perhaps the first company to establish aggressive goals to be carbon-free and even restorative, a tall task for a manufacturer of carpet—a product made with petro-chemicals. A growing number of corporate giants are now follow-ing Interface's lead and talking in similar terms:[8]

- HP has a program similar to BT's, called Net Positive. And in late 2013, Dell announced it's own value-chain goal, going further than BT, stating, "By 2020, the good that will come from our technology will be 10x what it takes to create and use it."

- Disney and Rio Tinto have set goals that shoot for a net positive impact on biodiversity and ecosystems.

- Korea's LG Electronics is aiming for a 50 percent cut in GHGs.

- Privately held candy giant Mars has committed to use no fossil fuels and emit no GHGs by 2040, and it says the decision was based on the science of climate change.

- Apple, BMW, IKEA, LEGO, Nestlé, P&G, and Walmart have all set "100 percent renewable energy" goals (most are open-ended, but IKEA has set a target date of 2020).

- Unilever's Sustainable Living Plan is filled with aggressive goals, and states up front in Paul Polman's CEO letter, "We will meet the United Nations' requirement to reduce GHGs by 50–85 percent by 2050 in order to limit global temperature rise to two degrees." You don't get much clearer than that.

- Similar to Ford's approach, Toshiba's strategy is to set detailed product targets based on one key assumption: that the world will only support billions of people leading affluent lives if we improve eco-efficiency (what the company describes as "mitigation of climate change, efficient use of resources, and management of chemical substances") tenfold between 2000 and 2050. Toshiba has set targets and metrics to track its progress on its "Factor 10" path.

- Tech giant EMC's carbon goal, an 80 percent reduction (absolute) from 2005 levels by 2050, was set "in accordance with the IPCC's Fourth Assessment Report." But, as EMC exec Kathrin Winkler realized, a 2050 goal leaves an awful lot of wiggle room to put off action. So, she says, EMC set aggressive shorter-term goals that would be elastic enough to adjust to changes in the business and still achieve a peak in absolute emissions by 2015 (another science-based target).[9]

All of the companies that are setting zero-waste goals—and that's a very large number now—are listening to science, or just to reality. To support 9 billion people with a decent quality of life, we'll need a closed-loop society where we capture nearly all materials to reuse in new products. So logic dictates we shoot for zero impact. Sony's Road to Zero plan takes this goal to its logical conclusion by shooting for zero impact across the company's value chain by 2050. That's the kind of goal that moves a company toward the Big Pivot.

HOW TO EXECUTE

Before diving into a list of quick prescriptions on execution of science-based goals, it's worth exploring one more detailed case study that reveals some helpful methods.

The Diageo Example

In late 2012, I was speaking to Roberta Barbieri, the global project manager for environmental sustainability for spirits giant Diageo. As we talked about how to set aggressive goals on carbon emissions, she casually mentioned that Diageo's North American

Context-Based Metrics

Science-based goals fall under a larger category of what some describe as context-based metrics. The scientific imperative to cut carbon emissions by 80 percent, for example, gives us a context for making decisions about our energy use. Mark McElroy from the Center for Sustainable Organizations makes the case that all sustainability reporting currently fails "because it does not measure performance against ... thresholds for what performance would have to be in order to be sustainable."[10]

Bill Baue, another context-based metric advocate, writes frequently about companies setting these kinds of goals. Kevin Rabinovitch, an executive at candy giant Mars, told Baue that it makes no sense to "base your decision to have a greenhouse gas emissions target on the fact that climate science has identified a problem, and then ... set a target that doesn't reflect that science."[11]

Whether you call it science, context, or just plain reality, the result is the same. If you're heading toward a cliff, and you're figuring out how quickly you want to reduce your speed, it helps to know how far away the drop-off is.

---

division—a group with $5.6 billion in sales and 14 production and manufacturing facilities—had already cut emissions by 80 percent.

The first thing I said was, "Excuse me?!" followed quickly by, "When can I come and talk to you?"

It started in 2008, when top Diageo execs decided to set some big goals. Before committing themselves, they ran the numbers on what it might cost to go entirely carbon-free. The back-of-the-envelope calculation was daunting (hundreds of millions of dollars) and included the building of bioenergy plants to power some of the company's largest distilleries. The executives settled on a still-aggressive goal of 50 percent, made it public, and, remarkably, crossed their fingers.

Environmental exec Richard Dunne took responsibility for meeting the target in North America. He suspected that building an expensive bioenergy plant was not the only way to get there. His team implemented a rigorous process of collecting ideas for emissions cuts and estimating the costs. Then they sorted the results, ranking ideas by net gain on environmental improvement and *then* by financial investment, grouping the ideas into three expense buckets: (1) low or no cost, "the no-brainers"; (2) some increase in operating expense; and (3) significant capital expenditures (like the bioenergy plant).[12]

Diageo's leaders initially thought that only major capital projects would reduce emissions significantly. But Dunne's process revealed a surprising number of no-brainers. As a result, Diageo North America cut emissions 50 percent by 2012, mainly using ideas from the low-cost group of initiatives. The projects ranged from easy efforts—like lighting retrofits, boiler upgrades, and installing variable-speed mechanical drives—to larger, but still economical, changes such as switching from oil to natural gas and cutting back from two boilers to one in a small distillery.

The next step—getting from 50 percent to 80 percent reductions—makes for another critical Big Pivot story, and we'll come back to it in chapter 9. But Diageo's example, along with other leadership stories, provides some guideposts on how to make big goals happen.

Executing Big, Science-Based Goals

Setting and achieving radical efficiency goals can be easier than it sounds. After all, Diageo made it happen pretty fast. But it takes focus and trust in the best science available. Here are a few guidelines.

Understand the Science and Global Goals When They're Clear

On carbon, the IPCC continues to lay out recommended goals, and scientists like Jim Hansen and Michael Mann help convey these goals to the public. An 80 percent reduction by 2050 (from 1990 emissions) is the latest *minimum* goal as of this writing.[13] On a range of biophysical concerns, the Stockholm Resilience Center is doing fantastic work on our global system boundaries. And on social issues, the UN Millennium Development Goals are a combination of scientific and moral imperatives, all grounded in real social and ecological limits.

Assume the Scientific Recommendations Will Become *Less* Flexible

The effects of climate change are moving faster, not slower than expected, so the 80 percent goal may soon be considered insufficient. In one year, PwC's Low Carbon Economy report went from recommending a 5 percent annual carbon intensity improvement to 6 percent—a sizable difference when the world is only reducing intensity at the rate of 0.7 percent today. Or on other issues, water is not becoming more available in dry regions. And when was the last time we saw a chemical of concern get the "all clear" from scientists? No, much more likely is a widening uneasiness resulting in ever-stricter regulations.

Collaborate with Others When the Science Isn't Crystal Clear (But Is Indicative)

For example, EMC developed its action plan on phthalates, the controversial chemical appearing in plastics and electronics, "based on recommendations from consortia such as ... the EPA Partnership on Alternatives to Certain Phthalates."[14]

Understand Where Context Matters

Are we talking about water? If so, then setting a goal for a global organization may be useless. Water will be a critical issue in drier regions, and less so in others. And what matters is how everyone in an area uses water, not just your company, so the metrics and goals need to cover the whole watershed. How about carbon? In this case, global science is the guideline. As context-based metrics champions continue advocating for change in how we measure environmental and social performance, keep an eye on the influencers that they're targeting, including the Global Reporting Initiative, the Global Initiative for Sustainability Ratings, and other standards-setting bodies. All have incorporated or will be adding more context-based thinking over time.

Set the Goal from the Top

This may be the hardest part—harder even than making the cuts. But it's not much more complicated than this. Diageo's executives set the 50 percent global reduction target because they "wanted to do something big."

Visit PivotGoals.com, and Keep an Eye on the Competition

If your peers aren't setting the big, science-based goals, it's an opportunity; if they are, better get going. The searchable database I'm providing at PivotGoals.com should help you get started (see the sidebar "PivotGoals.com" for more info).

Generate a Lot of Ideas

Use employee engagement tools to ask the people closest to operations. Then use open innovation to ask customers, suppliers, stakeholders, NGOs, and everyone else for good ideas.

Go for Scale and Quick Payback

It may seem obvious, but this was the secret of Diageo's success. Sorting all the ideas by largest carbon impact first and then by ROI hits both targets. And it's an important step for building buy-in since the quick return on the early projects will convince people in the organization to go further. In a study of 260 large emitters by the CDP (formerly Carbon Disclosure Project), carbon reduction efforts yielded an average ROI of 33 percent, with less than three years to payback.[15]

Use Available Tools to Create Your Targets

EMC went for something a bit more complicated than Diageo's Excel spreadsheet and worked with Autodesk's Corporate Finance Approach to Climate-stabilizing Targets (C-FACT) tool. C-FACT, much like McKinsey and PwC's work discussed in chapter 1, "calculates the annual percentage reduction in intensity required to achieve an absolute goal."[16] Basically, it helps companies create their own glide path as Ford did. See appendix B for more on tools and how to think about what your company's targets should be.

Believe That Massive, Radical Reductions Are Not Only Possible, But Also Profitable

This last point is critical. The opportunity is vast: according to the International Energy Agency, "four-fifths of the potential [of eco-efficiency and carbon and energy reductions] in the building sector and half in industry still remains untapped."[17]

PivotGoals.com

In an effort to understand better what kind of goals the world's largest companies are setting, my firm created a website, PivotGoals.com, to capture those targets and make them searchable. Companies can use this tool to benchmark and see who has set the bar on targets for carbon, water, waste, biodiversity, community involvement, safety, and much more (a similar site, cloudofcommitments.com, covers some companies, but mainly country and regional targets on carbon).

So how are we doing on setting science-based goals in companies? Not good enough. Of course, judging whether a goal is really based on science or works within the limits we face is not an exact process (see appendix B for more on setting science-based goals), but we can tell if a company is in the ballpark.

And most firms have not even entered the stadium. Of the world's 200 largest corporations, 56 have set a clear goal for carbon reduction in a major part of their business—manufacturing, product use, or supply chain—at the required pace (about 6 percent per year in carbon intensity improvement, or 3 percent per year in absolute reduction). It's a higher number of companies than I expected we'd find when we started the research, but it's clearly fewer than we need.

A few final, critical points here. First, as discussed earlier, don't be a fast follower. This is about being bold. We have to bail a lot of proverbial water, and we can't afford to be timid. And best of all, big goals drive big performance. The CDP study of large emitters discovered that "companies that set absolute emissions reduction targets achieved reductions double the rate of those without targets with 10 percent higher firm-wide profitability."[18]

Second, we need to set goals not just for our own operations, but for the full value chain (like BT's approach). And third, we have to be honest about whether we're really heading in the right direction, especially if we're setting what seem like solid, but ultimately ineffective, goals. Mike Brown, CEO of the South African bank Nedbank Group, says that if you know you need to go north, "then heading south, even more slowly than the rest of the pack, is still heading south." Our north star here has to be science. Brown continues: "The hard limits imposed by planetary boundaries define not only the direction of travel, but also the required rate of progress."[19]

To make the Big Pivot, we must create value through radical efficiency, reduced risk, heretical innovation, and stronger brands. That's the direction we should go. But it is only through science that we know how fast we must go.

CHAPTER SEVEN

Pursue Heretical Innovation

As mentioned earlier, Albert Einstein once said that we can't solve problems with the same old thinking. But he also reportedly said something even more enlightening: "If I had an hour to solve a problem and my life depended on the answer, I would spend the first 55 minutes figuring out the proper questions to ask."[1]

To tackle challenges as vast as climate change and resource scarcity, we need to ask the right questions. We need to pursue a deeper level of innovation that challenges our own long-held beliefs about how things work. In my last book, *Green Recovery*, I introduced the concept of heretical innovation to capture this idea of exploring what we take for granted. If the questions we come up with don't make us uncomfortable or seem odd (or even impossible), then they're not going far enough and we won't make the Big Pivot.

Heresies can be small or large, from redesigning a single process or product to rethinking the whole business model. Don't discount the smaller heresies—the vast majority of people in a company don't have the mandate to rethink strategy, but anyone in an organization can ask disruptive questions that profoundly change one aspect of a business. What makes it heretical is how deeply it challenges the conventional wisdom.

Consider the brief, enlightening story of UPS's "no left turns," a classic tale in the sustainability world and one I've told many times (including in previous books). The catchy phrase was a rallying cry for mapping out new delivery routes that avoided crossing traffic and idling at stoplights. UPS is saving time, money, and energy—85 million miles and 8 million gallons of fuel annually at last count.[2] The story wasn't unique to UPS—FedEx, Waste Management, and other fleets have similar approaches—but it is memorable and demonstrates the heresy idea. Imagine the meeting where someone suggested not taking left turns. Uncomfortable? Yes. Odd? Surely. Profitable? Absolutely.

Seven Kinds of Heretical Innovation

We can ask heretical questions in so many ways. Here are some categories to consider, along with some quick examples of the questions some companies have already asked.

Constraints Drive Innovation

The techno-optimist in me sees the mega challenges as simply constraints on a system. And as they say, necessity is the mother of invention. Jim Crilly, SVP of Unilever's strategic science group, describes the company's strategy of setting really big goals that force new thinking as "challenge-centered innovation." Similarly, Rohan Parikh, the head of green innovation at the Indian tech giant Infosys, talks about "unreasonable goals" as a spur to new thinking.[3]

Process or Operations: Could We Dye Clothes without Water?

Eco-efficiency is incredibly popular and profitable, so there are countless examples of companies using less energy, water, or material. But a heretical innovation goes further than incremental eco-efficiency (see the sidebar "From Incremental to Heretical").

Take the example of dyeing clothing, a shockingly water-intensive process. Adidas released an eye-catching statistic, which I double-checked because it sounded absurd. Picture the Mediterranean Sea, extending 2,300 miles from the Strait of Gibraltar in the west to Turkey, Syria, Lebanon, and Israel in the east. Now imagine this: every two years, just to dye our clothes, the global apparel industry uses that much water.[4]

Clearly this level of resource use can't continue in a hotter, scarcer world. So Adidas asked a heretical question: Could we dye clothes with no water? The answer was yes, but the company needed to partner with a small Thailand-based company, Yeh Group. The DryDye process Adidas is now piloting uses heat and pressure to force pigment into the fibers. The process cuts energy and chemical use by 50 percent and *uses no water.*

Nike has also asked many heretical questions about shoe production, looking for ways to reduce toxic chemicals in adhesives and to cut back on material use. During the 2012 Olympics, a new design—the Nike Flyknit—made its global debut. The upper part (not the sole) of this flashy shoe is knit from one strand of fabric, not assembled from different cut-out pieces. Compared with typical running shoes, some models of the Nike Flyknit reduce material waste by 80 percent.[5]

Product: Why Do Toilet Paper Rolls Need Cardboard Cores?

In 2010, Kimberly-Clark, the $21 billion company behind major brands like Kleenex and Scott, questioned the simple assumption that toilet paper rolls must have cardboard tubes to hold their shape. It developed instead the Scott Naturals Tube-Free line, which offers this household staple in the familiar cylindrical shape, but with no cardboard core—just a hole the same size.

The rolls go on dispensers as usual and hold their shape until the last few sheets. It may not seem like much, but this product required innovative new rolling technology, which the company hides under a big tarp when people tour the factory. It's been a successful product launch, part of the now $100 million Scott Naturals brand.[6]

So, does eliminating cardboard cores save the world? Of course not, but if it became industry standard, we could eliminate the 17 billion tubes we use in the United States every year and save fuel from shipping lighter rolls. It's a good example of heretical thinking since the core-less rolls don't use incrementally less cardboard—they use none. This may be a small example of the kind of change we can create, but that's the point—heresy comes in all sizes.

Even so, deeper heresies are waiting for most products. For many more product categories than we ever thought, the thing we buy could be turned into a service or eliminated altogether. Remember HP's reimagined server technology called Moonshot (see chapter 3). HP claims that their new product is the first "software-defined server," and that it cuts energy up to 89 percent and lowers cost by 77 percent. Or consider barefoot running as a heretical approach that goes even further than Nike's Flyknit innovation (asking, do we need shoes?). Or look at the business model innovation at TOM's Shoes, which sends one pair of shoes to the developing world for each pair you buy. The company has its critics, but it certainly shakes up the entire shoe sales model. Car-sharing companies like Zipcar—and all the new collaborative consumption start-ups—are all asking different questions about products and ownership.

We're beginning to go even deeper and reimagine products and services that are regenerative and improve the world with each use (such as, again, homes that generate more energy than they use). These ideas can sound out-there today, but what was once heresy can become standard very fast.

Packaging: Why Do We Need It?

Shoes always come in cardboard boxes, which are then placed in a larger plastic bag when you leave the store. In a creative piece of redesign, Puma eliminated the top of the box and slipped the shoes (in their topless box) into a tight-fitting, biodegradable sleeve called the Clever Little Bag. It's both a stylish and a functional way to carry your purchase out, and it reduces cardboard use by 65 percent.[7]

Kimberly-Clark sells the Neve brand of toilet paper in Brazil. In a strange, little heretical moment, product managers decided to reduce package size by just squeezing the rolls flat(ish), which shrank the dimensions of the multiroll package. At zero extra cost, the simply named Neve Compacto cuts out 13 percent of the plastic wrap and fits 18 percent more packages on a truck (which saves fuel), on retailers' shelves, and in customers' pantries.[8] It's a small, but interesting, brand heresy to purposely warp the shape of the product—until, that is, the customer squeezes it back into shape to put it on the dispenser.

Working with Walmart, HP ran an interesting experiment with its laptops. Instead of shipping the computers the normal way—with foam and cardboard pieces wrapped around both the computer and all the accessories—HP put all the components into a messenger bag that consumers could use to carry the computer. The company wrapped each messenger bag in a small plastic bag for security and placed three of these bags in a single cardboard shipping box. This outer box was the lone piece of packaging that retailers had to manage. From the consumer's perspective, the packaging was just that little plastic security bag, a total reduction of more than 90 percent.

HP came close to eliminating all packaging—now that's heretical.[9]

From Incremental to Heretical

I'm a fan of incremental, linear thinking, and action. Regular, consistent progress can yield amazing results. In strategy guru Jim Collins's *Great by Choice*, he describes one relentless commitment that helped Roald Amundsen win the first race to the South Pole: no matter what the conditions, his team marched 20 miles every day.[10]

In mega-challenge terms, we know how fast we need to go on some issues. We need to reduce carbon intensity (carbon produced per dollar of GDP) globally by 6 percent every year until 2100. It sounds clear, but there are three important reasons to think that incremental approaches are sub-optimal and won't get us there.

First, even 6 percent is a big number. If Amundsen had to trek, say, 100 miles every day to reach his goal in time, he might have rethought his entire strategy of using sled dogs—or waited 28 years for the invention of the helicopter. Second, companies often discover that slashing some input or impact by 80 or 100 percent is cheaper than making 10 cuts of 8 to 10 percent. The marginal costs of stepwise improvements tend to rise fast. Third, going for the big, leapfrog reduction also drives innovation—P&G recently developed a new plastic injection molding technology that they say will make their plastic packaging 75 percent thinner. And it could save them $1 billion in material costs annually.[11] Quite often, a complete rethink with a systems perspective is the better path.

Market: Why Can't Innovation Come from the Bottom of the Pyramid?

The bottom of the pyramid refers to the billion or so people who make up the near bottom of income distribution globally—those who have *some* disposable income and may move into the global middle class soon. For years, companies like P&G have been trying to crack this market by creating less expensive versions of their products, such as smaller, cheaper single-use packages of shampoo. But there's a growing recognition that the innovation required to serve a lower-income population can ripple back up the income ladder. GE, for example, built a simplified electrocardiogram that sells for $1,000 in India (instead of $10,000 in the West). Why can't the company take what it learned about using less material and simplifying design to sell a less expensive model globally? Given the natural-resource pressures we face, this form of what professor Vijay Govindarajan has called "reverse innovation" can be a powerful tool.[12]

Innovation Itself: Can We Invite Everyone into Our Innovation?

The whole idea of open innovation is heretical. R&D has always been a highly proprietary pursuit, and most organizations have a deep vein of the "not invented here" reaction to outside ideas. But some companies are realizing that we can't solve global challenges alone. As GE's chief marketing officer Beth Comstock told me, "We're looking for new models of innovation. We don't have all the answers or all the capabilities."[13]

GE jumped into the open waters with its Ecomagination Challenge, which were open calls for ideas on how to better "power the grid" and "power your home." Five thousand business plans later, the company and its venture-capital partners have invested $140 million in the clean-tech start-ups that they invited to the open party. Comstock said the initiative was eye-opening in that it "challenged our assumptions … Many ideas came in, and we thought, 'This is not scientifically possible,' but then we looked closer and figured out why it was."

Open innovation and its close cousin, *cocreation*, are great tools for bringing new entrepreneurial voices to the table to ask heretical questions. Programs like GE's Ecomagination Challenge may be our best hope for marrying big companies with small innovators, capital with ideas, seasoned hands with young voices, and practicality with heresy.

Consumption-Driven Business Models: What If We Asked Customers to Use Less of Our Product?

I've written often about how Waste Management (WM) was facing an existential threat to its business from customers' zero-waste-to-landfill goals (another business practice quickly moving from heresy to the norm). So WM is morphing into a company that helps businesses recycle and reduce waste. Or consider how Xerox, HP, and other printing companies now help customers reduce the number of printers they buy, which reduces paper use and cost. It's the deepest, and often the most productive, heresy to ask your customers to use less of your core product (before someone else does).

Unilever is also challenging core precepts of the typical consumer products business model. The company's Sustainable Living Plan is a clear, strategic set of targets aligned around the one big goal of doubling sales while halving its footprint. But this plan for improving Unilever's environmental and social performance—and for helping billions of people improve their health and reduce their own impacts—is not separate from Unilever's strategic plan. Most other companies that have any stated goals or strategies to manage mega challenges keep these plans distinct from the corporate vision. For Unilever, however, the Sustainable Living Plan *is* the company's strategic plan.

A few companies, like Patagonia, are pushing even further to ask whether selling so much stuff makes sense in a resource-constrained world at all. The company already guarantees its clothes indefinitely, offering to repair any Patagonia item no matter how lovingly used. But it's pushing even further than that, asking people to buy less. This is an even deeper challenge to the normal business model and to consumption-led capitalism.

Systems: Can We Work with Our Fiercest Competitor?

What makes the mega challenges like climate change and resource constraints so different is their scale and interconnectedness. We have to tackle these problems holistically, understanding the system we're a part of, and working with others facing the same challenges.

For years, beverage and food companies have been looking for alternatives to refrigerants that damage the ozone or otherwise contribute to global warming. Coca-Cola has worked closely with Pepsi and their shared suppliers to explore new technologies for vending machines. Think about that for a second: Coke and Pepsi working together (more on this partnership in chapter 12).

Just this one problem—keeping drinks cool—crosses many competitive, sector, and value chain lines. For bigger challenges, we're dealing with even larger, more complicated systems. Hannah Jones, Nike's VP of sustainable business and innovation, is a loud, clear voice in the call for systems innovation: "If we don't achieve systems change, then we might as well go home."[14]

Signs of the Pivot: Max Burgers

With more than $200 million in revenues, Swedish fast food purveyor Max Burgers is an unusual company. Starting in 2000, the company examined every ingredient to improve nutrition, reducing fat, salt, and sugar and eliminating genetically modified organisms and trans fats. The menu became healthier and broader than just burgers. On the heels of the popular *Supersize Me* documentary about the dangers of fast food, Max Burgers launched a tongue-in-cheek Minimize Me campaign. A customer, much like Subway's famous spokesperson Jared, ate only at Max Burgers for 90 days and lost 77 pounds. Max Burgers has continued to encourage customers to eat less meat, partly for health reasons but also because of the large carbon footprint of industrial, factory-farmed meat. The burger chain's mix of nonbeef products is now 30 percent higher than before it started these efforts, and profit margins run much higher than the industry average.[15]

HOW TO EXECUTE

Operationalizing the Heretical

It's easy enough to say, "Ask heretical questions," but not as simple to implement. Here are some top-line ideas, drawing from my own work in *Green Recovery* and from conversations with clients and innovators.

- **Think big and set big goals.** Again, when we set science-based, large-scale goals, it compels people to search for larger opportunities.

- **Start with value-chain data to identify big risks and opportunities.** With solid data—even if it's directional

analysis that identifies "hot spots" of large impacts—
managers can focus heretical questions on the right parts
of the value chain.

- **Formulate the right problem statements.** What are your
  biggest hurdles to achieving big goals and drastically
  reducing impacts? Unilever has posted online an open
  discussion under the heading "Challenges and Wants."
  The company is seeking solutions to big problems such
  as bringing water to the developing world (a critical issue
  not only because it's a deep moral concern, but also for
  practical reasons—because if there's no water, there's no
  market for Unilever's shampoos).

- **Take innovation ideas to extreme, but logical conclusions.**
  Managers running data centers can ask operationally
  heretical questions like, "Why can't we use outside
  air instead of air-conditioning?" but they can take it
  even further. Microsoft is experimenting with placing
  equipment outside under a tent (why do we need a
  building?), and many companies are outsourcing their
  processing to the much more efficient cloud (do we even
  need our own data center?).

- **Assume that any aspect of operations is open to heretical
  innovation.** UPS, according to exec Scott Wicker, sees
  its "brown delivery fleet as a rolling laboratory—we're
  experimenting with every technology you can imagine."[16]

- **Use open innovation and cocreation.** Invite employees,
  customers, suppliers, and the rest of the world to help solve
  big problems. Cocreation is meant to be smaller in its scope
  of participants, bringing together broad perspectives into a
  deep conversation. Make sure to get your newer, younger

employees involved—they take much less for granted and have deeper convictions about global challenges.

- **Show personal leadership (walk the talk).** Have senior execs take part in innovation jams and brainstorming. They should publicly generate wacky ideas and support pilot projects to explore them.

- **"Systematize" innovation.** Build formal structures around informal idea generation. Make green innovation someone's job within R&D, but also make it everyone's job informally. Emulate 3M and Google, both of which famously set aside a portion of everyone's time for whatever strikes the employee's fancy. But go further than this; make innovation part of the culture. As design expert Valerie Casey likes to say, "I'd prefer to be innovative all the time, not just setting aside time for it."[17]

- **Create competition.** Sharing data on sustainability performance internally can drive real competition and learning across divisions or products. Or utilize public prizes, like the X Prize or the $1 million Netflix Prize, which challenged anyone to find a better algorithm for movie recommendations.

- **Make little bets.** It may sound counterintuitive, but a heretical idea can start in a small part of the business, then be expanded rapidly if it shows promise. It's the core idea in Peter Sims's *Little Bets* and shows up in a similar way in Jim Collins and Morten Hansen's *Great by Choice*, which advises, "Fire bullets, then cannonballs." Try something different in a smaller way (one brand or one process), and then get ready to blow it out quickly.[18]

- **Reward the wackiest ideas, and celebrate failure.** Some public pats on the back and recognition for employees who show bravery and try new things can go a long way. Software maker Intuit once bestowed its Swing for the Fence Award on an employee who had developed a new campaign to reach out to young customers—although the initiative failed miserably. In the words of author and nonprofit expert Beth Kanter, "take a failure bow." Kanter also relates the story of Dosomething.org, which holds a FailFest once a quarter, "an off-the-record session open to all staff, interns, and board members designed to send a message: Failure isn't something to be ashamed of."[19]

- **Fail fast.** We don't have a lot of time to waste. If you're creating a culture where failing is OK and are making little bets, you should also be able to pull the plug on ideas quickly.

An Idea for Heretical Innovation: Build a Skunk Works

Companies should get comfortable with disruption and try to bring it on themselves. Any strategy that could cannibalize a core business will run into powerful resistance, so you should set up a separate unit to challenge business as usual. Call it a heretical innovation hub. Bring together cross-functional experience, as well as long-term and new employees. Charge them with (1) developing new products and services that help customers deal with global mega forces, (2) finding radical efficiencies in operations, (3) discovering deep supply-chain opportunities, and (4) redesigning the organization and culture to support profound change. Use the savings from the efficiencies to drive buy-in and fund the larger ideas.

The whole concept of accepting failure and shooting for deep, heretical innovation is tough for many organizations to embrace. But think about what you're saying if you *don't* pursue this strategy.

Ed Catmull, the president and cofounder of animation pioneer Pixar, points out that when you're doing something new, you're by definition doing something you don't know very well, and that means mistakes. If you don't encourage mistakes, he says, you won't encourage anything new: "We're very conscientious about making it so that mistakes really aren't thought of as bad ... they're just learning."[20]

Even with a forgiving attitude, it's a big challenge to overthrow the status quo. They used to burn heretics at the stake, after all. We'll need to be smart *and* brave. As Einstein reportedly once said, "Any fool can make things bigger, more complex, and more violent. It takes a touch of genius—and a lot of courage—to move in the opposite direction."

VALUATION PIVOT

The Big Pivot Strategies

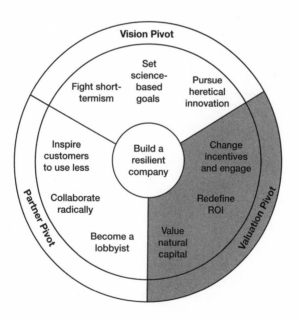

CHAPTER EIGHT

Change the Incentives, Engage the Whole Organization

It matters if employees are engaged at work. It matters a lot.

A Gallup study showed that companies whose workers are the most engaged outperform those with the least engaged—by a significant amount: 16 percent higher profitability, 18 percent higher productivity, and 25 to 49 percent lower turnover (depending on the industry).[1] The last benefit can save real money. Software leader SAP calculated that "for each percentage point that our retention rate goes up or down, the impact on our operating profit is approximately €62 million [$81 million]."[2]

Tony Schwartz, an expert on peak performance, describes an engaged workplace as an "environment that more fully energizes employees by promoting their physical, emotional and social well-being … and more specifically, the added energy derived from … a strong sense of purpose."[3]

Working toward the Big Pivot and solving the mega challenges facing our companies and our world are particularly good motivators. It's inspiring to work on something that's both profitable and for the larger good. Strategy guru Michael Porter talks about a key benefit of his shared-value framework: "You get a tremendous burst of energy in the organization ... people feel proud of what they're doing ... they feel like they're really making a contribution ... they're not just making money ... they're making money *and* ..."[4]

The "and" is critical—but how do we create this level of engagement? To boil it way down, there are two fundamental drivers of motivation. First, there's the intrinsic or internal reward that people feel from having a sense of achievement, being valued, or finding meaning in the work itself. It's about what executive coach Mary Gorham describes as "how much people connect with their own sense of purpose through their work."[5] Basically, people work harder and better when they care about what they're doing. Second, there are the external motivators, mostly direct rewards such as recognition, awards, cash, and promotions. I include both kinds of rewards in the general category of *incentives*.

People do what they're motivated to do, either through their own sense of reward or by what they're paid to do. Ideally both the intrinsic and the external incentives work in harmony. Before getting into what drives individual behavior, let's look quickly at one big driver of organizational behavior—its culture.

The Role of Culture

Culture is an amorphous idea, but it infuses every organization and deeply influences how people act and how they feel about their work. Andy Savitz, a consultant and an author, writes a lot about culture in *Talent, Transformation, and the Triple Bottom Line*. Savitz describes it this way: "When employees say, 'That's just the way we do things around here,' they are often describing the influence of culture. When they carry out some management dictates with enthusiasm, quietly ignore others, and actively resist or even sabotage still others, they are likely reflecting the values and assumptions of a corporate culture ... that 'feels right' to them."[6] Culture, in his description, seems to be a "you know it when you feel it" kind of thing.

Savitz pointed me to a well-known model developed by Edgar Schein from MIT's Sloan School of Management. The Schein model describes corporate culture in three categories, which Savitz paraphrases as follows:

1. What we do (the observable part of a company, its processes and actions)

2. What we say (the explicit statements like "Safety is our top priority")

3. What we believe (the "underlying assumptions," the "unconscious, taken for granted beliefs ... the ultimate source of values and actions")[7]

This simple but powerful model captures some of what stands in the way of the Big Pivot. In most organizations, the goal of maximizing profits is clear on all three levels—it's what's done and rewarded, it's what's stated, and it's what most execs believe. But when it comes to environmental or social performance, there's a breakdown.

A growing number of organizations, but not all, are taking some actions to reduce impacts (level 1), and many are making statements and putting out sustainability reports (level 2). But the belief system in many companies (level 3) still questions the whole endeavor. In my experience, many executives still believe that these mega challenges are overblown or will work themselves out. And most think that tackling these issues will be expensive.

In the short run, it would seem that the what-we-believe level trumps the other two. But how do you change beliefs, either personal or cultural? Perhaps changing the top two levels aggressively and consistently enough can gradually move the third. If you put in place the specific incentives that drive behavior toward greener operations and—this is critical—if people start to see the benefit and the value to the company, then beliefs will change.

The first step, then, is changing incentives to encourage longer-term thinking and pay people for different priorities.

Direct Incentives for Long-Term Thinking

We could talk at length about whether the absolute level of executive pay has grown to absurd heights. But for this discussion, what really matters is whether C-level execs are incentivized to do the right things. Top execs are paid mainly through bonuses and loads of options, and nearly all are rewarded for performance on short-term earnings and shareholder returns, neither of which necessarily ties to real value creation.

As Alfred Rappaport, author of *Saving Capitalism from Short-Termism*, says, "executives may choose to delay or forgo value-creating investments to achieve their bonus targets. These vital investments include research, new product development, brand building, and product and market extensions." Even multiyear incentive plans contain the same flaws: shockingly, only 10 percent of the largest 250 companies include *any* nonfinancial measures of success like quality, safety, or new business development.[8]

To solve this major problem with incentives, Rappaport offers a range of solutions, which I'll summarize in a few main ideas. We need longer vesting periods on options; delayed payout on those options (e.g., if options vest in three years, you can't sell the shares for five more years); and indexed options, which only pay off if you outperform a benchmark of peers.

These are good ways to change the time horizon on stock incentives, but there's also cash. Changing what bonuses are based on, from the very top down through the organization, can go a long way to changing priorities and indicating what the company really cares about.

Rappaport recommends paying bonuses to operational managers for driving long-term value: "Leading indicators look to the long term but demand accountability in the short term." He uses the example of a driver for PepsiCo's Frito-Lay. This employee's incentive pay could be based on metrics that measure how much shelf space Frito-Lay gets per store on the delivery route or on overall customer satisfaction and retention. For other roles in a company, the bonus could tie to the launch of a new product or to employee satisfaction.

Direct Incentives to Motivate the Big Pivot

Bonuses should encourage managers to take action on the mega challenges, not just day-to-day results. If they don't, what signal does that send about what the organization believes? Worse yet, when a company says it's committed to environmental and social issues, but does not connect compensation to those statements, the gap between rhetoric and reality may be more de-motivating than saying nothing at all.

Paying people for actions that support the Big Pivot sends the right signal as a direct reward, but it also triggers that sense of purpose that drives true engagement. I suggest linking pay to concrete actions such as reduction in material or carbon intensity (for a manufacturing manager), or how well suppliers do on the same issues (for procurement execs), or the number of open-innovation ideas collected (for R&D).

But what percentage of the total bonus or incentive pay should tie to these mega challenge actions? The more the better. One midsize company in the sand and mining business, Fairmount Minerals, has pushed the envelope on this topic. After employees suggested the idea at an internal innovation event, Fairmount made performance against key performance indicators (KPIs) for sustainability a whopping 50 percent of *everyone's* bonus.

As CEO Chuck Fowler told me, "We felt like we'd get exponential benefits by embedding sustainable development in our everyday work-life." And the incentives are working. In 2012, the company spent $6 million on its sustainability program and achieved about $11 million in direct savings and cost avoidance—a net benefit of $5 million.[9] Fairmount has also built deeper relationships with communities and with customers, who often ask for advice on how to build a similar program.

Fairmount has set the bar with 50 percent of bonus tied to sustainability strategy: I know of no other organization that has come anywhere close to that figure. But some large companies are starting to pay for Big-Pivot action as well—including the largest of all, Walmart.

Walmart's 100,000 suppliers know that the retail giant wants them to improve their environmental performance. The pressure has changed how thousands of products are made, packaged, and sold. But suppliers have repeatedly voiced one critical and legitimate complaint: Walmart's "merchants," the procurement managers with billions of dollars in purchasing power, didn't take sustainability into account when they made their buying decisions.

According to Walmart exec Jeff Rice, suppliers have essentially told the company, "It's great to ask us questions, but it only matters if you do something with the information." In their view,

Walmart was still buying mainly on price. But now, in addition to Walmart's laser-like focus on cost, its merchants must include environmental and social performance in their buying decisions or risk a weak performance review and lower bonus.[10]

Using data from The Sustainability Consortium (TSC), Walmart has mapped out footprint hot spots along the value chain of different product categories (for example, with a product like soda, the best place to target water and energy reduction efforts is upstream with sugar growers). Walmart then uses TSC's category-specific metrics to evaluate how suppliers are handling those hot spots. Based on both the heat maps and on supplier performance against category peers, the buyers must now create sustainability targets to include in their annual performance reviews.

The first merchant who designed a performance target was Walmart's computer laptop buyer. One clear hot spot in the computer lifecycle is energy consumption during the computer's use. For most laptops, a default power management setting determines how quickly the computer goes to sleep (if at all) or when the screen dims. But only 30 percent of the laptops that the merchant had been buying came preinstalled with the best energy-saving settings. This wouldn't matter much if we consumers changed the factory default settings ourselves, but Walmart's own research shows that most of us never do.

So the laptop buyer set a new target for herself: increase the percentage of laptops sold with the advanced power settings from 30 percent to 100 percent, a goal she achieved in 2013. Walmart has rolled out data-guided, footprint-aware performance targets to three hundred categories and hundreds of buyers covering 60 percent of US sales volume (about $165 billion in revenue).

The change in incentives is not minor. Walmart's Rice told me that a buyer's performance evaluation includes just a handful of targets, and all are discussed thoroughly at annual reviews.

Sustainability performance won't determine the entire evaluation, but it's high profile enough that it will affect behavior.

Incentives matter, and cultures shift over time. Hard-won operational changes like modifying performance reviews may not be sexy, but the results can be profound.

"Gaming" the System: Paying People with Fun and Valuing Their Input

I grew up playing the first generation of video games—hours upon hours spent with my Atari and, later, Nintendo. And if you call forgetting to eat being "engaged," then yes, I found games engaging. But what was once geeky is now chic—and mainstream. "Angry Birds," the popular game for the iPhone and iPad, has been downloaded a stunning one billion times.[11] The most popular video games now outsell the biggest movies.

The business world notices a large phenomenon like this and then figures out how to use it. For example, Toyota and GE have made a game out of searching for energy savings, bringing cross-functional teams together for "treasure hunts." GE has found $150 million of savings in its own operations and has also helped others do the same. GE Capital conducted a treasure hunt with ExoPack, a midsize packaging company, and found $453,000 in annual energy-saving opportunities.[12]

Companies are now transferring the tools and addictive qualities of gaming to other settings. This means using "game mechanics in a non-game context" (thanks, *Wikipedia*) and leveraging techniques like points, badges, levels, progress bars, or virtual currency to reward people for actions they take. The strategy, called *gamification*, is increasingly becoming big-business.

Organizations are using games to teach people new skills, encourage innovation, motivate employees, and attract new hires—the US military created an online recruiting game "America's Army." Practically Green (PG), a startup in the gamification world, describes itself as a sustainability engagement platform for encouraging employees to do more green things at work and at home. Employees can check into the system, take credit for their actions, receive kudos from peers, and earn rewards.

Susan Hunt Stevens, the founder and CEO of PG, is a keen observer of the gamification phenomenon and has a good view on what will make engagement programs like this really work for companies. "A great program has to be accessible (both on computer and mobile), measurable, and engaging," Stevens told me. "If you can't measure, you can't justify the investment. And you need to tie the program to the business results you're trying to drive."[13]

Appropriately enough, one of PG's clients is gaming giant Caesars Entertainment, which has used the platform as part of its CodeGreen engagement program. Yes, casino dealers are getting points to make their lives and workplaces greener. Caesars exec Gwen Migita told me how the company used the program at first to encourage employees to reduce energy and water at home, saving participants an average of about $400 a year on their utility bills.[14]

Then Caesar's used its CodeGreen program and PG's platform to gather ideas for improving the business. The company awarded employees points for two specific actions: "Submit a big idea for energy savings in the workplace" and "Lead an energy audit of your area." The first one, a good example of open innovation, yielded some great new programs. One employee suggested the company create a virtual warehouse, where properties that were getting rid of lightly used equipment—like refrigerators, furniture, or flatware—could post it for other properties to take for free. It's a cool form of corporate collaborative consumption that's up and running today.

Getting employees on board and contributing is important to Caesars. The company's CEO, Gary Loveman, has written about the challenge of integrating environmental and social priorities "into a company's DNA," and the importance of employee engagement to that goal. "True integration takes champions," he says.[15]

Gamification does a good job of getting people involved and creating champions, so it isn't just fun and games. Caesars has conducted studies that show an important correlation: the hotels with higher CodeGreen participation also have higher guest satisfaction and loyalty scores.

Intrinsic Rewards: Finding Meaning at Work

Direct pay incentives obviously matter. People do what they're being paid to do at companies. But at a deeper level, what if they know that what they're being paid to do is not quite right? Or to flip that, when you align people's values with their incentives, what kind of performance—and happiness and fulfillment—is unleashed? More specifically, consider the Walmart computer buyer again. Does she feel better about her job, or work smarter and harder, when she knows her actions have resulted in millions of people using laptops that save energy and money?

The answer is pretty obvious. The challenge is to align organizational values, the third level of the Schein model described above, with the personal values of employees. A single path to change, the external motivation that comes from shifting bonuses and key performance indicators, is not enough. Many companies now try to connect to a larger purpose and attract people because of that purpose. The B Corps are good examples of these more morally focused companies, but we can see big guys going down this path as well. Savitz highlights PepsiCo with its "Performance with Purpose" mission statement and Starbucks, which attracts employees with its stated values and its actions that support those values.

The agenda for change will need to include some softer culture efforts to create workplaces that cause no disconnect between home and the job, or between internal values and external behaviors. This means building meaningful work, a sense of teamwork, and ownership over the larger agenda—both through actual incentives and by really valuing people's opinions and letting them generate new ideas and new businesses. These shifts will build deeper engagement than will bonuses alone.

But what happens if you set out to change the corporate focus and values, in part by changing the "what we do and say" levels first, and the new beliefs don't fit some people? Well, in the words

---

Little People, Big Impact

Kids can be an important pivot motivator. So encourage people to talk to their children about the mega challenges. Consider Doug McMillon, the new CEO of Walmart. Back in 2007, when he was running Sam's Club, he read a few books on sustainability that influenced his thinking (including one of my own, *Green to Gold*). One day, McMillon asked his 11- and 14-year-old boys whether Walmart should care about this green stuff. The answer that came back: "Duh. We're going to need the planet." That was pretty much the whole conversation, and it helped McMillon connect his values at home to what he did at work.[16] I've heard similar stories from many executives. These personal moments with family can be profound.

---

of Jim Collins in *Good to Great,* you may have to get the "right people on the bus (and the wrong ones off the bus)."[17] Indeed, a few of the leaders I spoke with talked about losing some personnel when they started to pivot.

The CEO of one small company told me that a few key salespeople were uncomfortable with his new strategy of making nontoxic products and drastically reducing impacts. But most of the staff made the transition. And in one case, even when one longtime employee struggled and took early retirement, he still recommended the company to his son.

Changing the Culture by Force: Holding a Wake

A few years ago, executives at Nike knew they were making progress on environmental and social issues, but they felt it wasn't fast enough. They knew that to go further, they should embed green principles in the center of the company's innovation agenda. To move away from old ways of thinking, they pursued a "deliberate narrative shift," a Big Pivot in their approach.

The corporate responsibility team went to a jazz bar and held a wake for their current incarnation. Rising from the ashes, they renamed the group Sustainable Business & Innovation and then marketed the new shift internally. The team felt energized by a strengthened mandate to hardwire sustainable innovation into the business.[18]

Clarke Environmental, a midsize pesticide and mosquito control business, began its profound Big Pivot in 2008. Lyell Clarke, CEO and grandson of the founder, knew that things needed to change. He didn't have the words for it at the time, but he wanted to put his company on a new, cleaner, better path. But first, he gathered his management team, took them to the edge of a pool (in bathing suits, thankfully), and asked them to take the plunge with him—literally. It was mental reset by dunking.[19]

Through that meeting and a subsequent first-ever all-hands event, including reps from small offices around the world, the people of Clarke looked inside their business and culture. They thought hard about what they wanted to be, and considered what might stop them.

Preparing for the Big Pivot means knowing where you are now, roughly where you want to go, and what hurdles stand in your way. Not everyone needs to hold a wake or jump into a pool, but those two symbolic actions certainly prepared people for a new way of thinking.

HOW TO EXECUTE

Every company will likely follow a different path on driving engagement. Each organization will need a different mix of rewards that are external (concrete incentives) and internal (cultural shifts that create a sense of fulfillment and purpose). Some companies will naturally connect their operations to a broader set of goals and will need to call on specific rewards much less. But everyone should shift some of the structural incentives. The list of to-dos on that front is not overly complicated, even if there are some challenges to actually implement them:

- **Change options and bonuses for C-level execs.** Reward broader thinking with longer-term incentive payments at the top of the company (longer vesting, delayed payouts, indexed options).

- **Build green and social issues into key performance indicators and bonuses for everyone.** Fairmount Minerals sets the pace at 50 percent, but Shell has sustainability KPIs at 25 percent of executive bonuses. The percentages most likely need to be this substantial to effectively make the Big Pivot.

- **Require operational managers to add a sustainability target to their performance reviews.** Also tie operational bonuses to performance on "leading indicators" of long-term value creation and footprint reduction.

- **Create rewards and incentives for deep, heretical innovation.** Give an award for wackiest idea or deepest heresy—even if it fails. Remember Intuit's Swing for the Fence Award.

- **Try a lot, and promote fast failure.** Try a lot of heretical things, but in smaller settings with low risk first, then invest heavily in the things that work. Again, as Jim Collins and Morten Hansen describe it in *Great by Choice*, "Fire bullets, then cannonballs."

- **"Gamify" to engage all employees, and use competition.** Ask employees to contribute ideas and take action to improve the company's performance and make it fun. People like to win. PepsiCo's Chicago offices ran a floor-by-floor energy reduction competition over three months. Electricity use dropped 17 percent in total, and 31 percent on the winning floor.[20]

- **Connect employee actions to larger issues.** Caesars' Migita told me about her efforts to engage housekeepers and help them understand why a small action—collecting used soaps instead of throwing them out—mattered to the larger world: "We showed them a video of the soaps

being repurposed in Haiti and Mexico to help people stay
healthy—they were brought to tears."[21]

- **Ask for everyone's ideas.** Being valued and heard is a prime
  driver of job satisfaction. The best ideas often come from
  those closest to a challenge, so ask the front lines for their
  opinions.

- **Track progress to celebrate wins and give credit.** The US
  Postal Service careful measured all employee-led initiatives
  that reduced energy, waste, water, and so on. It was able
  to credit employees publicly with finding $52 million in
  annual savings.[22]

- **Get human resources involved early and often.** I've probably
  given this point too little attention, but almost none of the
  above can happen without strategic thinking and guidance
  from HR, the group that is, in Savitz's words, "considered
  the stewards of culture, the facilitators of organizational
  change, and the experts on shaping and motivating
  behavior."[23] We need HR to make environmental and social
  thinking a part of recruiting, training, job descriptions,
  reviews, and bonuses and incentives.

I'm often asked how to get people to take green issues seriously.
I generally respond by asking one simple question: "What are
people in your company paid to do?" It's an oversimplification,
for sure, but it's at the heart of level 1 in Savitz' version of Schein's
model: "what we do." And it offers a peek into the beliefs lying
underneath the surface. But more importantly, if we *don't* pay
people to tackle the mega challenges, doesn't it tell everyone that
these issues are just not that central to business success? It's an
issue of putting your money where your mouth is.

We can change beliefs over time by changing the external incentives, actions, and statements first. Many studies on changing habits—eating, exercise, and so on—show that you make a pivot in your life by starting with a concrete change. Get up early to take a run, do it consistently for a couple months, and the odds are better that you can turn it into a habit.

Besides changing the external incentives, connecting people at work to a larger purpose also—and perhaps even more so—drives change. The *combination* of extrinsic and intrinsic motivation is key. As proof of how a Big-Pivot-type organization can attract people, consider the list of LinkedIn's most in-demand employers, which the networking colossus tabulates from billions of member interactions. Unilever, which I've discussed more than any other company in this book, is the third-most in-demand employer—it falls just behind two of the hottest, most valuable companies in the world, Google and Apple, and ahead of very popular employers like Disney, Nike, Coca-Cola, and McKinsey.[24]

So if we start paying people to think about the longer term and to solve mega challenges, and if we make connections between what they do and a larger purpose, we will build organizations that regularly manage for the long term. Over time, all the other rewards of having an aligned organization will kick in. The companies that make these connections will become formidable forces in the marketplace. When people are freed up to do their work with no cognitive dissonance around their values, watch out.

CHAPTER NINE

Redefine Return on Investment to Make Better Strategic Decisions

A few years ago, Unilever hired rapper Eminem to endorse Lipton Brisk Iced Tea, created a Claymation spot featuring the mega star, and ran it during the 2011 Super Bowl. What was the total cost of talent, animation, and airtime? I'll go out on a limb and say it was a lot.

What was the return on investment (ROI) on the marketing effort? What, exactly, was the payback? It's an unanswerable question, which tells us something.

What's the ROI on a Super Bowl Ad?

Companies spend enormous sums of money on important business initiatives without knowing precisely how the investments will pay off. Consider marketing, R&D, or entering new markets—what was the internal rate of return (IRR) on opening the first Starbucks in China? We have no clear idea, but we accept the uncertainty as a normal part of strategic decision making and budgeting. So why, when we label a project as sustainable or green, do executives usually require an exact ROI calculation and business justification? Green is usually guilty until proven innocent.

But many green investments should get *more* than the benefit of the doubt. As Suhas Apte, a former exec at Kimberly-Clark, points out, "an energy reduction project is a sure thing." That is, the paybacks are entirely predictable while the results of a marketing initiative are incredibly *un*certain. So why, Apte asks, are we using the same cost of capital for both marketing and efficiency projects? Mark Buthman, Kimberly-Clark's CFO, agrees that there are important differences in types of investments: "The IRR for renewable energy investments can reflect a lower risk profile than the company's typical capital projects."[1]

So back to the Super Bowl. I use Unilever (and Eminem) to make a small point: even the companies I laud for their Big Pivot leadership are still typical in many ways. They often make large investment decisions without knowing whether the gamble will pay off. These blind investments have been normal for a long time, especially in marketing—as the nineteenth-century department store merchant John Wanamaker reportedly said, "Half the money I spend on advertising is wasted; the trouble is I don't know which half."[2]

As a former marketing manager, I have nothing against spending money to build brands. But I have to ask, why do some big-ticket items receive enormous budgets with few questions asked, but strategic investments in the long-run viability of the firm—particularly those tied to tackling environmental and social issues—get so much scrutiny?

This question dances around the core issue of this chapter and the next. In business, there are many contributors to value that we fail to put a number on. This oversight presents a big problem when it comes to challenges like climate change or resource constraints.

The Unvalued

If something is free, we'll overuse it. And if we don't have a way to put a number on something, we'll undervalue it. We're then much more likely to miss big opportunities or to ignore risks until they sneak up on us.

In figure 9-1, I propose a simple framework for thinking about the unvalued in business. On the one side sits the range of things economists call externalities—the impacts, negative and positive, that we have on the world and for which we don't pay or receive money. The market does not value them. Pollution is the

FIGURE 9-1

What we don't value

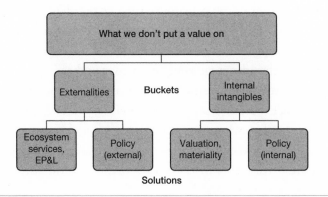

classic example on the negative side of the ledger, and providing employment or the ripples of (unpatented) technology—such as the creation of an "app" economy for programmers on Apple's operating platform—are positive externalities.

I see two broad solutions to the problem of not valuing externalities. First, we can use relatively new estimation tools to put a number on the value or cost to society. A prime example is the "environmental profit-and-loss" statement (or EP&L) that apparel maker Puma developed (with some outside help). It was a solid attempt to put a value on the natural capital that the company draws on, for free, to make its products. Second, we can lobby and otherwise work with governments to put an actual price on externalities (think carbon tax) which makes these external costs both internal and tangible. I'll dive deeper into these two solutions in chapters 10 and 11, respectively.

On the other side of the "unvalued" framework are the things that create real, internal value (or risk), but are currently unmeasured. This compelling category includes brand value, customer loyalty, license to operate, and the ability to attract the best talent. And this unmeasured value is now the majority of the market cap for most organizations. I recently asked a group of 200 financial executives from the world's largest consumer product companies a simple question: Do any of you believe that more than half of your company's total market value comes from traditional, tangible value (that is, financial and manufactured capital)? Not a single hand went up.

Imagine the advantage your company could capture if it were better at measuring, investing in, creating, and reaping intangible value (which becomes tangible through, say, higher prices and sales, or workers who are more productive and more creative). Or if your firm avoided business continuity risk better than others. What are investments in resilience worth when the unexpected happens, as it always does?

There are two primary ways to put a value on these "internal intangibles." First, we could use valuation techniques pioneered in some industries with long investment paybacks, such as pharma or utilities, and the new tools and thinking around determining what is "material" to the business (especially around environmental and social issues). Second, we could change our internal "policy" or the rules we use for making investment decisions, in particular return on investment (ROI).

To be blunt, the first path is not yet very well developed. The creation of new tools is being led by organizations such as the Sustainability Accounting Standards Board (SASB) on the materiality question, and by the big accounting firms, including my business partners at PwC, on how to apply valuation techniques to a company's environmental and social initiatives. The best recommendation for now is to watch this space carefully and get involved in the working groups that are trying to answer these tough materiality and valuation questions. I will explore these areas further outside the confines of this book (in blogs and white papers) as best practices evolve.

In this chapter I'm focused on the second path, the part that's much more in a single company's control. Let's look at how to change internal policies to make better strategic investments.

We Need to Reinvent ROI

ROI is broken. Phew, there, I've said it.

The practice of putting investment choices on equal footing to compare them fairly has utility. But most companies use ROI as a blunt tool, without measuring the full spectrum of value. ROI and its close cousin, internal rate of return (IRR), have migrated from being useful decision-making aids to being mental straitjackets.

Companies set absolute "hurdle rates," with inputs and outputs measured solely in actual cash flows. In the process, these organizations lose out on making strategic investments that might miss the hurdle rate, but create much more value than just what is immediately measurable in cash.

Energy innovation, for example, presents business leaders with a dilemma: they may want to reduce carbon emissions and increase their use of renewable energy, but they can't always justify the level of investment needed to make renewables a truly significant portion of their energy demand. For example, installing your own renewable-energy systems *does* pay off in traditional financial terms, but it may take longer than a typical company's two-year hurdle rate (although the payback period on renewables is dropping fast).

But the investment also creates value that doesn't often get measured. By lowering reliance on fossil fuels, you reduce energy price risk and make planning easier since variable costs on energy will be about zero (a CFO-heartwarming number). Investments like this increase your resilience to big changes in energy markets or to sudden shifts in energy availability during extreme weather (if you move some of your energy demand off the grid). Making a smart bet on clean energy creates a kind of risk reduction that Mark McElroy, founder of the Center for Sustainable Organizations, calls "eco-immunity."[3] The value of this resilience is not currently included in traditional ROI calculations.

The investment in renewables (or other green initiatives) can also create additional direct value by increasing sales—by demonstrating to consumers and business customers that you're keeping costs and carbon use low, it can improve your odds of being the vendor of choice. A majority of multinationals now say they will select suppliers based in part on carbon performance. And 39 percent of the CDP Supply Chain members—global heavy hitters with far-reaching value chains that include Carrefour, HP, Johnson & Johnson, Nestlé, Pepsi, Sony, and Unilever—report that they will actually *de*select suppliers that don't adopt good carbon management practices.[4]

Or what about employees? In the global war for talent, companies that are doing the right thing attract the best and brightest. So we're not talking about bad investments, but ones that often suffer by comparison only because the total value to the enterprise is not normally calculated. The value of reducing risk, building your brand, increasing sales potential, and attracting the best people is no less real for being hard to measure.

Yet none of these additional buckets of value—resilience, risk reduction, increased sales potential, or easier hiring—are recognized in an ROI calculation. In short, we're really good at the *I* side and horrible at the *R*.

The dilemma, however, is not unresolvable. What if businesses found ways to adjust the ROI process or definition so that the metric guides decisions better for the long term?

HOW TO EXECUTE: FIVE WAYS TO SHIFT ROI

How can companies make better strategic decisions about long-term investments that have a broad range of unmeasured benefits? Here are five approaches:

Set Aside Dedicated Funds for Green Investments

It's a simple tactic, but it can work well to dedicate funds specifically for investments that make your business more sustainable. For example, DuPont and building materials company Owens Corning allocate a portion of their capital expenditures budget (from 1 to 10 percent) for energy efficiency initiatives. Johnson & Johnson created an internal carbon-reduction fund, with about $40 million per year set aside.[5] Managers apply for money to invest both in efficiency projects and in renewables. Without a set-aside like this, efficiency efforts often take a backseat to issues that seem more urgent—something broken that needs fixing or a new, sexier manufacturing process. Mandating that some money goes to less exciting projects will unleash innovation and uncover ideas. And in this way, the important (and profitable) does not always lose out to the urgent.

Use a Portfolio Approach

A few companies have found a powerful way to invest more money in greener projects by grouping them together. The cleaning products company Diversey, for example, established two hurdles for projects in its carbon reduction plan: a three-year payback and a cost per megaton of carbon avoided. Out of 120 possible projects ranging from lighting retrofits to solar photovoltaic systems, only 30 cleared both hurdles. But about 60 of the other ideas could reach *one*.

An expanded 90-project portfolio, all added together, met the double hurdle. The combined portfolio, by including ideas higher up the efficiency tree, made more money than just taking a smaller segment of the lowest-hanging fruit. Diversey was able to increase its carbon reduction goal from 8 to 25 percent and generate a higher net present value.[6]

A portfolio approach is critical for hitting really big efficiency targets, such as an 80 percent reduction in carbon. Think of it this way: if you don't combine projects and you only do the ones with the quickest payback, then the next year, you're stuck. The next batch of projects, the higher-hanging fruit, doesn't clear the hurdle in simplified ROI terms. As Auden Schendler, VP of sustainability at Aspen Skiing Company, says, "because of your success picking the low-hanging fruit, you can't make additional progress."[7]

Change the ROI or Hurdle Rate Officially

Some leaders are experimenting around with lower ROIs. For capital investments, Unilever requires an environmental profile, which may trigger a lower hurdle rate. Industrial giant 3M will often slash the hurdle rate for pollution-prevention projects from 30 to 10 percent.[8] One major food and beverage company lowers the hurdle rate on sustainability investments from 20 to 10 percent (but maxes out the use of the lower rate to 15 percent of capital expense). Clearly these kinds of internal policies don't just happen; they need to come from the top of the financial organization.

These commitments will pay off over time. A decade ago, Swedish furniture retailer IKEA started allowing 10- to 15-year paybacks on solar investments (paybacks on renewables are much shorter today). The company now produces more than 150 gigawatt-hours of renewable energy, about 12 percent of the electricity needed to power its stores and distribution centers.[9]

Signs of the Pivot: AkzoNobel

At European chemical company AkzoNobel, all capital budget requests above $5 million go to the controller and to the chief sustainability officer (CSO), who conducts an environmental review.[10] Giving the CSO some CFO-like powers over investments is a very good indication of the Big Pivot.

Change the ROI or Hurdle Rate Strategically

Walmart, a famously frugal company, has purchased renewable energy for 75 percent of its stores in California. The company usually says that it only does projects that meet a two-year hurdle. But here's how Fred Bedore, Walmart's senior director of business strategy and sustainability, describes Walmart's approach to investments in green power: "There is an ROI calculation on all sustainability investments, but we look at where the investment gets us. The longer-term payback on solar helps us get to scale down the road."[11]

In essence, Bedore is saying that Walmart knows it can help the solar market scale up, thus lowering the company's future costs, all while reaping the immediate variable-cost benefits of free power. The company has tweaked its ROI requirements for green power initiatives to reflect a broader sense of value.

Whether it's done officially or informally, changing the hurdle rate requires leeway from the top. Top execs must recognize that some worthwhile investments take longer to payoff. Sprint Nextel CEO Dan Hesse has said, "A lot of environmental investments are still NPV [net present value] positive, but you have to make exceptions for payoff period."[12] Again, there's nothing really new here—companies make exceptions all the time for areas like marketing and R&D. What's new is applying the strategic logic to green projects.

Price Carbon Internally

In 2012, Microsoft started charging all its global offices and data centers a fee for every ton of carbon they produced (which came mostly from "indirect" emissions from the electric grid). By mid-2013, the company had collected about $10 million, which went toward carbon offsets, internal efficiency projects, and the direct purchase of renewable energy—Microsoft contracted to buy all of the power from a 110-megawatt wind farm near Fort Worth, Texas (for the next 20 years).[13]

Three years earlier, Disney implemented a similar program with two goals: (1) reduce the company's carbon footprint and (2) incentivize all of its businesses to innovate. The company charges each business between $10 and $20 per ton of direct emissions, mainly from onsite energy used by parks, studios, and company buildings, as well as fuel from company vehicles.[14]

"The more you emit, the more you pay. The less you emit, the less you pay," says Beth Stevens, Disney's senior vice president for environment and conservation. "This internal fee incentivizes our people to think creatively about new approaches and cutting-edge technologies that reduce both carbon and the charge."[15]

So far, Disney has collected more than $35 million and invested it in certified forest projects around the world, from Inner Mongolia to Mississippi. With these projects, Disney offset half its 2012 direct emissions, well on the way to its long-term goal of zero net direct emissions.

A few other companies use internal carbon pricing and trading, but these are shadow prices, not actual fees. For example, Shell models all investments with a $40-per-ton price on carbon. Microsoft and Disney, on the other hand, collect real money. As Rob Bernard, Microsoft's chief environmental strategist, says, "if you run one of our offices and you choose to use carbon-based power, we'll charge you more for your energy."[16] The fee will, in theory, move managers to make greener choices. Even though it's less than the $40 used at Shell, a smaller, real tax should have a much bigger impact than a larger, pretend one.

These carbon-fee programs do a good job of blurring the lines between the unvalued categories shown in figure 9-1: pricing the "un-priced" is a core solution to the problem of externalities, but the process also creates internal value. The higher carbon cost spurs managers to reduce energy use, which saves money, and using renewable energy reduces both operational and input price risk. Microsoft spent some of the funds to improve efficiency and change the ROI on some investments by accelerating the projects. But it was the creativity boost around energy reduction that was most interesting. T. J. Dicaprio, the Microsoft exec running the program, told me that the carbon fee has been "especially helpful in driving innovation."[17]

It Comes Down to Leadership

Let's revisit the story of Diageo from chapter 6. After top global execs set a big goal—a 50 percent reduction in global carbon emissions by 2015—the North American division got there years ahead of schedule, all through projects with "low or no cost." But it was turning out to be much harder to make the cuts economically in other parts of the world. So North America needed to go further to help the company reach its global goal. To cut more, something out-of-the-ordinary had to happen. And it did.

Gene Ruminski, Diageo's North American sustainability manager, proposed that one of the company's largest distilleries contract with the local utility to supply natural gas harvested from a landfill. This net-zero-carbon solution would reduce the carbon footprint for North America by another whopping 30 percent (to 80 percent in total). But there was a big catch: energy costs would go up more than $1 million per year. This expense was more than the single plant could justify.

Then a senior exec named David Gosnell, the president of global supply and procurement, got wind of the idea. (Gosnell sits on the company's internal sustainability council—an important point, demonstrating the benefits of aligning incentives and building buy-in.) With his global perspective, Gosnell realized that even though the landfill gas solution would increase operating costs for this one plant, it was actually a relatively cheap way to deliver a large reduction in emissions. So he gave the go-ahead, and also provided some much-needed financial leeway for the plant manager who would take the hit to his facility's bottom line.

As it turns out, the plant's ongoing cost-cutting initiatives had already identified millions of dollars' worth of savings, so Diageo reduced that distillery's target for total cost savings to allow for this massive carbon-reduction project. In short, as Diageo's Roberta Barbieri told me, the decision to go with landfill gas "wasn't painless, but it happened."[18]

And given the extent that the leaders in the company were willing to go to make this big goal happen, it's not surprising that Diageo's CEO Paul Walsh has said, "Sustainability has moved from something that's feel-good, to something that's far more integrated with what is required for our future success."[19]

This was a strategic choice, and real leaders make strategic choices that don't meet the typical ROI requirements all the time. Tom Falk, CEO of Kimberly-Clark, told me, "We don't make every decision on a present-value basis." He used an example of making an improvement to Huggies diapers: "We measure how the change scores with moms, but we don't do an NPV on it—it's artificial to try and estimate the effect on market share—you can make the analysis say anything you want it to."[20] So they look at the general benefit to consumers, measure the capital expense required to implement the change, and make a call.

Clearly, leadership matters. With a more strategic attitude, you can invest in longer-term value, both tangible and intangible. Most of these ROI-modifying tools are, let's face it, mental games.

At any time, leaders could say, "Don't combine projects into one portfolio of investments—just do the ones that hit every hurdle on their own," or ask, "Why do we need to set aside funds for green spending? Let them compete with every other investment."

Those attitudes would certainly be in keeping with how companies normally operate. But Big Pivot companies will take a broader view. Shifting away from an attitude of "maximize profits this quarter at all costs" does not mean you leap right from capitalism to communism; it just means you take into account a broader definition of value to the organization and community. As clean tech and impact investor Charles Ewald said to me recently, "the gap between capitalism and so-called philanthropy leaves a lot of room for creativity."[21]

These mental and organizational tools and tricks are meant to free up your organization to get creative and reap the value that's real but not easily measured. Another great opportunity awaits those who put a value on things that don't necessarily create internal value or risk. We'll turn to these externalities now.

CHAPTER TEN

Put a Number on the Value of Natural Capital

In an old joke, one fish asks another, "How's the water?" The other fish answers, "What the heck is water?"

I first read a similar metaphor in the pioneering book *Natural Capitalism*, by Paul Hawken, Amory Lovins, and Hunter Lovins. For years, these authors—as well as other scientists, ecologists, and economists such as Gretchen Daily, Robert Costanza, Herman Daly, and E. F. Schumacher—have explored the value of everything the world provides our economy and lives, all called *natural capital*. Forests give us timber for homes and clean our water; fisheries and healthy soil feed us; the earth's crust offers up its metals for cars, cities, and electronics; coastal wetlands and marshes protect us from storm surges and floods … I could go on (see the sidebar "Trillions of Dollars' Worth of Value" for more info on nature's worth).

These benefits are quite tangible even if we swim through it all blithely unaware. At its core, the Big Pivot is about seeing the water we're in. Our society and economy sit within the natural world, not the other way around. Again, looking back at Ray Anderson's simple view in figure P2-1, we're the "business" square inside the "environment" circle, which is a bounty of natural assets that we can't replicate and depend upon completely. The idea may sound corny, but there truly is only one spinning blue ball.

In some sense, the question, "What's the business case for valuing nature?" is moot (and a bit silly). We live in an integrated network on a single planet with a finite amount of resources. Either we manage these assets well, or we don't survive. Constantly asking about the business case is like a starving arctic explorer worrying about how much his dwindling stash of canned goods cost to buy—the expedition's finances won't matter if he dies of starvation.

We're currently, and effectively, knocking down pieces of our own support structure, the load-bearing walls of our home. In business terms, we're drawing down assets from the balance sheet of the world. A key failing of our market-based system is the awful job it does in valuing the assets and services our home provides.

Deep misperceptions remain about these issues. I was talking to a senior executive from a large food company that works to protect fisheries (to ensure its own supply chain). He said it was nice his company was doing this, but it wasn't necessary— markets would take care of it since, he thought, when supplies got low, prices would go up and everyone would buy less or pay more.

Besides being bad business (so you're OK with the price of a major input rising rapidly?), his view is deeply and dangerously out of touch with reality. We can easily fish a species to extinction long before the market price reflects the shortage (and we have). It's a classic externalities issue most commonly called *the tragedy of the commons*, which describes a situation where everyone maximizes their short-term self-interest by grabbing as much of a resource as possible. The irony is that individuals, by acting rationally, deplete the common resource, a result that undermines everyone's best interest.[1] And this profound problem is why we need to put numbers on the real value of shared resources (like air, water, climate, fish, and so on)—prices *not* currently reflected in the marketplace—even if it's not easy.

As Robert Mattison, CEO of TruCost (which specializes in environmental data and natural capital), has pointed out, "just because it's difficult to do doesn't mean we shouldn't do it. Oil companies find it quite difficult to accurately state their reserves, but it would be ridiculous if they didn't actually report on their calculations of what those reserves look like to their shareholders, because otherwise, how would you value the company?"[2]

Many of the world's largest companies in a few key sectors (oil and gas, mining, chemicals, and some consumer-facing businesses like tourism) are now working on valuing natural capital in their businesses.[3] But communicating the value of this work to Wall Street won't be easy.

One person qualified to bridge the natural and financial capital worlds is Mark Tercek. After twenty-four years working at Goldman Sachs and climbing the ranks to partner, Tercek took an interesting career turn in 2008 to run the international NGO The Nature Conservancy (TNC). In his book, *Nature's Fortune*, Tercek says, "we need to get business, government, and individuals to understand that nature is not only wonderful, it is also economically valuable. Indeed, nature is the fundamental underpinning to human well-being." By putting some numbers on natural capital and "by making the connection between nature and basic human and business needs," he says, we can help "spread the word on why everyone should care about maintaining a diverse, resilient environment."[4]

In a hotter, scarcer, more open world, we will face some choices, region by region. Do we use limited water resources in a given watershed for agriculture, give it to cities, or just leave it for the fish? "These are the kind of trade-offs the communities,

Trillions of Dollars' Worth of Value

The purification of our air and water; flood control; and the provision of timber, metals and minerals, food, and medicines—all called *ecosystem services*—must be worth something, right? The most quoted estimate of the total value that nature provides is $33 trillion annually (about $48 trillion in today's dollars). A slightly different analysis estimates that the global economy is consuming or damaging natural capital, for free, to the tune of $7 trillion dollars every year.[5] That's quite a subsidy to our economy and businesses. But these numbers can seem kind of moot. The value of everything we rely on for our society to function is basically infinite. When you have no water, the first drop is priceless.

---

governments, and businesses will face with increasing regularity," Tercek says. "A market-based approach, guided by science and ethics, can provide a basis for making these hard choices."[6]

He's right of course, but for markets to work, they needs prices. This chapter looks at new, exciting attempts to value the natural world. Two companies, Dow and Puma, have taken the early lead in figuring this all out.

The Business Case for Protecting Nature: Dow and The Nature Conservancy

A few years ago, Dow announced a five-year, $10 million partnership with The Nature Conservancy to, in the chemical company's words, "work together to apply scientific knowledge and experience to examine how Dow's operations rely on and affect nature."

The partnership is examining Dow's facilities, products, and supply chain to identify and accurately value the risks and opportunities related to natural capital. Where does the business depend on water, for example, and how much is that worth to the company? Dow's CEO Andrew Liveris described the collaboration as a way to "help us innovate new approaches to critical world challenges while demonstrating that environmental conservation is not just good for nature—it is good for business ... Companies that value and integrate biodiversity and ecosystem services into their strategic plans are best positioned for the future."[7]

A couple years into the effort, Dow's executives and TNC's scientists have done some tough and excellent work. They have focused mainly on Dow's Freeport, Texas, site, the world's largest chemical and refining complex, which manufactures 20 percent of the company's global sales. The facilities sit at the junction of the Gulf of Mexico, the lower Brazos River, and a large network of freshwater, marsh, and forest ecosystems. This web of water systems provides critical services to the region's human communities and its wildlife.

Dow faces at least three core water-related risks: (1) damage to assets from being on the coast, in the frequent path of hurricanes and storm surges; (2) business interruptions from lack of water; and (3) longer-term risks from rising seas and incursions of salt water, which is not good for Dow machinery—or for local drinking water or agriculture.

Dow and TNC have placed the options for reducing these risks into two broad categories of infrastructure, the *gray* and the *green*. Building a levee system to protect against surges or a desalination plant to provide water are gray (human) infrastructure solutions. Alternatively, green options leverage natural processes and include building reefs to blunt storm surges, or preserving the coastal lands that both cleanse the water and protect the inland regions from storms.

Both the gray and the green options work well. As TNC's Michelle Lapinski told me, "while it may vary depending on the marsh land available, the cheapest option—on both upfront capital expense and ongoing operating expense—is a combination of both natural infrastructure and some levees."[8] As we keep finding out, nature provides many services more efficiently that we can. It's very often cheaper to safeguard natural capital than to pay for what happens when you don't protect it.

Dow is always planning expansions and capital expenditures, and it has ways to model most input costs, like employee time or fuel. However, the lack of numbers for natural capital like water creates a blind spot. As Dow's Mark Weick describes it, "our dream is to value ecosystem services in the same way we value labor or a barrel of Brent crude."[9] The Dow-TNC partnership is estimating what it costs to provide a gallon of water using both gray and green infrastructure. These calculations will help Weick achieve his dream.

But is this partnership really working on valuing externalities? Yes and no. On the one hand, TNC and Dow are estimating concrete costs and benefits—ones we haven't put good numbers on before. So the partnership has been incredibly useful in translating into hard numbers the real value that green infrastructure provides and in creating an incentive to manage natural capital. Lapinski says, "Businesses take care of what they value. The more they see nature as an asset, the more they'll work to protect and restore it, just as they would any business asset."[10]

But on the other hand, investing in natural capital creates more value for society than direct benefits to a particular company. Green infrastructure investments reduce storm risk for everyone in the region, sequester carbon, and protect fishing and other recreational activities people value. These positive externalities in the Freeport area alone are worth $150 million to the broader community (which Dow and its employees are, of course, a part of). But none of these benefits are currently valued in the marketplace and they're not really included in Dow's business decisions … yet.

To explore how one company is attempting to include these true externalities in business planning, let's turn to Puma, the athletic apparel company.

The Cost of Natural Capital for One Business: Puma's Environmental P&L

The growing field of valuing natural capital owes a great deal to Jochen Zeitz, the former chairman and CEO of athletic apparel company Puma. Inspired by the work of the United Nations and The Economics of Ecosystems and Biodiversity (TEEB) study, Zeitz set out to value natural inputs and assess the toll Puma's business took on nature.

He asked two consultancies, TruCost and Pricewaterhouse-Coopers (PwC), to help him create something entirely new, an *environmental profit-and-loss statement (EP&L)*. The idea sounds simple: put a monetary value on all natural capital inputs and impacts of Puma's business. As Zeitz put it, the key questions were these: "If our planet were a business, how much would it ask to be paid for the services it provides to a company in order to operate? If nature accepted pollution, what would it charge for the damage that a company leaves behind?"[11] In other words, what's the real cost of every gallon of water used, every acre of land used, and every ton of carbon emitted?

To answer these tough questions, Puma, TruCost, and PwC used the best available science on the *social cost of carbon*, for example. Every ton of carbon emitted into the atmosphere costs society something through pollution, human health effects, property damage from floods, climate change, reductions in agricultural productivity, and so on. Governments approximate the social cost of carbon when assessing projects or regulations, with the estimates ranging from a few dollars per ton up to $100 or more. Similar calculations can help gauge the value of water (much as Dow and TNC estimated), waste, and other environmental impacts.

The EP&L revealed that Puma would have spent about 150 million euros, or about half its profits, on natural capital. About 94 percent of that cost was actually upstream with suppliers. A stunning 96 percent of the water cost was attached to suppliers *four* steps back in the chain—that is, the farmers growing the cotton that Puma eventually turns into shirts and shoes.

Puma learned a great deal about its business from the exercise, which exposed some tough realities. In particular, how should the company manage these value-chain issues outside its direct control? As Zeitz told me, "when you know the problem is in someone else's P&Ls, you realize that fixing it will cost money."

So what needs to happen next? This externality valuation game is still very young, but Zeitz described the need to invest

Signs of the Pivot: Natura

Brazilian cosmetics company Natura is estimating the costs of natural capital and impacts in its supply chain. Its Strategic Sourcing Triple Bottom Line program, which is saving this Big Pivot company real money, puts shadow prices on externalities like carbon, water, and waste. These prices help Natura decide which suppliers can deliver the lowest financial *and* environmental cost.[12]

in innovation and to shift the mind-set of managers so that they think about systems and value chains more. Doing this well requires "breaking it down to the functional level," he said, such as giving product designers better information. At the tactical level, it means comparing material X with material Y on value-chain impacts and costs. The EP&L is a tool to foment a larger discussion about the environment, social, and fiscal costs of the operational decisions we make.

Puma's project brings up a very good question: why should any company do this? Externalities are, well, external: on the surface, it appears that you don't have to pay for them. But it's not that black-and-white.

Why Do This?

Why put yourself and your organization through the significant effort, and some cost, to put a value on something the marketplace does not? The adage that anything worth having takes hard work probably doesn't suffice as an answer. Put aside for the moment the logic that preserving natural capital is profoundly in our own interest, since nature provides everything our lives depend on. Or the connection we have to the inspiration and beauty of the natural world. Even without those reasons, there is a strategic logic to valuing the hard-to-value:

- **Deeper knowledge of the business and identifying hot spots.** For Puma, the work was largely about understanding what resources it relies on and currently gets for free. In general, better data helps us focus limited resources on the highest leverage opportunities to reduce impacts and risks. Let's say Puma wanted to reduce the threat of water shortages disrupting its ability to operate.

With the EP&L in hand, the company might determine that the best option would be to lower its demand for cotton in general or from water-scarce regions specifically.

- **Improved business planning.** As Dow's Weick says, the company wants to "understand what the real costs of doing business are going to be. We wouldn't build a chemical plant without estimating the cost of labor and feedstock like crude oil."[13]

- **Expectations of future pricing (and getting ahead of the curve).** As Dow's Neil Hawkins told me, "managing and pricing ecosystem services will become a key part of running a business and running the world." Weick adds, "The Texas legislature is talking about how, if we can't guarantee water, we may struggle to attract businesses … so maybe taxing water is not so far-fetched, even in [tax-averse] Texas." Dow executives believe that it's smart to treat future costs like current costs since, as Hawkins says, "early adopters will be advantaged."[14]

- **Identification of emerging risks.** Pricing aside, some natural inputs are basically binary in value. If there's no water for your factory, you can't operate. In key watersheds, companies like SABMiller work with communities, farms, municipalities, and other businesses to manage the shared resource. The companies take this collaborative approach not because it's easy, but because water availability represents a serious and shared business continuity risk.

- **The necessity of valuing natural capital, even if the practice costs money.** Not everything we do to keep our economies and society viable will fit the simple and easy business case of eco-efficiency and cost savings. Zeitz told me, "We're kidding ourselves if we talk about all sustainability issues only fitting the bottom line … Some of this will require capital, and to believe we can find every solution free of charge is wishful thinking. That's why valuing and measuring is so important."[15]

- **The radical practicality of understanding natural inputs and trying to price them.** Our only other "choice" is to run through our resources until we have far less available than we need. By then, building gray infrastructure to replicate the green will become prohibitively expensive if not impossible. Using one ecosystem service as an example, Zeitz says, "If you want to pollinate your crops yourself, you can try, but the costs will be tremendous."

- **Moral responsibility.** When I asked Zeitz point-blank why he was doing this, he said, "Because I care about the future." *The Big Pivot* is 99 percent focused on the deep practicality of managing our mega challenges, but we do have a responsibility to future generations, to all other species, and to nature itself. Self-preservation provides plenty of ammunition for the Big Pivot, but it's not always about pure self-interest.

HOW TO EXECUTE

Execution on something so broad and hard to define as managing natural capital is not easy to describe. But I can suggest some priorities and actions:

- **Assess your key hotspots and dependencies on natural capital.** This risk and opportunity assessment needs to extend to your suppliers and customers as well. How do they interact with natural inputs? Which suppliers are energy-intensive, for example, and would struggle with rising energy costs?

- **Use available tools to figure out risks and potential value.** The Aqueduct tool from the World Resources Institute can help you map global water availability, which you can then overlay on your own operations (Coca-Cola conducted this exercise on its own years ago). Other organizations, like the Global Environmental Management Initiative and World Business Council for Sustainable Development, offer localized water mapping tools. The council has also created Eco4Biz, a toolkit and source for different approaches to measuring natural capital. And check out the Corporate Ecosystem Services Review from the World Resources Institute, a "structured methodology that helps managers proactively develop strategies to manage business risks and opportunities arising from dependence and impact on ecosystems."[16]

- **Understand and leverage REDD+.** The program called Reducing Emissions from Deforestation and Forest Degradation, or REDD+, was one of the only concrete initiatives to come out of recent global climate negotiations. While the execution will be challenging, the idea is relatively simple: since cutting down trees—for farms, cattle, mining, infrastructure, or other human uses—produces up to 20 percent of global carbon emissions (more than all cars and trucks), why not provide incentives for leaving forests standing by valuing the carbon storage services they provide?[17] At this point, REDD+ projects are transacted on the voluntary carbon market, but the system is evolving into a more formalized framework.

- **Find and join key coalitions.** Sometimes, peer pressure is a good thing. Momentum is building to value natural capital. Jochen Zeitz has reduced his role at Puma to work with Richard Branson. The two men launched the B Team, a group of business and public sector leaders hoping to change capitalism, in part by scaling up EP&L efforts in many more companies. Also check out the TEEB for Business Coalition; a partnership called Wealth Accounting and the Valuation of Ecosystem Services; and the Valuing Natural Capital Initiative (a coalition of the Corporate EcoForum, TEEB, and dozens of the world's largest companies, including Alcoa, Coca-Cola, Dell, Disney, Dow, GM, Kimberly-Clark, Marriott, Nike, Patagonia, and Xerox).

- **Partner with those you share resources with.** Around every facility, there will be communities, other businesses, and local governments that you'll need to comanage natural capital with. If you're worried about water availability, you're surely not alone. Again, look at key points in your supply chain as well.

- **Listen both to experts and to your critics.** So recommends TNC's Tercek. Work with the environmental NGOs, global and local, that have deep knowledge of natural capital and possible trade-offs. Share your knowledge of your operations and dependencies as well.

- **Analyze options for green infrastructure to replace or supplement gray.** Expand your horizons on the options available to protect your operations.

- **Understand and study how other business leaders manage limited resources.** For example, look at the ways that

Coca-Cola, Dow, Puma, and SABMiller manage and
prepare for constraints on shared resources.

- **Support and lobby for increased conservation and the
development of green infrastructure.** Lead the discussion
about shared resources, or risk spending much more alone.

- **Put enough resources into all your efforts.** I may sound like
a broken record on this point, but it bears repeating. Hire
someone, or expand someone's responsibilities, to manage
all of these activities. It's not easy work; it requires focus
and resources.

Call it what you like—nature, biodiversity, natural capital, the
earth's bounty. They're all similar concepts that speak to something much more than just that pretty stuff we visit in national
parks. Natural capital is the platform and foundation for every
human endeavor.

Nature and human systems (especially markets) are the two
most powerful forces on the planet, but make no mistake about
which is the strongest. But we can use our tools to help preserve
natural capital, put a value on the priceless, and ensure that we
thrive and flourish.

As Puma's Zeitz says, some greener choices may cost more
today, but that's only because we don't price the externalities for
everyone. So it's up to the real leaders to start paying for some
things—like healthier products made in ways that are safe for
workers and that use far less energy, water, and other materials—
before those benefits are priced fully into the market. In parallel,
these leaders must demand a level playing field and policies that
do put a value on the things that benefit us all. And that brings us
to the Partner Pivot and lobbying.

The Big Pivot Strategies

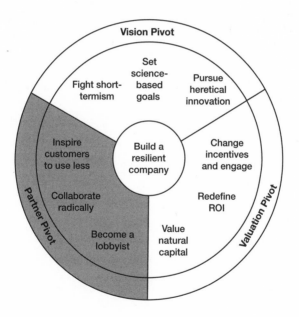

CHAPTER ELEVEN

Become a Lobbyist

Is it possible that CEOs don't know what their own lobbyists are doing? It's a reasonable question when you look at how companies address issues like climate change in public versus what they—and the trade associations they fund—actually fight for or against.

A study by the Union of Concerned Scientists found a major disconnect between the public rhetoric at 28 large public companies ("all expressed concern about climate change," the study says) and how they acted behind closed lobbying doors.[1] The nicest interpretation of this gap is that one hand doesn't know what the other one's doing. A more cynical view would say these companies know exactly what they're doing.

I'll be generous and say it's a bit of both. But either way, it needs to stop.

Left Hand, Meet Right Hand

In a more open world, it's harder to speak one way and act another. As one *Fortune* 100 executive told me, "if we say these are our values, then we don't get to do it only when convenient. We have to talk to government in the same voice."

Political action and lobbying are absolutely critical to making the Big Pivot successfully. The other nine strategies, which reflect mostly a company's own actions, are not enough. We can set big goals or estimate the price of externalities over and over, but until we change some of the rules of game, create a level playing field, and cap or price carbon, we won't invest enough in big solutions.

We can't wait for government to set new policies that enable the Big Pivot. The US government is effectively broken on these issues, so the private sector must lead. As the same *Fortune* 100 exec said, "the debate is so polarized; it's time for companies to get off the sidelines and help make progress."

Unilever CEO Paul Polman has also called for a change in business lobbying as usual: "The business voices that whisper to politicians in private ... are those who are opposed to ambitious action on climate change ... This strategy has outlived its usefulness." He goes on to paint a picture of a much better interaction between the private and the public sector, suggesting that "many companies are waking up and realizing that they can be inside the tent, shaping solutions, future-proofing their businesses."[2]

I hope Polman is right. But what should companies ask for instead of taking the normal, more defensive crouch of fighting the government? This chapter discusses five key policies that companies need to lobby for, roughly in order of importance, and a few other ideas whose significance may vary, depending on industry or region. This is not a full list of what the government can do, but it focuses on what the private sector should push for. Admittedly, the list is US-centric, since some of the policies are already in place elsewhere. Overall, these policies will dramatically shift the economics of energy and business investments in favor of cleaner options, enabling companies to use the power of markets and competition most effectively.

A Price on Carbon

Here's how economist Gernot Wagner deftly explains the externality problem with carbon: "Every time I fly back-and-forth across the United States or across the Atlantic to Europe, I spew a metric ton of CO_2 ... I cause at least $20 of damage and 7 billion people pay for it—that's socialism—I'm privatizing benefits, and socializing the cost!"[3]

We need to price these impacts in some way. One method would be a *cap and trade* policy, which would set a limit on carbon and allow trading between companies, industries, or states (depending on the program). It's in place in the European Union, California, a group of states in the US Northeast, and parts of China.

Despite the advantages of a market-based system like cap and trade, a carbon tax is a better choice. It's the cleanest and most efficient method, and economists of all stripes generally agree. Aparna Mathur, from the conservative think tank American Enterprise Institute, has said, "I think most economists—on the right and the left—think a carbon tax is a good idea." One of the leading conservative economists, N. Gregory Mankiw (an adviser to President George W. Bush and presidential candidate John McCain), has repeatedly called for a carbon "fee" that would "in economics jargon ... induce people to 'internalize the externality.'"[4]

Yet who doesn't have at least some visceral distaste for taxes? In the economic culture wars, taxes are equated with socialism and talked about as anticapitalist. But a carbon tax is a very different animal. It's not antimarket; with externalities it's the *lack* of a price that distorts markets.

There's another good reason for the consensus among economists: the carbon tax is a great revenue and deficit-reduction opportunity. The US Congressional Budget Office estimated that a "modest" carbon tax ($20 per ton), scaling up gradually, could generate $1.2 trillion over ten years and cut the deficit in half.[5] The countries that have already acted are cutting emissions without sacrificing growth. Sweden, Denmark, and the Netherlands have had carbon taxes in place since the early 1990s, and on a per-person basis, Sweden produces roughly one-third of the carbon dioxide produced in the United States—at the same level of wealth.[6]

More recently, Ireland, devastated by the 2008 financial crisis, implemented a carbon tax. The *New York Times* reported that the tax "played a crucial role in helping Ireland reduce a daunting deficit." In 2011, emissions dropped nearly 7 percent while the Irish economy *grew* a bit in recovery. China has been experimenting with regional cap-and-trade schemes and announced an intention to put in place a carbon tax as well.[7]

This is all basic economics. We humans need price signals, and a price of zero tells us to use something, like our atmosphere, with no regard for the consequences. But to do this right, we need to shift taxes in a revenue-neutral way, by raising the price of the thing we want less of, carbon, while lowering taxes by the same amount on the things we want more of, like income.

Former Secretary of State George Shultz has said, "We need to make all forms of energy bear these costs, and a tax on pollution—on carbon—is a good way to do it. Doing it on a revenue-neutral basis is a good idea because then you're not creating any fiscal drag on the economy."[8]

An End to Fossil Fuel Subsidies

The International Monetary Fund has called for ending energy subsidies (which are mostly for fossil fuels), estimating that these market distortions add up to $1.9 trillion globally, or 8 percent of all government revenue and 2.5 percent of global GDP. The logic for supporting fossil fuels made sense about 100 years ago. But fossil fuel companies don't really need the help today—in the first decade of the 2000s, the big five oil giants' combined net income neared $1 trillion.[9]

But what about subsidies for renewable energy, which could in theory level the playing field? Since subsidizing both fossil fuels and renewables may be inefficient, some people are calling for an end to *all* energy subsidies. And this includes my friend Jigar Shah, founder of the innovative solar installer SunEdison. He makes a fair point that putting everything on an equal footing will unleash capital that's sitting on the sidelines—$10 trillion, he believes—with investors that don't like the uncertainty of businesses that need ongoing government subsidies.[10]

I admire Shah's bravado and confidence that solar will win in a straight-up economic battle with dirty fuels, and the capital flow issue is important. But there's also a strong economic logic for subsidizing cleaner energy for a while. As economist Wagner says, "just as there's a negative externality called 'climate change' that merits a tax on carbon, there's a positive externality called 'learning-by-doing' [or economies of scale] that merits subsidies for renewables, financial assistance that should start strong and almost immediately decline."[11]

Renewable energy is quickly becoming cheaper than fossil fuels, even with the distortions in the market in favor of the older options. But I keep coming back to climate math and physics. Since we know we have a relatively short time to eliminate carbon—in infrastructure terms, a few decades is not much—it seems prudent to accelerate the transition by ditching dirty-fuel subsidies and increasing clean ones. The case is even stronger if you consider the externalities, which are negative for one kind of energy and largely neutral to positive for the other.

Again, it's all about price signals. Unilever's Polman has said, "We know that without proper pricing of externalities, including carbon and water, and an end to perverse subsidies that encourage the production and inefficient use of these resources, we will always face an uphill battle to persuade consumers to change their behavior."[12]

Could there be some increase in energy prices in the short or medium run if we priced carbon and ended fossil fuel subsidies? Perhaps, although efficiency improvements could easily offset the increase in price—if over time the gas price doubles, but you drive a vehicle that gets twice the miles per gallon, you come out the same. In reality, some additional cost may be unavoidable if we want an energy system that's safe (as in, not creating dangerous climate change). In a different context, would we accept a food system that regularly made people violently ill just because that system was less expensive?

Public-Private Investment in the Clean Economy

In 2010, Google announced that it would invest $200 million in building a 350-mile transmission line off the Atlantic coast to spur development of offshore wind power.[13] While it sounds cool, and Google will likely make money, from a societal perspective, it's absurd. The private sector alone cannot build the infrastructure we need for a modern, clean economy. Most of our business leaders know this.

The American Energy Innovation Council is a group with some big names—including Bill Gates, GE's Jeff Immelt, Xerox's Ursula Burns, and Chad Holliday (formerly DuPont's CEO and now chairman of Bank of America)—pushing for American leadership on energy. The council made a pronouncement on the current state of

US energy policy: "America's energy system is deficient in ways that cause serious harm to our economy, our national security, and our environment. We must make a serious commitment to cleaner, more efficient technologies … including both robust, public investments [and] policy reforms to deploy these technologies on a large scale."[14]

This group is saying we need "and" solutions, not false "or" choices.

Economist Jeffrey Sachs describes the public-private logic very well: "A clearly laid out federal program to support [the clean economy], backed partly by public money, would unlock hundreds of billions of dollars of private investments."[15]

But it's not just investments in specific projects. We also need basic research into energy (storage in particular), water technologies, green chemistry, and sustainable materials. Who's going to do basic research at scale? Companies face pressure to cut back on "nonessential" science spending.

The United States has done this kind of thing many times. As Sachs says, "the United States government has a strong track record of success in long-term public-private investment programs. Federal agencies helped support and guide the birth of the computer age, the Human Genome Project, the federal highway system, the GPS revolution, the global fight against AIDS and, of course, the space program."[16] So companies should encourage a combined public-private investment in new, clean-economy solutions.

One big concern about government investment that many people express is the idea that government shouldn't pick winners. On the one hand, it's kind of silly—we pick winners all the time, and I'd rather pick ones with positive externalities than negative ones. But the real way around the concern is to invest broadly and to set high standards on performance or outcomes, not specific technologies. Which leads me to the next policy companies should lobby for.

Higher "Clean" Product and Production Standards

I recently sat in a meeting with the head of government relations for a big tech company. At one point, he mused, "You know, we make the most energy-efficient products in our market ... I should really lobby for higher energy-efficiency standards." Well, of course.

If your product makes strides toward building a clean economy by, say, using less energy or leveraging green chemistry to lower toxicity, then you're already ahead of the game. Why not encourage a higher standard for all? If it costs more to make a cleaner version, then you'll level the playing field. Either way, you'll put your competitors in a tough spot (see the sidebar "Signs of the Pivot: Broad Air").

Alternatively, there are some issues that companies should not compete on, like labor conditions. In those cases, it still makes sense to lobby for higher standards for the good of the whole sector. For example, all tech companies suffer when scandals erupt about worker conditions in one part of the supply chain. Or when toxic, discarded electronics pile up somewhere in the developing world, no computer company wins.

Higher efficiency standards have a tremendous benefit: they drive innovation, keeping companies competitive globally. After President Bush passed the 2008 energy bill that raised the standards on new light bulbs, the industry got to work. Sales of compact fluorescent light bulbs took off, LEDs are rising fast, and, most interestingly, Philips innovated to create incandescent bulbs that met the new standard—the company made a technology mostly unchanged for one hundred years about 30 percent more efficient.[17]

Signs of the Pivot: Broad Air

Broad Air, a leading manufacturer of absorption chillers, a much more efficient kind of central air-conditioning, has pushed the Chinese government to set higher efficiency standards. Does Broad Air and its billionaire CEO Zhang Yue benefit from tighter standards? Of course. But Zhang has set his sights on something larger: "I have completely shifted the focus of this business towards the direction of reducing emissions. I've taken on the challenge of climate change." He also walks the Big Pivot talk by, ironically, setting his office thermostat to 81 degrees in the summer.[18]

Transparency

In the elections of 2012 and 2013, in two different states, voters narrowly rejected two very similar ballot initiatives. Proposition 37 in California and Proposition 522 in Washington State would have required food companies to label packaging if the product included genetically modified organisms (GMOs). While on the surface, these votes were about science and health, the real battle was over transparency. Companies that were against the law—nearly all the large food and agriculture businesses—were on the wrong side of history.

If companies think the defeat of Prop 37 will stem the transparency tide, they will be sorely disappointed. It's not good for these big brands to be against transparency. When companies fight so hard, it's easy for consumers to wonder, regardless of the science, "If GMOs are safe, then why hide it from me?"

The defeats are a blip. The power of big data and transparency is a relentless tide. Even if current law doesn't mandate disclosure, there will be workarounds as companies like GoodGuide provide more information about products, in real time, on any mobile device. There may be legitimate concerns about using package labeling as the means of transparency, but the information will get out there somehow. So instead of playing the little Dutch boy, putting their fingers in the proverbial dike, companies should become proactive and promote the change. And again, those with a better story will win with more openness.

Additional Ideas

For other topics, the key issues worth a lobbying effort will depend heavily on the industry, the level of government you're talking to, and other factors. There are too many issues to enumerate them all. But here are a few additional categories to consider supporting:

- **Removing the money from politics.** It's incredibly hard for politicians to support longer-term investments in new sectors like the clean economy when vested interests hold the purse strings. Doing this right may require a constitutional amendment in the United States.

- **Increased conservation and the development of green infrastructure.** Among these measures would be a change in the priorities of the US Farm Bill.

- **Renewable portfolio standards.** These rules, in place in seventy-six countries, states, and provinces (and growing fast), mandate that utilities generate a certain percentage of their electricity from renewables.[19] These laws can help a company reach its own value-chain carbon goals as the grid gets cleaner, and they help bring the cost of renewables down through market demand and scale.

- **Deeper research into chemicals and their interactions.** If companies—US companies in particular—don't want to adopt the precautionary principle that dominates European chemical legislation, then they should work with their governments to research chemicals and accelerate the green-chemistry movement. They should help develop alternatives long before legislation forces their hands. And companies can set the bar high for their suppliers as well (see the sidebar "De Facto Regulation").

- **Exceptions to antitrust rules.** Some very well-meaning laws may stand in the way of companies' working together across industry and competitive boundaries to solve the mega challenges (the focus of Chapter 12).

- **Support for new macrolevel metrics.** We need much better measures of national well-being than the blunt instrument of GDP. For example, Bhutan has developed the gross national happiness metric, and economist Joseph Stiglitz has been exploring the issue for years. Newer entrants into the alternative-GDP game include the Alliance for Sustainability and Prosperity and Michael Porter's proposal for a social progress index. Explore these options, and help your government develop and support these new metrics.

- **Support for new microlevel metrics and accounting.** The laws that push for disclosure of material risks are straining under the weight of new issues like climate change. There will be changes at the US Securities and Exchange Commission and at accounting standards bodies like the Financial Accounting Standards Board. (I'll discuss efforts to change the conversation on "materiality" issues, led by the Sustainability Accounting Standards Board (or SASB) in chapter 14.) Big companies, particularly the accounting giants, can play a proactive role in helping these standard-setting bodies develop better tools for measuring natural capital and emerging risks.

De Facto Regulation

At a meeting we both spoke at, Cal Dooley, former US congressman and president of the American Chemistry Council, talked bluntly about how business customers are reducing toxicity in their supply chains: "Walmart and Target are de facto regulators." It's exactly the phrase I often use, and it's a real and growing phenomenon. Dooley was referring in part to policies like Walmart's restriction on the amount of lead in toys on its shelves. The Walmart standard was 85 percent stricter than the US government's rule at the time. In September 2013, Walmart proved Dooley right again by targeting ten specific chemicals, demanding more transparency about their risks and pushing for safer options.[20]

Walmart's revenues, if it were a country, would rank it twenty-seventh in the world in GDP (above Austria). So the standards it sets create markets and can push the agenda on many issues. When the retail giant established a goal for its suppliers to reduce carbon emissions by 20 million metric tons, people noticed. They're not alone anymore: in October 2013, tech giant HP set an aggressive goal for its suppliers to cut emissions 20 percent by 2020 (versus 2010 levels).[21]

This kind of thing should happen a lot more. For example, why couldn't all the members of the Consumer Goods Forum, representing trillions of dollars in revenue, mimic governments and set rules for their suppliers on renewable energy use?

Examples of Corporate Action

It's a rare sight, but companies do occasionally lobby for stricter regulations to seek competitive advantage. The most famous example is DuPont's role in promoting regulations on ozone-depleting chemicals in the late 1980s. After it developed profitable substitutes, the company pivoted and lobbied for the creation of the global agreement called the Montréal Protocol, which phased-out chlorofluorocarbons (CFCs).

More recently, industrial giant 3M expanded its Novec product line to create more sustainable chemistry for fire suppression and extinguishing agents. These products help protect control rooms, data centers, and other areas where you wouldn't want to use water to put out fires. 3M's newer, nonflammable options don't deplete the ozone and have a drastically lower impact on the climate. In technical terms, they have a *global warming potential* (GWP) of 1, compared with alternative products, which have a GWP of up to 7,000.

3M's customers are already asking for greener options, but the company wants to nudge the market along faster. Herve Gindre, a 3M general manager, describes the company's subtle approach as "environmental advocacy" (or what I'd call lobbying), and adds, "We have dedicated resources focused on moving regulations and markets in the right direction for the environment."[22]

These are powerful niche examples. But some companies have been lobbying for broader goals such as continued government support for renewables. Starbucks, Ben & Jerry's, Johnson & Johnson, the Portland Trail Blazers, and a dozen other organizations have together lobbied Congress to keep the tax credit for wind power development going. At the local level, eBay lobbied the Utah state legislature to let it buy power directly from a wind farm (not from the utility) for a big new data center, making their pitch in pure business terms. The founder of the NGO Ceres, Mindy Lubber, wrote in *Forbes* that eBay and other companies "didn't need to convince Utah that a change in the law ... would help protect the environment and reduce greenhouse gas emissions. They only needed to make the case that providing access to renewables would mean new economic growth and jobs for Utah."[23]

The logic for these leaders is clear: their investments in clean energy will pay off faster with government support. Companies could do more to further their own short-term investment interests, but they need to collaborate.

Group Action

In a few interesting cases that are worth reviewing quickly, groups of companies across sectors have pushed for government action together, almost always with large NGOs playing a coordinating role. Groups like these represent the future of green lobbying.

US Climate Action Partnership

The US Climate Action Partnership, formed in 2007, joined together key NGOs—Environmental Defense Fund, Pew, Natural Resources Defense Council, and The Nature Conservancy—with a range of large companies, including Dow, Duke Energy, DuPont, Johnson & Johnson, GE, NRG, PepsiCo, Shell, Siemens, and many others. The group was publicly in favor of policies to "slow, stop, and reverse the growth of U.S. Emissions." But the group failed when the climate bill collapsed in Congress in 2010. Even so, the partnership was a good example of a business/NGO collaboration to lobby for pro-environmental laws, and it spurred others to create what may end up being more effective groups.

Ceres

The NGO Ceres formed the Business for Innovative Climate & Energy Policy (BICEP), with Nike in the lead corporate role. BICEP is growing, gaining traction, and calling for much more specific, tougher policies, including in essence the five key policies listed above. Nike exec Hannah Jones describes the group as coming along at a tough time after the US climate bill failed and providing a much-needed counterbalance to the "generally held perspective in media that all business hates climate action."[24]

In 2013, the group issued the following joint statement, which anyone could sign on to: "Tackling climate change is one of America's greatest economic opportunities of the 21st century." A growing list of leaders have signed this Climate Declaration, including Avon, Diageo, eBay, EMC, Gap, GM, IKEA, Intel, Jones Lang LaSalle, Microsoft, Nestlé, Nike, Owens Corning, Patagonia, Starbucks, Swiss Re, Timberland, and Unilever.

Prince of Wales's Corporate Leaders Group

Other groups are lobbying for action on a global scale. The Prince of Wales's Corporate Leaders Group created the "2°C Challenge Communiqué," a statement to the world's governments, signed by 400 of the world's largest companies from 40 countries. The letter called on governments to pass laws to hold emissions to the 2-degree warming level and "secure a low carbon-emission economy that is more resilient, more efficient and less vulnerable to global shocks." The group then added a more specific appeal, "The Carbon Price Communiqué."[25]

These groups and other smaller lobbying coalitions may need to come together to have real impact. As Nike's Jones put it, "we need more coalitions of coalitions, an even greater coming together of different voices saying the same thing."[26]

She may be close to getting her wish. CEOs are starting to realize that given the scale of our mega challenges, they need government action. Accenture's 2013 survey of one thousand global CEOs, conducted for the UN Global Compact, was eye-opening. A large majority (83 percent) saw a critical role for government in enabling the private sector to advance sustainability, 55 percent called for governments to use regulations and standards (like auto fuel efficiency), 43 percent thought subsidies and incentives would be effective, and 31 percent wanted "intervention through taxation."[27]

That's right: a third of global CEOs basically said, "tax us."

HOW TO EXECUTE

There's no easy list of to-dos here, but after talking to a range of people about the hurdles of shifting the lobbying culture, I'd suggest a few big themes. It's important to do some internal housekeeping first—that is, figuring out what issues and policies you're supporting now. Then you can develop a more proactive lobbying strategy.

1. **Gather data on your own lobbying efforts.** Find out first how much money you're spending in Washington, Brussels, and state and regional government headquarters and on what issues.

2. **Take stock of your trade associations.** Which organizations are you in bed with, how much money are you spending with these groups, and what are they lobbying for? Does their agenda help or hinder yours? If you're a smaller company, an association may be your only voice.

3. **Conduct an "alignment" assessment of all lobbying with your overall goals.** Are you or your trade groups working against rules that could help some of your business units or products? Do you make more energy-efficient products than your competitors do, but lobby against any government increase in energy standards, calling it an "intrusion" in your business? Lobbying *for* stricter standards is strategic and proactive, but that's not really in the job description for government relations; so make it the job.

4. **Realign the role of the lobbyist.** As Nike's Jones says, "many government affairs functions have been focused on playing defense and minimizing the impact of regulations. That's not a judgment; it's often what makes someone *good* at government affairs."[28] This reactive approach toward government needs to change. Recalibrating the public policy office in the company will not be easy, but try to pivot government relations toward collaboration and proactive lobbying for changes that create advantage for your company or sector.

5. **Publicly distance yourself from trade-association positions that are at odds with your own.** To be blunt, a few very powerful actors, including the US Chamber of Commerce and the National Association of Manufacturers, have been relentless in their attacks on climate-related policies. They don't even remotely represent everyone. After the Chamber took a strong position against climate action, Coca-Cola issued its own letter saying the Chamber did not speak for it. I'd like to see more companies pull out of the Chamber of Commerce and other regressive groups over climate

policy, as Apple and Nike did in 2009 (Nike didn't leave entirely, but resigned from the group's board).[29]

6. **Identify potential partners and existing groups to join or support.** Sign on to communiqués, join BICEP (or just sign its declarations), and work together. The voice must be large, loud, and coordinated.

7. **Get involved at the regional and local level.** If you have connections in state and city governments, do all of the above steps on a smaller scale. I hear repeatedly that companies that want to engage on climate policy, for example, get further in local conversations than with national or continental governments.

With enough leaders taking the leap, we can change the norms of what's an acceptable attitude toward green policy. As Harvard Business School professor Rebecca Henderson says, "it has to be illegitimate to lobby against some of these changes. It's not cool to chain kids to looms anymore, and we should make it not cool to lobby against carbon regulations."[30]

In short, the relationship that companies have with governments must change. Business needs to treat government—which is the representation of our collective wills—as a partner, not an enemy, and work "inside the tent." This leads us into chapter 12, which discusses the larger idea of opening up and collaborating for deeper change.

CHAPTER TWELVE

Collaborate Radically

A friend once asked me, "Does it really matter if I use green cleaning products or drive a hybrid car?" I answered the way I always do. "You're one of seven billion people on the planet, so of course it doesn't *literally* matter ... but of course it does."

Strength in Numbers

Everything we do adds up to collective impact, so it all matters. The weird dichotomy of impact versus no impact is hard to grasp; we feel small in the face of global challenges. But surprisingly, companies as large as countries ask the same kinds of questions: Does it really matter what we do? Can we really have an impact alone? Even an entity the size of Walmart, with US revenues nearing 2 percent of US GDP, cannot unilaterally transform the things it needs to change—from the price of solar power to the availability of local food—to be more sustainable.

The mega challenges are exactly that—mega. Clearly, no single person, organization, or country can solve them alone. We're all in this together. This is not some call for a group drum circle, but just a radically practical observation that we have to collaborate.

As consultant Eric Lowitt points out in *The Collaboration Economy*, "said simply, problems held in common will require solutions developed and agreed on in common."[1]

Working together challenges our normal mode of cutthroat competition. But the leading companies, realizing that the problems are too big, are learning to partner with governments and communities, with their suppliers and customers, and even with longtime rivals.

In this chapter, we'll take a look at a few examples of these new collaborations, while keeping an eye on critical questions: what can you safely collaborate on? That is, what do you really compete on?

The Sustainability Consortium: Collaboration with the Value Chain

The Sustainability Consortium (TSC) is an unusual organization. Established with funding mainly from Walmart, the group is a collaboration of eighty of the world's largest retailers; consumer products companies like Coca-Cola, Clorox, Colgate-Palmolive, P&G, PepsiCo, and Unilever; suppliers, including chemical giants Dow, DuPont, and BASF; and important NGO and academic partners.

Broadly speaking, the purpose of TSC is to reduce the impacts of global consumption by gathering much better data on the life cycle impacts (both social and environmental) of consumer products and then—this is the critical part—putting that information in buyers' hands. Using TSC's footprint data, retailers can decide what goes on their shelves. When TSC was first formed, there were reports that the group would produce information to help consumers make better choices. But for now, it's truly a business-to-business effort.

According to Kara Hurst, TSC's CEO, the group is developing four tools for hundreds of product categories (from milk to plastic toys):[2]

1. A "huge dossier of information" on product impacts—data drawn from academic journals and other scientific sources

2. A strategic summary document highlighting the value chain's hot spots, where the impacts are the largest, and outlining opportunities for improvement

3. A set of key performance indicators on life-cycle impacts for each category

4. A data platform, built by TSC member and software developer SAP, that allows product manufacturers to answer one set of questions that all the retailers can access to help them make their own choices

The second tool is critical. Identifying hot spots helps companies along the value chain work together to reduce impacts in the most efficient ways. Remember, we should be guided by data, but not obsessed with it. Ideally, this entire collaboration means that we zero in on the big issues and bring to the table those companies best able to effect change.

Another great example of value chain collaboration actually predates TSC. The Sustainable Apparel Coalition brings together an impressive mix of the entire clothing value chain, from manufacturers to retailers. This group has leveraged extensive data from Nike and the Outdoor Industry Association—as well as developed its own—on supplier performance on energy, water, toxicity, and other footprint issues. Through the coalition, the big apparel companies are sharing data and tools that help them both design cleaner and greener products and also identify the best suppliers to work with.

All of this effort creates a ripple of activity, a gathering of data and best practices along lengthy value chains. And it requires natural competitors to put aside differences and work together for common solutions. Even the biggest rivals in the business world can do it.

Vending Machines: Collaborating with Competitors or Even Mortal Enemies

Name the biggest, most heated rivalries in corporate history. Boeing versus Airbus? Gates versus Jobs? IBM versus HP? When *Fortune* magazine made its own list of the top 50, it declared Coke versus Pepsi the number one rivalry.[3] So how bizarre is it that these two mortal enemies actually collaborate on big environmental and social issues? In one area in particular, refrigerants, they have worked together for years.

Most supermarket refrigerators and vending machines use chemicals called hydrofluorocarbons (HFCs), which were an improvement over chlorofluorocarbons (CFCs), the gases that were destroying Earth's protective ozone layer. But HFCs are potent greenhouse gases, thousands of times more powerful than carbon dioxide. One ton of the most commonly used HFC, when it reaches the atmosphere, creates as much warming effect over 20 years as about 4,000 tons of carbon dioxide.[4]

It's not a small problem—Coca-Cola alone has more than 12 million vending and cooling machines around the world. By a weird twist of fate, it looks like the best option for replacing HFCs is carbon dioxide, which, surprisingly, makes a good, safe refrigerant. In the world of cold, CO_2 is now somehow the good guy.

But switching over an entire industry of refrigerants and cooling systems to a new technology is not easy or cheap. Getting to scale is always a challenge—often called the "valley of death" in the world of clean-tech investing. Coca-Cola exec Jeff Seabright says that ten years ago, CO_2 compressors cost roughly twice as much as the comparable HFC models.[5] But over time, as with all investments in new technologies, per-unit costs are dropping.

Coca-Cola has been working with a range of partners, including Pepsi and other competitors. The companies have held summits coordinated by Greenpeace—under the banner "Refrigerants, Naturally!"—and with the powerful industry network, the Consumer Goods Forum. These organizations have really helped move the needle.

Today, with senior-level support, Coca-Cola has committed to buy the output from a new factory that is making compressor units with CO_2 refrigerants, paying a small price premium (single-digit percentage) for the climate-friendly alternative. As with Diageo's purchase of landfill gas discussed earlier, leadership sometimes means paying a bit more and requires top-level buy-in.

The effort is not solely out of the goodness of Coca-Cola's green hearts. Customers are demanding change. The UK-based supermarket chain Tesco has committed to using only HFC-free systems in all its new stores. Other retailers, including US supermarket chains, will surely follow.

But leadership and collaboration matter. Even with customer pressure, Coca-Cola would only go so far if it didn't know that Pepsi and others were going in the same direction. This very careful partnership to explore new technologies has given suppliers confidence that a market will be there for them. The Big Pivot means calling a truce with enemies on the big issues (see the sidebar "Antitrust and the 'Precompetitive'").

Antitrust and the "Precompetitive"

As I talked to companies about collaboration efforts, many leaders posed the same question: Wouldn't working together raise antitrust concerns and risk lawsuits from the government, suppliers, or customers? It probably depends on what you talk about in these partnerships. Clearly, Coca-Cola and Pepsi can't discuss exact demand volumes for vending machines and compressors and wouldn't want to, anyway. They have to stay on safe ground and talk about the technologies. The hot idea here is that many mega challenges require "precompetitive" cooperation, since the issues raise or lower all boats.

It's a thorny problem, no doubt. But companies regularly meet in industry forums, trade association meetings, and other events, reading out boilerplate noncollusion language at the start of the meeting. And they sometimes ask the government for antitrust exemptions so they can work together. I can see no reason that companies can't use similar approaches to tackle the mega challenges.

What Are You Really Competing On?
The GreenXChange Story

About five years ago, Nike, Best Buy, Yahoo!, and a few others launched a radical new organization, the GreenXChange, where members share patents for new methods of production that reduce energy, water, toxicity, and so on. For example, Nike had developed a "green rubber" that lowered production costs and slashed toxic emissions by 96 percent. The company offered this technology openly, and the Canadian retailer Mountain Equipment Co-op licensed it.

But isn't sharing clean technologies contrary to the idea that going green creates competitive advantage? Yes and no. It's certainly unusual to share patents, but does it hurt Nike's competitiveness to share green rubber technology? When I asked Nike execs why they would do this, two really interesting points came out: (1) when the company discovers a better technology like green rubber, its employees and other key stakeholders expect the company to do the right thing and spread the word, and (2) there are certain kinds of innovations the company would *not* share.

The ideal shoe, one exec said publicly at a conference, would likely be made from a single material, which would greatly reduce its life-cycle impacts and make recycling very easy (just a couple years later, Nike did produce the innovative Flyknit shoe I described earlier). Any new geometry and designs for a shoe with a smaller, well, footprint would be all Nike's, and a source of real advantage. In short, Nike is competing on design and athletic functionality, not on how rubber is made.

Here are a few other examples of different sectors and what topics may be safe for precompetitive cooperation:[6]

- Coke and Pepsi compete on taste and branding, not on the inner workings of vending machines.

- Semiconductor makers compete on chip designs and processor speed, not on water use or toxics used in production.

- Apparel companies compete on design and cost, not on the water footprint of cotton or on worker conditions at factories in the supply chain.

- Daimler, Ford, and Renault-Nissan are working together to codevelop fuel-cell vehicles, sharing the development costs of an expensive and new technology rather than trying to compete directly (for now).

- Twenty-three global hospitality companies are collaborating to harmonize standards for how they measure their carbon footprints.

- Delivery company UPS and the US Postal Service are sharing carbon data information to help track their emissions. The shippers are competing on package delivery speed and cost, not on greenhouse gases.

These fine distinctions are sometimes hard to get right. Some areas may become competitive over time—in a transparent world, everything becomes fair game and may be a source of differentiation. But a single company can't solve many of these issues by itself. I've seen big retailers share ideas on better lighting systems, for example, and here's why: reducing costs by implementing new technologies would be great, but if you can't move the market toward energy-efficient lighting systems alone, then the cost advantage of new technologies is not a source of competitive differentiation you can access—so you may as well work with competitors to pool demand and bring everyone's costs and footprint down.

One final point: sharing is clearly a challenge to how companies normally operate, particularly with intellectual property (IP). But as Nike's Hannah Jones says, "as you go from one end of the spectrum from owned (solo) R&D to shared, systems innovation, your proprietary IP goes down … but so does the cost."[7] Sharing ideas thus means sharing value and sharing costs. So the critical question is, What are you really competing on?

Band-Aids from Brazil: Collaboration with Communities and Governments

A majority of the world's Band-Aid bandages are made in Brazil. Johnson & Johnson, which produces the popular products for treating cuts and scrapes, has long wanted to increase the percentage of packaging that comes from postconsumer recycled (PCR) content.

But getting enough quality PCR locally has been a challenge, especially since much of what's recovered in Brazil comes from informal networks of waste pickers at landfills. This situation is unfortunately not unusual: the World Bank estimates that 1 percent of the urban population in developing countries makes a living from scavenging waste at garbage dumps.[8]

In Brazil and some other countries, the waste collectors have organized into loose cooperatives. Johnson & Johnson wanted to help one large group, now called Futura, become a more viable business. As part of what Johnson & Johnson called Project Phoenix, the company took two major steps to help turn Futura into a top-notch supplier.

First, it helped the company adopt an internationally recognized set of operating practices that help create safer, better-run, more decent workplaces—the SA8000 certification standard from Social Accountability International. SA8000 gives companies a management system with well-designed procedures—structures that were logically lacking in a co-op that had started informally on a landfill. Futura is now SA8000 certified, giving everyone in the value chain and community new confidence in its operation.

Second, Johnson & Johnson partnered with the city of São José dos Campos, Brazil, to help make Futura's transformation a reality. The municipality also needed confidence in Futura's viability before it would invest in the necessary infrastructure to support the cooperative's operations. Then the city and Johnson & Johnson connected Futura to local banks to provide investment capital to the cooperative. These loans were no doubt easier to secure with a multinational company and the city supporting Futura, making it a sounder investment.

Today, Futura is a growing business enterprise, with safer working conditions, and it's providing PCR that's higher quality and much more reliable. Johnson & Johnson now sources PCR from Futura for its Band-Aid brand boxes.

Johnson & Johnson took the lead in bringing together this diverse group—the city, the cooperative, the banks, and other stakeholders—to help build out an enterprise that now contributes to both the local community and the global economy. "For us," says Johnson & Johnson's Paulette Frank, "Project Phoenix fires on every cylinder of sustainability."[9]

Appreciative Inquiry: Employee-Led Collaboration

What if you invited your employees and a wide range of external stakeholders to really challenge your business? Imagine putting them in a room for a couple of days, wiping the slate clean, and asking heretical questions: What are we really about? How should we operate? What do we compete on? What can we be?

These kinds of questions can lead to profound business results. David Cooperrider, a professor at Case Western Reserve University's Weatherhead School of Management, has created a tool for squeezing the best out of a diverse group of people. He calls the process Appreciative Inquiry (or AI, which in this case is anything but *artificial* intelligence). Cooperrider has

Shared Value at Nestlé

Strategy guru Michael Porter has been promoting "shared value," a way for companies to solve the world's largest problems by collaborating to create value for themselves and society simultaneously. (The idea is similar to an earlier concept, Jed Emerson's "blended value.") Nestlé, the food and self-declared nutrition company, has dived into this philosophy deeply. CEO Paul Bulcke says, "creating shared value is the fundamental way we want to behave as a company and as persons ... a conviction that a company, to be meaningful and successful over time, has to intersect with society in productive and constructive ways."[10] Shared value is a nice bow to put around the idea that we're all in this together. As many have said, business cannot succeed in a society that fails.

Nestlé is seeking to create value for shareholders and the rest of society by addressing issues of nutrition, water, and rural development. At the concrete level, this undertaking translates into everything from reducing salt, sugar, and fat in products, to increasing consumption of whole grains, to working with farmers, to helping develop rural areas.

conducted these multi-day innovation and strategy sessions with everyone from multinationals to the United Nations and the US Navy.

What makes AI special is that it allows employees and other influencers to share their ideas as equals. And it considers the whole system of the company and its role in the world. This is systemic thinking at its best. Cooperrider describes his process for creating a "positive contagion": "Large groups of hundreds ... can unleash system-wide strategies, designing rapid prototypes and taking action ... [W]e excel only by amplifying strengths, never by simply fixing weaknesses. But the best in human systems comes about most naturally, even easily, when people collectively experience the wholeness of their system, when strength ignites strength ... [with] relevant and engaged stakeholders, internal and external, and top to bottom."[11]

I've had the pleasure of attending and speaking at a few of these summits—for a large utility, for a local government agency, and with Clarke Environmental, the midsize pesticide and mosquito control company discussed earlier. At Clarke's event, I got a real taste for what AI summits can do. Remember how CEO Lyell Clarke asked his leadership team to jump in a pool with him to signal commitment to change? He then called a series of all-company meetings that culminated with an AI summit to, as Clarke says, "break through this wall of sustainability."

Largely as a result of the meeting, Clarke Environmental embarked on an overhaul of its wellness and health-care programs, its offices and physical environment, its approach to partnerships, and its product development. For example, its Natular line of organic mosquito control products is its fastest-growing product ever and won the EPA Presidential Green Chemistry Award. Next-generation, greener products will be 25 percent of sales by 2014, the company's operational changes are saving up to $500,000 a year, and employee turnover has dropped.[12]

Fairmount Minerals, the midsize mining company discussed earlier, also used the AI method. Remember how 50 percent of the bonuses at Fairmount are tied to environmental and social performance? The idea for this level of commitment came from its 2005 AI summit. Using employee and other stakeholder feedback to change how everyone gets paid demonstrates a real openness to new ideas. But it also requires trusting a process that brings together a broad assortment of brains.

HOW TO EXECUTE

Collaboration is far too broad a topic for there to be one main path to success. Each partnership or multiparty relationship is unique—working with governments is very different from working with suppliers, which is different from working with your competitors. But some analyses and thought exercises can prepare your organization for real collaboration. Here are a few ideas:

- **Assess the biggest environmental and social challenges for your industry.** Take a broader view of the sector and the systems that your company is a part of, not just your own value-chain impacts.

- **Map out who else is affected by these challenges.** Is it just competitors, or are there parallel entities with similar issues? Say you're a business making paper-based products, for example, and sourcing virgin and recycled paper is getting tougher and more expensive. Perhaps companies that don't use fiber in their products, but need tons of packaging, would be natural allies.

- **Draw a model of the ecosystem of companies and stakeholders.** Who would need to be a part of any solutions? Who has to be at the table? For a big issue, the system may be very broad. For example, to better understand water issues and to develop solutions, Coca-Cola, Pepsi, SABMiller, and Nestlé formed the 2030 Water Resources Group both with public-sector organizations (The World Bank, USAID) and with government representatives from India, Jordan, Mexico, and South Africa.

- **Conduct a "What do we compete on?" analysis.** Assemble a cross-functional group of strategic thinkers, especially from sales and marketing, and try to lay out what your organization is selling. What is the real difference between what you do and what others do? What's your defensible differentiation today? Will the advantage remain stable? (It probably won't.)

- **Discuss with your legal team what might trigger antitrust concerns.** What issues can you safely talk about with your competitors?

- **For regional partnerships, understand local context and get expertise.** Like Johnson & Johnson working in Brazil, it helps to find NGO and academic partners who know the region and its issues.

- **Explore who might best convene the right players.** Which NGOs are tackling this issue (e.g., working groups assembled by Business for Social Responsibility or environmental groups)? Which coalitions have they already brought together? Check out the UN Global Compact Business Partnership Hub, a tool to match businesses and "facilitate collective action."[13]

- **Figure out where you and your partners are on the path to change.** Tackling mega challenges is about change, which is hard, and it's even harder when you're trying to work with partners. Ask yourself, where is our sector or group of competitors on a key issue? Are we still debating whether there's a problem, or are some players a couple steps ahead, piloting some solutions?

- **Establish a pathway, metrics, and a plan for maintaining the momentum.** Sally Uren from the UK-headquartered NGO Forum for the Future speaks about change and collaborations: "It's great to create a vision of an entire system, but you have to keep momentum and maintain the transition."[14] So what could cause the group to lose its way? Do you need commitments from key players to provide ongoing support (money and time mainly) or to guarantee volume to suppliers of new technologies (like refrigerants for Coca-Cola and Pepsi)?

- **Think big and envision the endpoint.** What would success look like for this problem or collaboration? Who would be there at the finish line together?

Collaborations today can take unusual, fun forms. In addition to its collaborative work around sharing patents (e.g., GreenXChange) and advocating on climate policy (e.g., BICEP), Nike started LAUNCH, a strategic collaboration with NASA, USAID, and the US Department of State to identify and foster innovation for a better world. LAUNCH has brought together designers, academics, manufacturers, entrepreneurs, and NGOs to "catalyze action around the sustainability of materials and how they are made."[15]

Nike's president and CEO Mark Parker spoke about the LAUNCH 2020 innovation challenge: "Innovation is most powerful when it's activated by collaboration between unlikely partners, coupled with investment dollars, marketing know-how and determination. Now is the time for big, bold solutions. Incremental change won't get us where we need to go fast enough or at a scale that makes a difference."[16]

To tackle our mega challenges, we can't compete on everything. In many cases competition will drive better performance and the creation of much better products. But to take some innovations to scale quickly enough to make a difference, we will need to work together. And we need to bring consumers along for the ride.

CHAPTER THIRTEEN

Inspire Customers to Care and to Use Less

The scene opens on a beautiful polar bear walking in the Arctic. The bear begins a long trek south, lugging itself to a suburban driveway in America. It stands up on its hind legs, and hugs a guy ... apparently because he bought the all-electric Nissan Leaf.[1]

The TV ad was gorgeous, but was it effective? I'd argue no, because of one simple, but harsh truth: *people don't care much about polar bears.*

I was born two weeks before the first Earth Day in 1970, so I know we've been holding the annual awareness-building event to celebrate our planet—and the polar bears—for over four decades. Earth Day itself has had real impact, demonstrating citizen support that helped legislators pass important policies.

But the general rhetoric of "save the earth" hasn't shifted the way we live our lives as consumers much, if at all. A study from market research firm Ipsos found that just 3 percent of Americans surveyed say they buy *only* sustainable, green, or otherwise eco-friendly products.[2] Outside of some high-profile and important exceptions, like the Toyota Prius or organic foods, the percentage of consumers that fall into the "deep green" segment—those that would regularly pay more for something sustainable—has not grown much.

That presents something of a problem for all of us. The mega challenges we face cannot be handled by government or business alone. We need the third leg of the stool—citizens as consumers—to make different choices, and we need the mass market to join in. As Adam Lowry, cofounder of cleaning products innovator Method says, "making green products for green people is totally pointless; we need to make them for everyone else."[3]

The good news is that while people may not pay more for green, they will increasingly choose the green option *when price and quality are equal*. Basically, green or social benefits are the "third button" marketers can press.[4] The part of the buying public that uses green as a tiebreaker is growing fast—the Ipsos study revealed that 40 percent of people will buy ecofriendly products when the items are easy to find and cost the same (or less). To reach this larger, more typical segment of the population, Nissan pivoted its marketing and ran a far more effective print campaign that showed how many miles a Leaf could go on $1.

But there's a larger issue here. In a scarcer world, it's not just about picking a less toxic product or even the car with better mileage. We need to examine consumption at a deeper level and use less stuff or, at the very least, use things much differently and make them to be recycled endlessly. A circular economy filled with smartly designed products can help solve some of our resource challenges, but that's a long way off. For now, and perhaps in the future as well, we may just need to do less of some things. Changing the nature of consumption is a heretical shift for companies that make their money selling more stuff.

The Big Pivot means both changing our thinking on how we make money and convincing consumers and business customers to come along for the ride. For a group of leading companies, working with customers to help them use less is, paradoxically, a path to growth. But that's because these smart marketers are not talking about sacrifice: the core message is not really "use less," but "get more value and live better." By using a blended brand message and building deeper customer relationships, they are taking more market share. They are leading a hard conversation about consumption, and nobody is doing it louder than Patagonia.

Patagonia Declares War on Consumerism

"Don't Buy This Jacket" blared the full-page ad in the *New York Times*. It was an eye-catching anticonsumption message from apparel maker Patagonia. It was particularly startling because it ran on Black Friday, the start of the 30-day Christmas shopping season.

Patagonia is obviously a different kind of company, but one with a rabid customer base. It was founded in 1972 by Yvon Chouinard, a man who would rather be outdoors than anywhere else (he titled one of his books *Let My People Go Surfing*). The company is probably the most financially successful enterprise so conspicuously uninterested in growth and profit. Patagonia has reached $600 million in annual sales almost in spite of itself; given the quality of its products and the devotion of its customers, the company could be far larger if it wanted to be.

Environmental concern is at the heart of the business. Its mission statement is simply, "Build the best product, cause no unnecessary harm, use business to inspire and implement solutions to the environmental crisis." Chouinard founded an organization, One Percent for the Planet, whose member companies, logically, commit

1 percent of sales to grassroots environmentalism. Patagonia became California's first registered Benefit Corporation when the state created the new status in early 2012. And the company recently set aside $20 million just to invest in green companies that have disruptive ideas in clothing, food, water, energy, and waste.[5]

Patagonia is so clearly out of the ordinary that I rarely use it as an example. Being privately held by effectively one mission-driven person means the company can take its own path and prioritize environmental initiatives over short-term profits (although it is quite profitable). But that very freedom means that Patagonia demonstrates what a Big Pivot company can do. It's playing around with new models, showing the way to more radically practical strategies that are profitable because, mission or not, only through ongoing profit does the company thrive and continue to fund its 1 percent passion.

But we should also look at Patagonia because traditional, large, profit-centered companies like Walmart are asking Patagonia and its "radical" leader to give them advice. Because the economic

---

Signs of the Pivot: Kingfisher

Kingfisher is Europe's largest home-improvement retailer, a public company with £11 billion ($16 billion) in sales and more than a thousand stores. The company's core vision is to "make it easier for customers to have better and more sustainable homes." Kingfisher envisions helping people build homes that generate more energy than they use, a restorative business model that it calls "Net Positive." This compelling mission, it says, "will unlock more customer demand and grow our business to the benefit of all our stakeholders, creating a more valuable business for our shareholders … and a more secure and brighter future."[6]

movers and shakers no longer write off what Patagonia does, we all need to sit up and take notice when it decides to question the consumption-driven model of profit.

And that's the point of the company's Common Threads Initiative, which included the "Don't Buy This Jacket" ad and a partnership with eBay to let people trade used Patagonia clothing. The company said it wanted to create a new deal with customers, with five statements or commitments, including, "*We* make useful gear that lasts a long time. *You* don't buy what you don't need."[7]

Some critics thought the jacket ad was some kind of twisted reverse psychology to drive sales. But Patagonia's VP of environmental affairs, Rick Ridgeway, tells me, "We were really serious about the content of that ad. Our motive was to start a conversation on the topic of growth. We don't have a picture (yet) of what business will look like when growth reverses. But we are convinced it has to reverse, and that business needs to start the conversation."[8]

A couple of years later in the fall of 2013, Patagonia started a new campaign based on the theme of the "responsible economy," calling on consumers and business to rethink the current model of consumption. The messaging tries to point out that an endless cycle of "see that thing … want that thing … get that thing … use that thing … discard that thing … forget that thing" is not going to continue—it can't.[9]

These initiatives demonstrate the core of what I call the *use-less heresy*: connecting with your customers about something larger and actually asking them to use less of your product (or, again, use it much smarter and then recycle it). The apparel industry in particular seems to be having a much larger conversation and trying to engage customers. Where Patagonia says, "Don't buy so much," others are adding on, in effect, "But when you do buy, bring back what you've already used."

Marks & Spencer Wants You to "Shwop" Your Old Clothes

Asking customers to use less is one thing, but they also need to be engaged in the mission of closing the loop and bringing stuff back when they're done with it. One company leading the charge is British retailer Marks & Spencer (M&S), which has been encouraging customers to recycle old clothing. The Shwop initiative, a collaboration with longtime partner Oxfam, asks customers to bring used clothing (of any brand) to M&S stores.

The Shwop program is part of the retailer's sustainability strategy, Plan A, so named "because there is no Plan B" (clearly, the company gets the we-have-no-choice Big Pivot logic). To spread the word about the clothing exchange initiative, M&S covered a multistory warehouse entirely with old clothing. The scale of the guerilla marketing effort was not random. The roughly 10,000 garments represented the amount of clothing sent to a landfill in the United Kingdom—every five minutes. As Adam Elman, head of Plan A, told me, "we wanted to bring the idea to life."[10] Mission accomplished.

The clothing-covered building got plenty of attention, but it was only the beginning of a multipronged effort to drive the initiative into the business and integrate it with all marketing. M&S is utilizing a range of new marketing techniques, from running temporary pop-up Shwop shops, with garments donated by celebrities, to gamification efforts that give customers Facebook points and "badges" for donating. The company is also leveraging star power, putting its Plan A Ambassador, the actress Joanne Lumley (most famous abroad for costarring in the sitcom *Absolutely Fabulous*), at the center of marketing efforts.

M&S has collected a lot of clothing—nearly 4 million garments in the first year—and it has raised more than £2.3 million

($3.5 million) for Oxfam to boot. The company has also used the clothes to start down the circular economy path, producing the "Shwop coat," which is made from recycled items that M&S collected. The garment is half the cost of a virgin wool coat.

In the realm of asking customers to do something, this program is low-key. Mike Barry, an M&S senior exec, adds that "consumers lose none of the utility of clothing (fashion, fit) nor the value (nothing costs more), but it does require them to do something different (donate unwanted clothing). Crucially it's a scalable program—a behavior change that you can imagine everyone adopting."[11] Without being as direct as Patagonia, M&S is sending a message that you shouldn't waste anything. At the same time, the company is building a deeper connection with customers.

Unilever's Water Efforts, Brand by Brand

The leading companies are figuring out how to tie individual brands, not just their corporate entities, to action on environmental and social issues. At the annual Sustainable Brands (SB) conference, big company marketers, academics, NGOs, thought leaders, and entrepreneurs gather to discuss how to embed sustainability into brands and connect more deeply with customers. The goal, SB founder KoAnn Skrzyniarz says, is building better brands for the future.[12]

It's a broad and fun mission, and one of the furthest along this path is Unilever. For the company to hit its aggressive goals (one of which, as mentioned earlier, is to double sales while halving the footprint of its products), customers will have to play a big role. There's no getting around it.

When the company measured the impacts (energy, water, waste, etc.) of its major products over their life cycle, it found that its own manufacturing footprint was only a small fraction of the total. Consumers were responsible for the lion's share. The water we use to shampoo our hair, and the energy we use to heat the water, dwarfs the resources needed to make the product.

With this data in mind, the company has been experimenting with new ways to engage consumers in the mission of reducing impacts. Unilever has run campaigns to encourage people to take shorter showers, for example. Such efforts are clearly a dangerous strategy for any brand, especially one in a sector that promotes pampering and long, luxurious showers (not to mention "lather, rinse, and repeat"). Unilever exec Jonathan Atwood describes the "feedback we heard from women saying, 'How dare you tell me to shorten my "me time" away from everything.'"[13]

The key to talking about consumption with consumers is really customizing the message to each specific brand. It's devilishly hard to do well. The first question they ask themselves, says Kees Kruythoff, Unilever's North America president, is, "What is this brand's purpose? What value does it deliver back to society?"[14]

The Suave shampoo brand led Unilever's water-saving messaging in the United States with a campaign (run with Walmart) to encourage people to use less water. As Kruythoff says, the program "fits the brand promise of 'affordable beauty'—if you turn off the tap earlier, you save money."

In contrast, the Axe men's products have a brand message tied to the "mating game" and logically took a very different route to the water discussion. Axe produced videos suggesting that we all "showerpool," which is like carpooling, but a lot more fun. The idea of taking a shower with someone to save water was clever and sexy, and it fit the brand well.[15]

But Kruythoff admits that the company is still experimenting since some messages are a stretch and the impact is hard measure.

Changing consumer behavior is, in his words, "unbelievably difficult—it happens one person at a time" until we hit a behavior tipping point (like what happened to smoking). In this spirit, the company launched a new campaign called Project Sunlight in late 2013 to motivate people, and parents in particular, to adopt more sustainable lifestyles.

To help its thinking about behavior change, Unilever developed its own model for shifting consumers: the five levers for change (figure 13-1). The first step is making people understand how their behaviors affect themselves and the world. The next

FIGURE 13-1

Unilever's five levers for change

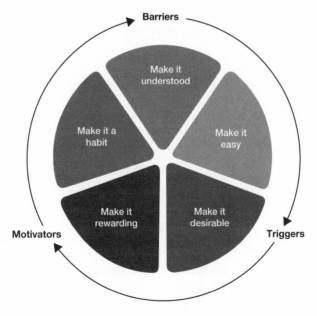

steps are making sure the change is easy, desirable, and rewarding. In the final step—the holy grail—the change becomes a habit.

Unilever is connecting brands to many mega challenges, not just water. The Lifebuoy soap brand is promoting hand-washing worldwide to improve health and drastically reduce the horrendous death rate of young children from preventable diseases (as CEO Polman has said, it's like "dozens of 747s full of children going down every day from childhood diseases").[16]

All of these experiments are in the service of both solving big problems and driving business growth. "It's not about doubling the business and *then* halving footprint because we have to deal with the consequences of growth," Kruythoff says, "but by connecting products to a larger purpose, we'll grow faster."

And so far it's working. Kruythoff says brands that struggle with how to connect to the Sustainable Living Plan are already struggling in general, and that "our purpose-driven brands that deliver something to society are growing twice as fast as the rest of portfolio."[17]

Does It Matter If Consumers "Care"?

Let's come back now to the discussion of whether consumers care about polar bears or any other environmental or social issues. To some extent, green has become a tiebreaker. All else equal, customers want products that are made responsibly and have a small environmental footprint.

But, let's ask the heretical question. *Do we need to wait for customers and consumers to care?* Companies create needs all the time—to be brutally honest with ourselves, it's a core competency of good consumer products companies. If dental hygiene were the only functional goal of a toothbrush, then how many styles and brands would there need to be? Certainly not hundreds.

When something is basically a commodity, like most consumer products, then differentiation comes from good marketing or the innovative creation of needs.

So when companies say they can't sell greener products because customers don't want them, it's a copout. Consumers haven't flocked to many green products because there's a lingering perception that these items are more expensive and lower quality. (It's hard to blame people: many early green products, like recycled paper that jammed copiers, did stink.)

There are two main paths to solving this green-product dilemma. First, you could build something so interesting along other product dimensions that customers *will* pay more, but will feel that the total experience is worth it. The Toyota Prius falls into this category. Some critics have noticed a certain smugness about Prius drivers (that includes my family). Could be, but perhaps it's just satisfaction, no different from the feelings of a proud owner of a fifty-inch television, the newest iPad, or a BMW. For the Prius driver, the satisfaction transcends the narrow question of whether the gas savings ever pays off (it probably won't, until gas prices are a lot higher). But really,

---

The Second Myth of ROI

If the idea that companies use exact calculations to make investment decisions is the first myth of ROI, then the second, and bigger one, is that we consumers use some hard calculation of utility (or *utils*, in classic economic terms) to decide what to buy. If we wanted pure functionality, we'd never spend more than $15,000 on a car or live in a 3,000-square-foot house. We spend much of our disposable income on many product attributes beyond utility.

have we ever bought products solely on payback (see the sidebar "The Second Myth of ROI")? We make emotional choices all the time.

The second path, a far more likely option, is something P&G has focused on. As former CEO Bob McDonald has said, "85 percent of consumers will not accept a tradeoff for the environment, and so [we have to] create products and services that do not involve tradeoffs."[18] In other words, why should we ask people to pay more? Instead, set the innovation bar high enough to create nontoxic, low-carbon, low-waste products that are better, more fun, and the same price as, or cheaper than, traditional products.

A big caveat here is that you *can* charge more up front for something that lowers total cost of ownership, like an LED light bulb that lasts much longer and saves more money than you spend on the up-front price premium. It requires a bit of consumer education and communication about the ongoing savings, but it can work. Or you could take a more forceful "education" path—just nudge consumers, hard, where you want them to go by giving them limited choices (this may not be the most popular strategy). After phasing out incandescent bulbs from its shelves in 2010, for instance, IKEA is already planning to get rid of CFL bulbs and to offer only LED bulbs by 2016.[19]

Asking consumers to use less is not easy—it's much simpler when you're selling to businesses. Talking to companies about saving money and using less is more natural, which brings me to the business-to-business (B2B) side of things.

Making the B2B "Use Less" Pitch: Kimberly-Clark Professional

As mentioned earlier, Waste Management and Xerox now help customers reduce their use of each company's core product (waste hauling and printing). In the B2B world, this approach isn't quite as unusual as it is on the consumer side. Helping customers lower their costs and environmental footprints builds deeper customer connections and can drive increased market share. But the company making this pitch may not think of it as asking the customer to use less, even if that's the outcome.

Kimberly-Clark makes the Scott and Kleenex brands, among others, but it also runs a multi-billion-dollar "professional" business that sells cleaning and paper products—disinfectants, soaps, towels, tissues, toilet paper—to commercial and government customers. When Kimberly-Clark Professional (KCP) develops a new, more absorbent line of towels, for example, the innovation might naturally lead to the customers' buying fewer cases.

I spoke with Elane Stock, the global president of KCP, about how the company works with customers. "We don't go out with the objective to help them use less, exactly," Stock says, "but we tell our sales guys to create value for customers and KCP. The number of cases they sell is only one indicator of value creation, and it's not a very good one—we think now about overall value and profitability of each customer."[20]

The pitch to customers has been migrating from cost per unit to something more subtle, the cost per customer use (each hand dried or surface cleaned), and now to an even broader message about employee wellness. KCP wants to avoid what the industry calls the "race to zero," a debilitating price- and margin-cutting war to drive volume. So it has launched the Exceptional Workplaces program, making the case that its products help keep employees healthy, which reduces absenteeism and improves productivity. Says Stock, "We move the discussion from 'How much is this roll of toilet paper?' to 'What's the value to your business that we can provide?'"

Elevating the sale to a larger mission is partly proactive and partly reactive to changes in what customers demand, including more questions about the total environmental impacts of their purchases. Again, it's about providing value and hitting all the customers' needs, which are evolving. Real market share is at stake. It sounds counterintuitive, but you can sell more by helping customers use less. Stock says, "When we talk to customers, they're looking for benefits for their employees, and if I can't provide that, they'll go with someone else."

HOW TO EXECUTE

Asking companies to talk to their customers about using less is a tall order, no doubt. But as Big Pivot companies are showing, it really can create value. You need to plan carefully and think through what your brand and product proposition really offers. Here are a few overall suggestions:

- **Understand the value-chain impacts of your product or service.** This suggestion comes up a lot (maybe it should be the first to-do in every chapter). Data matters, and you don't want to be talking about issues that have marginal impact—you'll lose credibility fast.

- **Think about the core brand promise of your product or service.** You don't need to be a consumer products company to have a brand purpose. Make sure you're clear on your brand's promise before asking how to tie it to sustainability.

- **Once you are clear on your core brand promise, connect it to mega challenges.** How can your products and services help solve our collective challenges around climate, water, and other resources?

- **Consider product end of life as an opportunity.** Can you create a closed-loop or circular conversation or process with your partners and customers? What value can you extract from the product's end of life? It's a good chance to reconnect with customers, solve a problem for them, and then sell them more (like the computer companies that will take back office electronics while selling the next generation).

- **Walk the talk—and communicate it.** Before asking customers to do more, make sure you're demonstrating sincere, measurable efforts yourself. But then talk about it. *Not* getting brand value from the work you do is its own form of waste.

- **Map out what a "use less" strategy would mean for your business.** If customers start wanting less of your core product or service, how can you still make money? Like Kimberly-Clark Professional moving from cost per box, to cost per use, to a larger pitch on health, what's your transition strategy?

- **Develop new business plans with your customers.** Many large companies, especially in consumer products, have business planning meetings with customers to map out strategies together. Map out your joint strategies for tackling the mega challenges.

- **Ask your consumers to help.** Be bold, and step off the heresy cliff. Ask your customers to use *less*, creating a deeper bond with them. It's risky but rewarding, and far better to do it yourself before your competitors do.

To make a go of really changing consumer behavior, we'll need all our marketing tools running full steam. Companies can get help now from an unlikely ally in rethinking consumption: advertising agencies. The largest ones are asking tough questions as well.

Ogilvy has built a practice, dubbed Ogilvy Earth, to help brands think differently. Martin Sorrell, the CEO of WPP, one of the world's largest agencies, has said, "Given population growth, the limitations on the planet, changes in the climate, and the scarcity of water, responsible consumption is critical."[21] And David Jones, CEO of global agency Havas, talks in terms of responsibility, saying, "If you do not do good, you will find it harder to compete and do well."[22]

The Big Pivot Strategies

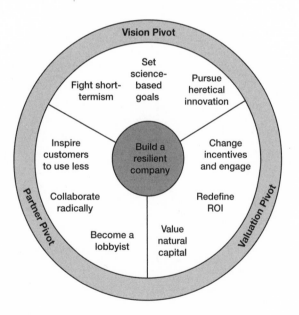

CHAPTER FOURTEEN

Build a Resilient, Antifragile Company

In the movie *Forrest Gump*, the title character is a simple man who stumbles into important moments in history, and everything goes his way. But when he tries his hand at being a shrimp boat captain, he fails miserably. Then a hurricane comes through, and although every other boat in the area is destroyed, Forrest and his shipmate, "Lieutenant Dan," somehow keep their own vessel afloat. After the storm, they have the whole fishery to themselves and make a fortune.

Forrest and his boat demonstrate resilience—an ability to survive in the face of a volatile world. But when he comes back even stronger after the storm, dominating his industry, he demonstrates a form of *antifragility*, a word coined by Nassim Taleb, the guru of uncertainty. In his book *Antifragile*, Taleb makes the case that robustness, another measure of how much stress a system can take and survive, is not good enough. We should aspire to actually get stronger when things get tough.

To help paint a picture of antifragile systems—ones that don't just survive as a merely resilient system would do, but get better—Taleb often points to the natural world. He repeatedly cites the example of our own bodies in particular: we stress our muscles when we exercise, and if we do it right, they get bigger. Our bodies react to stressors—be it exercise or a small amount of a pathogen in a vaccine—by getting stronger or developing resistance.

The key principles of the Big Pivot, particularly regeneration and circularity, are drawn from nature and demonstrate antifragility. Our planet is incredibly strong—it takes whatever is thrown at it and evolves, generally becoming more diverse and strong. A dinosaur-killing meteor? No problem, we'll just let mammals take over. This resilience in the face of change and stress is why all of our institutions should copy nature.[1]

With the mega challenges bearing down on us, I'd settle for building resilient or robust systems, but it's nice to imagine what antifragile economies, countries, and companies would look like. We know they would look very different than they do today.

It should be clear that none of our systems are currently antifragile, or even resilient. The global financial meltdown that cascaded from one class of bad assets, mortgage-backed securities, to infect the rest of the economy is proof enough. Or consider again how the storm surge from Hurricane Sandy caused a transformer to explode and took out half of New York City's power—that's not a resilient system. This is why former Mayor Bloomberg, before he left office, proposed a $20 billion climate resiliency plan for the city to prepare for rising sea levels and larger storms. The plan includes storm-surge barriers, dunes, revised building codes citywide, and much more.[2]

I'm not suggesting that we can perfectly prepare for all possible outcomes or know the future. Getting ready is not about better forecasting or detailed scenario planning. You don't build resilience into companies or economies because you know for sure how or when something bad will happen. You build it to protect yourself from the fact that you *don't* know what will happen.

We need systems that deal well with volatility and uncertainty—the only things in life, besides death and taxes, that are absolutely certain.

All of the radically practical strategies of the Big Pivot should help your company prepare for the future. But this final strategy is not just a result of the first nine; it's also about purposefully building the foundations you'll need to construct a resilient enterprise. In the face of climate change, resource constraints, and transparency, the most successful companies will specifically pursue resilience.

Foundations of Resilience

To create my list of foundational elements, I draw heavily on Taleb's *Antifragile* and, to a lesser extent, the book *Resilience* by Andrew Zolli and Ann Marie Healy. From these works and my own experience with companies facing deep challenges, I've zeroed in on five key foundations of resilience or antifragility.

Diversity

Throughout his book, Taleb shows a healthy respect for nature as a whole, which he suggests offers the best case study of antifragility. The earth has lasted for billions of years, facing planet-scale volatility, but as a system, nature generally comes back stronger or better.

Of course, Taleb warns, "nature is antifragile *up to a point* ... If a calamity completely kills life on the entire planet, the fittest will not survive."[3] It's is a tricky concept—an antifragile system actually desires stress, and it profits from it, but only to a certain extent.

In business, we're trained to reduce risk, not court it. But if your company mimics nature (remember, biomimicry should be a key operating principle) in products, processes, and strategies, you will survive better than competitors—nature-inspired resilience is a position of strength, allowing you to take advantage of the stresses that do come.

The key element that makes nature so strong is its diversity, which the authors of *Resilience* focus on quite a bit. The natural world is a rich tapestry of different life forms keeping a system humming, like the way a coral reef functions. Similarly, a diversity of ideas and perspectives makes an organization stronger; a variety of crops can reduce the risk of a single pest or blight wiping everything out (a serious problem with monocultures in agriculture); and a mix of assets in your investments can make for a relatively more shock-proof portfolio.

A company with just one product line, technology, or service that brings in the vast majority of its profits is at great risk. What Taleb calls a black-swan event (an unexpected occurrence with major, far-reaching consequences), or some other quick, fundamental shift in the industry, would threaten the company. Consider, for example, the beverage or candy giants that rely on sugar-based products for most of their profits. Nobody can predict how science and society will determine how best to manage health and wellness issues, but the discussion on sugar is following a path that looks a lot like what happened to tobacco 50 years ago (a steady drumbeat of scientific evidence of harm, leading to advertising bans and social stigma).

How will sugar-based product lines fare if the world turns away from sugar? Won't a company that has significant additional product lines, like healthier drinks or food, be able to ride out the storm better?

Think about what will happen to energy companies as society shifts aggressively away from carbon-based fuels. Or what will befall banks or funds with extensive loan portfolios or investments locked up in that same fossil fuel industry. The Big Pivot can come quickly, and those with multiple, diverse options and pathways will increase their odds of survival.

Redundancy, with Buffers

Perhaps the most important aspect of any natural system is redundancy: "Nature likes to overinsure itself," Taleb says. "Layers of redundancy are the central risk management property of natural systems. We have two kidneys, extra spare parts, and extra capacity in many, many things."[4]

Businesses don't tend toward having two of anything. But when things turn sour, running too lean can be a problem. The historic floods that ravaged Thailand in late 2011 had a deep impact on some very large industries when more than 1,000 factories filled with water. Hitachi and Western Digital, both large hard-drive producers with major facilities in Thailand, lost about half their production that quarter, and each suffered about $200 million in financial losses.[5]

In the auto industry, Toyota and Honda also ran into trouble during the flood, when it became clear that Thai suppliers were the only source for some of their parts. Industry watcher Edmunds estimated that vehicle production dropped by more than half a million units and pointed out that "only a few critical Thai-built parts laid Honda low."[6]

The devastating floods exposed some serious weaknesses in these companies' supply chains. Wouldn't it have been better to have multiple sources for these parts in different regions? A bit of redundancy in the system may be worth the expense if it avoids serious and expensive disruptions.

Or consider a more controversial example. When BP could not stop the gushing from the Deepwater Horizon oil well in the Gulf of Mexico in 2010, the company spent months building a secondary well to release the pressure, making it easier to plug the leak. Had the company built that relief well in the beginning, back when it dug the main well, the spill might have lasted minutes or hours, not months—and cut litigation and liability by decades and many billions of dollars.

That level of redundancy might seem ridiculous and expensive, but it wouldn't be unprecedented in the industry. After the famous *Exxon Valdez* oil spill in 1989, the oil industry was forced to build ships with double-layered hulls that reduce the odds of a breach when a ship runs aground. It's more expensive, but the hull redundancy has surely saved many spills and untold billions in liability.

If full duplication sounds like too much, consider the related idea of maintaining buffers and margins for error. In a white paper on resilience and risk, PricewaterhouseCoopers describes buffers as "the margins that provide the short-term breathing space needed to absorb shocks." The report describes how California utility PG&E "introduced a voluntary program for small commercial and residential customers who agree to shift their power use [to off-peak hours] in return for rate discounts." The 25,000 customers in the program allowed PG&E to cut back their power draw on hot days and during spikes, reducing the load on the grid by 16 percent.[7]

Redundancy is the critical factor in resilience. It may seem somehow weak to require a backup—the people who climb mountains with no ropes may be the most macho, but their margin for error is zero (one mistake can kill them). In business, however, as Taleb says, "redundancy is not necessarily wussy; it can be extremely aggressive … [I]f you have extra inventory of, say, fertilizers in the warehouse, just to be safe, and there happens to be a shortage because of disruptions in China, you can sell the excess inventory at a huge premium."[8]

Redundancy will be hard for the number-crunchers in us to accept. It seems wasteful. But in business, and life, we accept a certain level of expense to protect ourselves from risk—by some measures, insurance is 3 percent of the global economy. Why wouldn't we set up our businesses with some buffers to better handle extreme situations that seem to be happening more frequently? Taleb points out that "redundancy is ambiguous because it seems like a waste if nothing unusual happens. Except that something unusual happens—usually."[9]

So ask yourself, what's the single hull in our business?

Hating Risk … and Loving It

Taleb made his mark in the investing world by betting on the extremes that he says are inevitable. He talks about the benefits of pursuing an unusual investment strategy: put 90 percent of your portfolio in low-risk cash and 10 percent in extremely risky bets that can pay off 10-fold or much more (options that bet on volatility, for example). You can only lose 10 percent at most, and you have large upside. A normal portfolio with 100 percent "medium-risk" securities, Taleb points out, may actually carry higher total risk of complete ruin in market meltdowns.[10]

Companies operate much more in the latter mode, implementing low- or medium-risk investments and strategies across all parts of the business. Executives are inherently risk-averse and have incentives to be that way. Don't rock the boat too much and deliver predictable earnings in the short-run—that's the mantra.

But imagine what a company in the 90/10 mode would look like. It would use a safe, fast follower strategy with most of the business, but then take much larger risks in select pieces of the organization. This is where heretical innovation really matters and where the Skunk Works that I suggested earlier could come into play. It all makes for an interesting combination of extreme risk-aversion with a healthy dash of risk-seeking.

We're at a Big Pivot point globally, where we need some big bets. For some sectors and companies, the whole business model will shift—think again about Waste Management's move from just hauling waste to managing recycling and offering waste services. Or consider the fossil fuel companies with unrivaled power and profits today, but a deeply uncertain future as the world's governments, citizens, and investors realize we can't burn all of the fuels that the oil companies count as their main assets.

For many organizations, the Big Pivot can come in chunks, when the companies develop heretical innovations that pay off big but disrupt core pieces of the business (before someone else does). For that strategy to work well, we need to try a lot of things and find out quickly what's not going to fly. We need to fail fast.

Speed: Fast Feedback and Failure

My cardiologist friend, the one who told me that 40 percent of first heart attacks are fatal, also told me an amazing story about saving a man's life. During hospital rounds, my friend was talking to one of his patients who was hooked up to heart monitors. While the man was talking, my friend saw on the monitor that his heart had stopped working correctly even though the patient was unaware (there's a ten-second delay or so before he would feel it). My friend was able to turn to a nurse, call for the paddles, and get ready to resuscitate the man quickly, which he did.

The Materiality Challenge

Here's a short, but really complicated question: What's a material risk to a company? *Materiality* is an accounting term that gauges how important something is. Every public company must disclose risks to its investors, but which risks are big enough to mention?

The question is getting more thorny in the world of mega challenges—when does climate change, water availability, or possible legislation on toxic chemicals pose a material risk to a company or government? In March 2013, New York State issued a warning to bond investors that climate change would hurt the state's finances. Oddly, the ratings agencies Standard & Poor's and Moody's Investor Service—the same guys who gave AAA ratings to some very risky mortgage-backed securities—dismissed the idea and chose not to downgrade the state.[11] This disconnect can't, and won't, continue.

Climate change poses an unusual materiality challenge. It's a nonlinear risk that can present itself sometimes in larger storms. By the time parts of the Jersey Shore knew for sure, without a doubt, that climate change and extreme weather were material risks, some towns were wiped out. We can't wait until materiality is slapping us in the face.

In this general quest for better, more material information, one organization to watch is the Sustainability Accounting Standards Board, which identifies which environmental and social issues are truly material to business, sector by sector. The goal is for this new organization to have the same influence over accounting as the Financial Accounting Standards Board does, but it's early going.

Materiality is an enormous issue that goes to the core of the Big Pivot—if we can't value and identify the real risks and dependencies in our business, we can't manage them well.

Clearly luck played a part since my friend was in the room. But fast feedback—knowing what was going on with the patient at that moment—had a lot to do with it. Real-time feedback is powerful, even in less life-and-death situations. Energy meters that show homeowners their energy use, right now, change behavior. People flip off lights and air-conditioning, saving energy and money.

It's not just consumer behavior that's affected by quick data. The large oil refiner Valero used energy meters and real-time monitoring software from SAP to find inefficiencies. It optimized its tank temperatures and pressures, saving $120 million in the first year alone. Similarly, Dow Chemical used water meters to find a billion gallons of savings at the world's largest refinery in Texas, a state that's not getting wetter anytime soon.[12]

At both the global and the corporate levels, we need better feedback mechanisms—energy and water meters are easy, but how are we doing on the mega challenges? The Stockholm Resilience Center has developed a set of nine planetary boundaries that we can't breach for our own safety, in areas like climate change (measured as the amount of carbon in the atmosphere), biodiversity, ozone, ocean acidification, and water use. The center says we're already past the safe point on three of the nine.[13] And the people working on context-based metrics I discussed in chapter 6 are developing methods for thinking about similar issues at the corporate level (see Appendix B for more on this topic).

But again, we need to fail quickly, and even reward people for trying, no matter what the outcome. If we take 10 percent of our portfolio of businesses and make some wild, heretical bets, we should quickly know what works and what doesn't. The heretical bets require not only fast feedback, but also brave leaders who cut the cord on failed experiments and move on.

Modular and Distributed Design

In August 2003, the power went out all over the northeastern part of the United States, plunging 50 million people into darkness. On a personal level, I remember it well because my first child was 11 days old and we were stuck without refrigeration or air-conditioning. New parents are not in the most resilient mental place.

The story behind the blackout is absurd. The monumental cascade of power failure started when a single tree branch hit a power line in Ohio. The whole fiasco exposed a large security risk for the country. As the former head of the Central Intelligence Agency, Jim Woolsey, points out, it wouldn't take much planning to take out the grid on purpose: "Terrorists are a lot smarter than tree branches."[14]

A resilient system has not only redundancy, but also independent, modular, and distributed components. We would do ourselves an enormous service if we built distributed power systems, which means some combination of solar panels, wind turbines, and geothermal systems, for every home and office building.

My house has a seven-kilowatt solar system on the roof. In some months, we make more electricity than we need and ship the extra back to the grid. For now, we still need backup, but with a localized battery and microgrid—technologies that are on their way—we could save up on the sunny days and still have power when storms hit.

Companies can go even further. Those that rely on distributed energy and decouple themselves from fossil fuels and the grid can continue operating in extreme situations. Walmart understands the opportunity here. The company was already the largest on-site user of renewables and solar power when it committed to even more aggressive goals, including a 600 percent increase in the use of renewables. During the announcement event, Leslie Dach,

Signs of the Pivot: The US Military

The military has identified carbon-based fuels as a great risk to its mission. As an input to its operations, fossil fuels make for a vulnerable supply chain and one that basically funds the enemy. The reliance on these fuels threatens our troops: for every 24 convoys of fuel or water, one soldier or civilian contractor is injured or killed. They also cost a lot—the military spends $400 per gallon to get oil to forward operating bases. And they contribute to climate change, which a Pentagon-funded think tank identified as a "threat multiplier." In response, the US Navy in particular has taken action, running a US Marine forward operating base in Afghanistan on solar power, launching the USS *Makin Island*—a hybrid ship that runs on batteries and reaches speeds of up to 10 knots (the Prius of the seas, perhaps?)—and purchasing large quantities of biofuels for its planes.[15]

then the executive vice president of corporate affairs, described how Walmart's investments in energy efficiency and renewable energy would "help us keep our stores up and running no matter how bad the weather is or who else might be down."[16]

Like Forrest Gump's shrimp boat, the business that's left standing when the bad things happen will do very, very well.

The Challenge of Valuing Resilience and Risk Avoidance

We have a hurdle standing in the way of aggressively managing risk and building resilience, even if it's for competitive advantage: few people in any organization are rewarded for keeping bad things from happening (except maybe goalies). Sure, there are risk officers, but the leadership team and all middle management are generally praised for what they did do, not what they didn't.

It reminds me of all the pundits who made fun of the hand-wringing around Y2K, the expected meltdown of computer systems on New Year's 2000, when the date turned to 01/01/00. Not much went wrong that day, they pointed out. But that was because programmers around the world had worked hard to mitigate the risk. Both companies and governments invested a ton of time and resources to avoid problems.

In a meeting I had with the top management of a large company with manufacturing around the world, the CFO spoke about the expense of retrofitting factories for better fire protection. He talked about the supposed ROI of the project. But that's the problem—there really isn't an ROI. The "return" is the reassurance that something will not happen. Sure, you can put a value on what a fire would cost in physical assets (aside from human costs), but the number is counterfactual—posing a situation that doesn't or hasn't happened.

It's a good sign when management can see the "ROI" in these kinds of investments, but most of the time, risk control and management of the mega challenges are vastly undervalued by business. That is, until a company makes the Big Pivot.

HOW TO EXECUTE

This whole book is really about building a resilient, robust enterprise. Science-based goals that lead to radical efficiency and heretical innovation make your business more resilient—you're not as threatened by scarce resources if you use a lot less of them. Putting the right value on the inputs you use and benefits you gain from Big Pivot strategies builds long-term value and creates stronger companies. Collaboration means someone has your back and you're less likely to fail. Working with your customers to help them manage mega challenges builds longer-lasting, stronger relationships, which make the organization more resilient.

Beyond these points, I'd suggest asking a few key questions to start you on the path to building a resilient enterprise:

- Examine your value chain for impacts and risks—again. Then ask yourself, what's our single hull (that is, what's our prime vulnerability that can cause enormous damage and expense)?

- Where would redundancy truly help you? What would it cost to build it, or to recover from *not* having built it?

- What could you do to build buffers in your operations, in the supply chain, and in the organization (perhaps stockpiling critical skill sets in your people rather than always using layoffs as a path to cost-savings)?

- How can you make the various parts of your business less interdependent so that one area can fail without dragging down the rest?

- How can you reduce the risk for most of your business, but significantly ramp up the risk-taking in a part of it? Would a heretical innovation hub (chapter 7) help?

- How could you reward risk avoidance? When something happens to competitors or other businesses in a region, but your operations make it through, how are you rewarding the people who kept your business safe?

- How can you position your company for surprising opportunities when things turn ugly? What's your shrimp boat? What's your competitor's?

What roles do risk avoidance and resilience play in a company? Do we value it at all? Taleb criticizes businesspeople for often being narrow in their views: "[They] tend to believe that generating profits is their principal mission, with survival and risk control something to perhaps consider—they miss the strong logical precedence of survival over success. To make profits, it would be a good idea to, first, survive."[17]

Envisioning a Big-Pivot World

Change is coming, whether we like it or not. No company—and no person—will avoid the effects of a hotter, scarcer, more open world.

In a hotter world, businesses will face the constant risk of interruptions from storms, floods, and droughts. Companies will need to deal with rapid shifts in customer demands for climate-friendly products and services. They will also find employees and many other stakeholders increasingly expecting action on climate change.

In a scarcer world, businesses will have to manage rising cost structures as prices generally keep going up on most major inputs into the economy. Or they'll face an outright lack of availability of some critical input like water.

In a more open world, everyone will know how your business operates up and down your value chain. Customers, employees, and communities will judge you on whether you're part of the problem or the solution, on issues as diverse as climate change, water use, resource constraints, and worker safety.

The ten radically practical strategies that I've proposed in *The Big Pivot* may not cover everything we need to do to deal with our mega challenges and build a prosperous world. But for the private sector, they represent a broad agenda and they are a nonnegotiable package. There's really no partial version—as appealing as it would be, we can't undertake only some of the agenda, any more than we could embark on a partial plan to bail a sinking boat. These strategies, taken together, rethink how companies see the world (the Vision Pivot), what's important to them (the Valuation Pivot), and how they collaborate (the Partner Pivot). In total, the 10 strategies are necessary to tackle our mega challenges.

I know it's a lot to suggest that companies must act on all these fronts simultaneously. Organizations often park many of these issues in their "sustainability" departments and say they can't do it all—especially with the limited resources they've allotted to the group. We have to prioritize, they'll say soberly. But is this approach logical?

When it comes to the way you operate, is there some finite amount of doing the right thing for your business that you can handle at once? Imagine a CEO telling investors or employees, "This year, we're going to do a bang-up job on marketing. Next year, we'll pursue peak performance in product development, and in a couple years, we'll get to human resources."

There are different people involved in all major areas of the business, and every one of them is expected to excel and do what's best. The same is true of the Big-Pivot strategies. Different people will own separate parts of the agenda—government relations on lobbying, investor relations on some of the Wall Street conversation, product development or R&D on heretical innovation, HR on engagement, the CFO on investment decisions and valuations, and so on.

But make no mistake: the Big Pivot has to come from the top—from the C-suite. The captain and all the officers need to lead the charge. But once you have top-level buy-in, executing these strategies will involve some real, roll-up-your-sleeves work and new kinds of collaboration. Because the Big Pivot can require a lot of effort, it's fair to ask, what do we get out of it?

There is a tremendous upside waiting for those who are willing to make the profound shift. But I should be honest: some companies will not do so well in a Big-Pivot world. There will be winners and losers.

Most companies and industrial sectors will change profoundly, or they will disappear. Without a "clean-coal" technological miracle, for example, the coal sector will be gone. Fossil fuel companies in general will transform into renewable-energy giants or will become much, much smaller organizations. And yes, jobs in some areas will be lost. Just as we didn't artificially prop up horse-and-buggy or typewriter companies, we can't save some businesses today. No free-market economy has ever guaranteed a sector or any particular job. And true paradigm shifts, which are less rare than they used to be, come for us all.

Despite these important caveats, the vast majority of us will win in this new world, if for no other reason than the obvious fact that ensuring our very survival is a pretty big victory. Let's envision what we gain from making the Big Pivot and pursuing a more radically practical agenda.

A Big-Pivot World

Picture workplaces that are more open and inclusive, with engaged employees avidly pursuing a larger purpose. They will be designing, building, and providing products and services that stop contributing to our own destruction, and even restore our world, leaving it richer for the next generation of people and businesses.

We'll be innovating in new ways and redefining value within a company, freeing ourselves up for pursuits more exciting and fulfilling than just generating short-term profits. We'll stop running on the hamster wheel of quarterly earnings, allowing executives to build great companies that produce amazing customer experiences.

The leaders will be more profitable in every sense of the word, even as they redefine profit. Revamping our built environment, our transportation infrastructure, and our energy systems—as well as reworking consumption and what defines a good quality of life—will be multi-trillion-dollar endeavors with huge pots of gold for those who find the greenest ways to do it.

By helping build a more resilient, antifragile, prosperous world, corporations will establish a new role in society as a force for real progress, leading our ineffectual governments to better, more efficient, market-based outcomes. Business leaders will stop seeing governments—the only institutions that can marshal the collective will and resources at the scale we need—as the enemy. And governments, for their part, will become more than just regulators, but productive collaborators instead.

We will be investing in and deploying technologies and business models that make us healthier and less reliant on dangerous, inaccessible, and expensive resources that threaten the world's security. Our economy will decouple itself from material use as we build a circular economy—based in part on the ideas from books like *Cradle to Cradle* and *Upcycle*—where all safe materials are treated as "nutrients" that can be endlessly recycled.

And most significantly, renewable energy, delivered in a distributed way from every building and home, will power our world. We'll be betting on people and our future by building a more just, inclusive society that's also in line with nature's boundaries, leveraging the abundant, renewable forms of energy all around us.

Finally, we'll change our expectations about what's possible. Perhaps the biggest hurdle standing in the way of making the Big Pivot is not short-termism or silos or gaps in valuation; no, it's the lack of belief that we *can*.

We have to believe that we can change the direction we're headed. We must also realize that the shift will be easier the earlier we start. If you're sailing a supertanker across the ocean, a small change in trajectory early in the journey will shift which continent you ultimately reach. Wait too long, and you'll have a long way to go to correct your error—and your provisions may run out before you get there.

We're low on time to respond to many challenges—carbon in particular. It's easy to throw up our hands and say it's too hard. But changes in what's feasible politically, emotionally, financially, or socially come upon us with shocking speed. After years of what seems like no motion, with brave people working hard to shift perceptions, we hit a tipping point and the norm changes. Think of abolitionists and slavery; the civil rights battles for equality in race, gender, and sexuality; or the shift on views of smoking. When the change comes, it can come fast.

In the business world, we either change quickly with the times, or we go extinct. Our version of capitalism has its issues, but it's nothing if not ruthlessly efficient at casting out outdated models. The new way of doing business is upon us.

The Big Pivot will not always be easy, but that doesn't mean it's always hard, either, or that it's not fun. Improving our personal health and avoiding that fatal heart attack can be challenging at times, given the short-term demands of life. But we can build better, sometimes profoundly different habits into our lives. And the payback is immense. Personally, we can greatly increase the odds that we live longer and healthier. Surely we can accomplish the same thing for our species as a whole.

A client once asked me in a meeting with his peers, "Are we doing all of this green stuff because it makes business sense or just so we can sleep better?" Well, we probably all sleep easier when we know we've done everything we can to care for our own health, our children and families, our homes, our friends, and our communities. We can't know how everything will play out in the future, but we can work hard to build a better today. So, should we make the Big Pivot because it's profitable, or because we'll sleep better, or because we'll ensure a better future for all?

The answer is yes.

AFTERWORD

Thank you for picking up this book. I wanted to provide a quick perspective on the approach of the book, offer some information about my working relationships with some of the companies discussed, and answer some key questions that may come up.

Length and Approach

The era of the comprehensive "doorstop" book may be coming to a close. The amount of information coming into our lives is only expanding. So the burden is on any writer to cover issues that require some depth and contemplation and to do so as quickly as possible to respect the reader's time.

I've attempted to summarize the key points within some very large ideas (like the brutal math of climate change) and strategies (such as how companies can fight the short-termism that threatens business success) in a handful of pages each. *The Big Pivot* is intended to be relatively short, but still provide a solid roadmap to a new way of operating. I believe in the 80-20 rule, but I hope I'm conveying much more than 80 percent of what companies need to know to make the pivot.

In its approach, this book was not created as an academic series of case studies from which you can then draw your own conclusions. Instead, I've aimed to provide a framework for thinking about the mega challenges we face and the strategies companies need to employ to manage and profit from these challenges.

The stories I use are intended to support the scaffolding of ideas and strategies.

No book of this kind could lay out what these strategies mean for every sector specifically, so my goal is to—in a pithy way—create a sense of urgency and provide a roadmap, along with some key examples of companies that have begun the Big Pivot.

Transparency

In *The Big Pivot*, I focus on three mega forces changing the way business and society work, including the relentless drive toward transparency in all we do. Company operations are now open to public scrutiny in ways that managers could never before have imagined. So it would be inconsistent of me not to be transparent about my own business. I have had working relationships at some point with about 20 percent of the companies I discuss.

These consulting and advisory roles are one way I gain unique insight into what companies are doing. The strategies and themes in the book are enhanced by the knowledge I've gained through these relationships, but in no way is this book created to benefit any clients. In the interest of transparency, however, let me quickly list them.

Of the roughly 145 companies mentioned in this book (some of them in passing), I have consulted at some point with a handful. I currently sit on paid sustainability-focused advisory boards for Kimberly-Clark, HP, and Unilever (US division). I'm also on the unpaid advisory board for Practically Green. My firm has (or had) consulting projects (and sometimes speaking engagements) with Boeing, Caesars Entertainment, Coca-Cola, IKEA, Johnson & Johnson, Ogilvy, Owens-Corning, PepsiCo, Timberland, and Xerox. I also consulted to a multicompany working group that included Diversey, FedEx, and GE. In addition, I have an ongoing joint business relationship with PricewaterhouseCoopers (PwC) in the United States, which leads to consulting projects with some of these companies as well.

For another group of companies in the book, I've given paid speeches to groups of employees, executives, or customers. These companies are 3M, Clarke Environmental, Clorox, Diageo, eBay, Ford Motor Company, Hitachi, Jones Lang LaSalle, Marriott, P&G, SAP, Siemens, the US military, Walmart, Walt Disney Company, and Waste Management.

Answering a Few Concerns

A few overarching questions about the target audience and the companies I discuss may come up as you read this book. Over the years, I've heard some of these concerns about my first book, *Green to Gold*.

It would be impossible to fully cover every reader's industry or company type (size, culture, geography) perfectly. Nevertheless, a good discussion of strategies and principles can be applied across a range of businesses of all types. Some of the most useful business books have focused mainly on one sector or even one company. *The Big Pivot* tries to draw out lessons and ideas that the manager or influencer reading this can apply to his or her specific circumstances.

But it's worth addressing a few of the key concerns I often hear. First, in a discussion of corporate efforts on environmental and social issues, it can seem like the same companies come up a lot and that they are more consumer focused (B2C) than business to business (B2B). It's a fair point.

My goal is always to find the best examples of the principle or strategy I'm writing about. The companies that are taking the lead don't fall evenly across the spectrum of industry. Very early participants in the first phases of the greening of business—that is, the wave of environmental regulations that forced a focus on compliance in the 1970s and 1980s—were, logically, mainly in heavy industries (oil, mining, and so on). But today, more consumer products companies are leading the way toward new, more environmentally and socially beneficial ways of doing business. The sustainability agenda has become much broader and is now a core issue with customers, employees, and communities. The leaders in any given dimension of the new business agenda are who they are, and I'd rather tell a compelling story than force a false balance of business sectors.

Also, the line between B2C and B2B is often blurry. The consumer packaged goods (CPG) giants are trying to appeal to consumers. But these companies also have to answer to Walmart, Target, Tesco, and many others. On environmental issues, it's these business customers that are asking much more pointed questions than even government regulators. So these large CPG companies have a deep B2B sensibility running through their organizations.

Another issue that some readers might raise is that the book is US-focused. In addition to US companies, *The Big Pivot* features organizations from many other countries, such as Brazil, China, France, Germany, Holland, India, Japan, South Korea, Sweden, Switzerland, Thailand, and the United Kingdom. And most of the companies covered here, even those based in the United States, are multinational in scope, with often more than half their revenues coming from outside their home country. But, it may not seem like enough for the globalist reader.

There are a couple of reasons for this US slant. Admittedly, I'm an American and my work takes place mainly in the United States or Europe. But the other problem is a paucity of leaders—or at least transparent ones I can identify—in some regions. The top business experts I spoke with in China and India pointed only to a couple of large-scale examples of the level of corporate leadership highlighted in *The Big Pivot*.

Part of the problem stems from transparency and culture. In some of my other work, in particular a project to document the environmental and social goals of the world's largest companies (see www.pivotgoals.com), the stated targets of Chinese organizations were much less clear. I'm sure there is more going on in those regions, so I welcome readers to send me more stories of leadership from the developing world.

A final concern may be that the book seems to underreport on the world of small and medium-size business. Despite the use of mostly large companies as examples, much of what I present, especially the value-creation tactics, applies to small and medium companies equally well. Innovative strategies that save money, reduce risk, drive new products, or create brand value are not the sole domain of big companies.

Even so, there are clearly some important differences between what the small and large companies can do to improve environmental and social performance. For example, the pressure that large companies can put on their supply chains is unique (although the little guys can draft in the wake of rising standards). Additionally, the influence that large companies wield over government policy is also unique. And finally, some of the discussion here is squarely aimed at public companies, which are generally the larger ones (but all companies have investors with demands, even if those financial stakeholders are family members).

But primarily I focus on big companies because humanity has big, global-level problems to solve. We need scale to move the needle in a real way. The reality is that no matter how many people the small businesses of the world employ, the economic, environmental, and social impacts lie squarely with the giants. Just the largest 200 companies have revenues of over $20 trillion—that's about 29 percent of global GDP. As the famous line goes, you rob banks because that's where the money is.

I'm excited to share with you my thinking on the deep change in business that I believe we must make and are beginning to see. I truly welcome your involvement in the discussion and interpretation of the signs you see around the world. Please share them with me at www.andrewwinston.com, or talk to me on Twitter: @andrewwinston.

By taking this time to contemplate some big questions about the nature of business, together we can help bring about the Big Pivot, building a more prosperous future for all.

APPENDIX A

Sustainability 102

The Business Case for Green Strategy

As I discussed in chapter 4, the idea of the business case for managing our big challenges and finding ways to profit from them is increasingly surreal to me. But it's important that we have the basic logic at hand when we're making the larger pitch for greater, faster action. Many businesspeople are still skeptical that this pursuit isn't some anticorporate plot. Nothing could be further from the truth.

With all this in mind, let's review the basic business case, which is more than compelling. The key ideas here are based on my books *Green to Gold*, coauthored with Dan Esty, and *Green Recovery*. Additionally, I have developed a newer, "unified theory" to summarize the large forces coming to bear on companies (the main three I focus on in this book—climate, resources, and transparency—are part of this model). To start, let's quickly examine the basic green-strategy arsenal.

Value-Creation Buckets

One of the core frameworks of *Green to Gold* outlines four fundamental ways to create value: building the upside through (1) revenue and (2) brand growth, and reducing the downsides by (3) cutting costs and (4) reducing risk. In table A-1, I summarize some specific ways that managing environmental and social performance creates value.

TABLE A-1

Value creation from environmental and social performance

	Key value creators	In short ...
Revenue	• New products	Making more money
	• Increased sales ("vendor of choice")	
	• Higher prices	
Brand	• Product differentiation	Ensuring future money
	• Customer loyalty	
	• Employee attraction and retention	
Cost	• Eco-efficiency (less energy, water, waste)	Spending less money
	• Asset efficiency	
	• Insurance costs	
Risk	• Supply-chain reliability	More-reliable money
	• Lower volatility in input prices	
	• Business continuity and resilience	
Multi-category	• Business model innovation	Higher business value
	• License to operate and market access	
	• First-mover advantage	

Driving Revenue: Satisfying New Needs, Creating New Markets

We'll start with the upside. Helping customers reduce their impacts and limit their exposure to the risks posed by the mega challenges will drive sales. The strategy works in nearly any sector—construction and green building, telecom, retail, consumer products, energy, transportation, banking, consulting and other services, and so on. A number of companies have set aggressive targets—which they're hitting—for increasing the sales of more environmental-friendly products (see the sidebar "Green Product Sales").

The leading companies now see the revenue path as central to their strategy. Unilever CEO Paul Polman says that "businesses that make a contribution to society, make it part of their overall business model, will be very successful. So for us, it's an accelerator of our business." Unilever's core strategy, its Sustainable Living Plan, sets an aggressive goal of doubling revenues by 2020 while cutting its footprint in half. Polman often says that the company will reach this lofty goal, not *despite* its efforts to halve its footprint, but *because of them.*

Green-focused products and services can drive new sales and top-line growth, but they also help defend market share and maintain the customer base you already have. In many sectors, showing customers that you manage environmental and social issues well is becoming table stakes. For example, 75 percent of the requests for proposals (RFPs) that tech giant HP receives now include questions about green product attributes. Potential customers are asking about issues such as product energy efficiency, chemicals and toxics, and design for recyclability. These RFPs represent many billions of dollars of revenue that depend on HP's environmental bona fides.[1]

Green Product Sales

Many companies set revenue growth goals for their green products specifically. I've worked with both Kimberly-Clark and Johnson & Johnson on the internal-facing criteria they developed to spur the creation of products that are more sustainable. Both have established rigorous standards for which products qualify. Each company makes its product managers apply for the distinction and sets targets for the total percentage of sales coming from the better, greener products.

A few other companies have gone public with their goals, which are not small. Philips set a target that half its revenues would come from the greener portfolio—and in 2012 the company came close, with $15 billion in green product sales. Toshiba wants to sell $18 billion (1.8 trillion yen) worth of "excellent ECPs" (environmentally conscious products). In 2012, P&G surpassed its $50 billion cumulative sales target for its "sustainable innovation products." GE has sold more than $100 billion of ecomagination products and services since the program launch, and this part of its product portfolio is growing twice as fast as the rest of the business.[2]

Growing the Brand: Building Intangible Value, Loyalty, and License to Operate

Brand value is a concept that covers many ideas: customer loyalty and intention to buy; the ability to attract, retain, and engage the best talent; positive community perceptions; and many other things we can't measure very well. All of these intangible assets (or indirect value) quite often make up the majority of a company's value.

Just because soft value is difficult to measure doesn't mean that the value is low—far from it. HP surveyed IT execs, consumers, and other stakeholders to better understand what drove its reputation. About 40 percent of the company's reputation stemmed from a cluster of factors that included HP's environmental strategy, recycling efforts, supplier responsibility, employment practices, and community engagement. The company's research also tied these issues to "important business outcomes" like customers' purchase decisions and employee recruitment and retention.[3]

This latter value creator—the ability to attract and retain talent—may be the most important. The former CEO of P&G, Bob McDonald, described what he hears during recruiting trips to business schools and undergraduate programs: "Wherever I go on college campuses, people want to talk about the purpose of the company, because they want to work for a company that tries to make a difference in the world ... And secondly, [they ask about our] sustainability strategy."[4] I've heard similar stories many times as well from service-oriented businesses like banks and consulting firms. Even in a rough job market, potential employees are asking tough questions.

We can't always put perfect numbers on brand and engagement value. But no company can operate profitably without the willing and enthusiastic participations of its employees, communities, and customers.

Slashing Costs: Getting More from Less

Synonymous with eco-efficiency, cost reduction cuts in energy, waste, and water in the whole range of company operations, including buildings, IT, manufacturing, and fleet and distribution. The paybacks in these areas can come quickly—in months, not years. There are countless examples of companies slashing costs: Unilever saved $395 million over four years through eco-efficiency. From 1994 to 2005, Dow Chemical cut energy costs by $4 billion with less than a $1 billion investment—and then found another 20 percent in energy cuts over the next eight years. Walmart has improved the fuel efficiency of its distribution fleet by 69 percent since 2005.[5] These examples of so-called incremental changes have added up to billions of dollars in value.

Reducing Risk: Making Business, and Cash Flows, More Predictable

In old-school environmental thinking, risk management was mainly about complying with the law and perhaps changing operations and reformulating products to avoid regulations. But you can also reduce risk in more subtle ways, such as investing in onsite renewable energy to reduce reliance on traditional energy resources with incredibly volatile prices. Or you can manage the rising and serious risks to business continuity from increasingly extreme weather. Or you can protect a company's "license to operate," something of real value granted by communities, employees, and society at large.

In the mining world, for example, demonstrating your intention to minimize damage to the land and surrounding communities, and then to remediate the area when you're done digging, can make the difference between opening a mine or spending years and many millions *trying* to open a mine. British miner Vendanta, for example, ran into intense resistance from a local community in India and has repeatedly failed to obtain the clearance to build a bauxite mine. The aluminum giant Alcoa took a different tack to get a mine up and running in Brazil. According to one exec, the company "spent several extra years working with the local community before building a mine, which we now look forward to running for 100 years."[6]

Reducing risk can create short-term benefits such as lower borrowing and compliance costs, fewer regulatory hassles, and lower risk to earnings flows (a stability that investors love). But the conversation is now turning to a much deeper view of enterprise-level risk—the hot term is *resilience*, and the growing question is, "What's a material risk to our business?" (See chapter 14 for more on these issues.)

These four buckets of value creation overlap and interact in nice ways. For example, PNC bank has been building green branches at a furious pace, all of them LEED-certified (the US Green Building Council's rating system, Leadership in Energy and Environmental Design). Greener buildings reduce ongoing

---

The Integrated Bottom Line

The four main value buckets outlined in table A-1—revenue, brand, cost, and risk—are not new. But recognizing that tackling mega challenges actually creates value in these traditional ways is new for most executives and is key to the Big Pivot mind-set. Corporate adviser and thought leader Hunter Lovins was one of the first to see this deep truth and has made the business case for sustainability for 30 years. Recently she developed an approach to strategy she calls the *integrated bottom line*, which "enables managers to use more sustainable practices to build core business value, integrating sustainability into every aspect of enhancing shareholder value."[7]

---

operating costs and lower risk by cutting reliance on unpredictably priced energy (PNC has a net-zero branch that makes more energy than it needs). The buildings also improve brand value by speaking to customers' values, which then drives more sales. When PNC compared its LEED branches with regular ones, it calculated that the greener ones were generating $463,000 more revenue per employee per year. That's a nice payback on a building.[8]

The Total-Forces View

Part of the business case for sustainability strategy is the argument that companies don't have much choice—they face enormous pressure to manage environmental and social issues. This pressure comes from three main categories: key stakeholders that apply specific pressure on organizations, tectonic shifts in how the world works, and biophysical and social sustainability challenges (from climate change to global inequality).

Stakeholder Pressure

Green to Gold provides a framework for thinking about 20 different stakeholder categories in five groups.[9] But in my newer, three-level model, I focus on six key stakeholder groups:

- **Business customers.** Companies are asking more questions of their suppliers and setting their own standards, often stricter than what the government is demanding (see "De Facto Regulation" in Chapter 11).

- **Consumers.** People are conflicted, but growing more conscious and concerned about the story behind everything they buy (What's in it? Who made it? And so on).

- **Governments and NGOs.** These two groups of rule makers maintain their regulatory and watchdog roles.

- **Investors.** Some of the institutions providing capital, especially those with longer-term perspectives, are growing concerned about the risks to companies (and their earnings) from the mega challenges.

- **Employees.** Especially true of the rising new group of millennials, workers today demand much more of companies as they look for meaning in their work.

Understanding these six groups, what they want, and how best to work with them is critical to bringing about a Big Pivot. The expectations being set by your largest stakeholders are rising fast—meet their needs, or risk becoming irrelevant.

Tectonic Shifts

A quartet of deep changes in how the world works is sweeping through the business world and society. First, the world is becoming more globalized as customer demands become common around the world and capital and talent can move fluidly. Second, everything is getting more transparent as technology allows everyone to share more information (this is the "more open" part of the story). Third, hundreds of millions of new consumers are coming online, creating vast new global middle class (rising demand is a key part of the "scarcer" story). The stress that this growth in demand is placing on all our resources and on our planetary support structures (air, water, climate) has caused one very good development. The world is now investing serious capital to create a clean economy, the fourth tectonic change.

Sustainability Issues

Finally, there's the group of pressures that explain why we're even discussing all of this—the set of environmental and social challenges that stakeholders are very concerned about and that the tectonic shifts can make worse or better. In this simplified view of what companies are dealing with today, climate (the "hotter" part of our agenda here), water, toxics, waste, and biodiversity make up the big five on the environmental side. The social set of issues is long, but I suggest that equity (income, gender, racial, geographic), labor, freedom, and wellness cover the big bases. These issues are broad, thorny, and both local and global.

The core point is that these big, societal challenges are now on the business agenda. The government, especially in the United States, is largely dysfunctional. The annual global meeting of world leaders to address climate change has a nearly unbroken record (19 years at this writing) of agreeing to virtually nothing. It's up to the private sector now. The business community has the management skills, resources (trillions in cash sitting on the sidelines), and innovation capacity to tackle these issues. We are being asked to take the lead, and that's a good thing. The companies that can solve many of these problems for their customers will profit greatly.

Figure A-1 shows how various pressures might interact when a business is trying to manage environmental and social issues.[10] Imagine spinning the three wheels shown to line up a topic or issue from each rung, and explore how they interact. For example, look at the line of issues at about ten o'clock on the chart. Consider how business customers, leveraging the tools of transparency, might ask for more information about chemicals and toxics in the

FIGURE A-1

Forces wheel

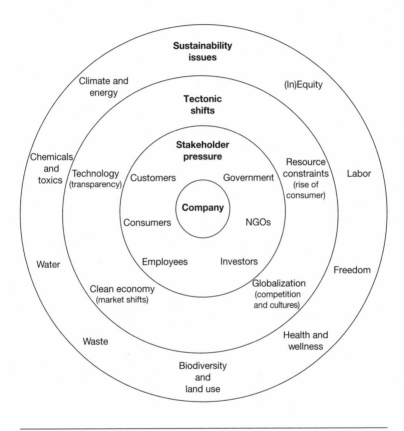

supply chain. This particular interaction is already playing out in mandates from retailers about chemicals like bisphenol A (BPA) and phthalates in plastics, and about certain toxics in electronics. Spin the wheel, and think about how issues may unfold over time, and who will win and lose.

Key Principles

Many companies have taken on some or most of the *Green to Gold* agenda and are trying to take part in a clean and green movement (the key principles of which are described in table 4-1). As I laid out in *Green Recovery*, business leaders are getting lean, smart, engaged, and creative. These companies have developed some identifiable attributes:

- **Value-aware.** In addition to cost-saving initiatives and risk reduction efforts, a wide range of companies are now seeking the other buckets of value, pitching their sustainability story to build their brands, and innovating at the product level to drive revenues. They're increasingly seeing the upside opportunities in managing environmental and social issues well.

- **Eco-efficient.** Companies are saving billions by getting lean, mostly through projects that meet normal hurdle rates.

- **Value-chain-focused.** Leaders are looking beyond their "four walls" to understand impacts, risks, and opportunities upstream with suppliers or downstream with customers. They're starting to close loops, use more recycled material, and innovate to provide products and services that help customers reduce *their* impacts.

- **Data-driven.** Companies are getting smarter and, if exact numbers are unavailable or too expensive to collect, they are figuring out the directionally correct answer about their biggest impacts (that is, where the hot spots in their value chain lie).

- **Risk-averse (precautionary).** Much of this agenda is still centered on reducing risk, particularly legal and compliance risk. Given the scale of the challenges we face, a healthy dose of risk avoidance can go a long way—after all, what is resilience if not a path to reduced risk?

- **Employee-engaging.** When companies ask employees to make operations greener and to contribute to a larger mission, it excites and galvanizes the workforce.

- **Collaborative (but not radically, yet).** More companies are moving from a war mentality with competitors and outside organizations (NGOs) to a truce mind-set so they can work together to tackle larger challenges.

- **More transparent.** My research shows that 89 percent of the 200 largest companies in the world now produce some form of report on environmental and social performance. It has become the norm, and companies are sharing more data with the outside world every year.

These are great developments, but to be realistic, large companies still view environmental and social issues in some less productive ways. Most top executives I engage with see sustainability as somewhat optional, incremental, short-term-focused (mostly about the "gold" from eco-efficiency), and perhaps idealistic or naive. They may have put someone in charge of focusing on mega challenges or at least on making the company more efficient and less vulnerable to attack. But these sustainability execs are usually off in a silo and are largely understaffed, underfunded, and working very hard to build a matrix of influence across organizational boundaries. For many companies, these issues are a check-box exercise, not a core driver of value and innovation.

Even if companies took on the *Green to Gold* agenda fully, embraced a value-chain view that was collaborative and more innovative, and pursued the four value-creating categories of strategies, it would not be enough to deal with today's mega challenges. Bridging the gap between where we (barely) are today and where we must go next is critical to the Big Pivot.

Setting Science-Based Goals

I'm aware of the irony here, but setting science-based goals is not always, well, an exact science. Knowing the precise limits we face is not easy when we're working with enormously complex systems like our climate. And the right goals, especially at the corporate level, will vary depending on the problem.

With water, for example, we have good numbers on the total amount available for human use around the world. But the global picture doesn't really matter when operational goals are being set; the reality in each watershed will dictate the right goal. And for carbon, it's almost the exact opposite. All we really care about is the total number of molecules of carbon emitted globally.

So let's start with carbon, where our need for science-based goals is most critical. The estimates of the global carbon budget are getting clearer. As discussed in chapter 1, organizations like Carbon Tracker, McKinsey, and PwC have used the IPCC data to estimate the pace of change we must achieve to reduce our chances of devastating climate change impacts.

In short, the world's total carbon intensity—the amount of carbon we emit for every dollar of GDP—needs to drop by about

6 percent per year for the foreseeable future. But what does that mean for an individual company? This is where it gets tricky, and not even for the political and economic reason that there is no mechanism—like a carbon market—to force a budget on any private enterprise. No, it's just tricky mathematically, and this is why I say it's not an exact science. But it's close.

The best methodology right now for coming up with a corporate-level carbon budget (something undertaken on a voluntary basis for now) is to start with a company's contribution to, or percentage of, global GDP. So, to oversimplify, with a global GDP of about $75 trillion, a company with revenues of $75 billion (about the size of Hyundai or Home Depot), would get a budget of about 0.1 percent of total carbon emissions.

There are a couple of great tools that help companies dig deeper than this simplification, starting with a company's contribution to global GDP and then, accounting for the global reductions we need, generating a company-level carbon emissions goal. First, check out Autodesk's *A Corporate Finance Approach to Climate-Stabilizing Targets*, or C-FACT for short (see http://autode.sk/q38bXd).

Another helpful tool is available from Mark McElroy's Center for Sustainable Organizations. McElroy's approach starts with a company's "value-added contribution to GDP," which has specific definitions in accounting and economics and provides the basis for value-added taxation in different parts of the world. His site provides a very handy (and free) spreadsheet that compares a single company's value-added contribution and emissions to the global numbers (see http://bit.ly/SIIvRr).

Business as a sector of the economy, and companies individually, need to match the global goals of cutting absolute emissions of carbon by 80 to 85 percent by 2050 and cutting carbon intensity at a rate of 6 percent per year. Each company should then adjust its target to reflect its own expected growth rate.

The tools described here can lead to a surprising outcome: if you grow fast enough, your budget may allow for an actual *increase* in carbon emissions. While this is dangerous thinking given the fact that global emissions continue to grow while we need to be slashing them quickly, there is inherent logic in it. Some sectors, such as parts of the IT world, should grow more, as long as they help the rest of the economy reduce emissions.

So the simple approach here is to start with the goal of a 6 percent per year drop in carbon intensity and then consider your company's expected growth (be honest … no "hockey stick" projections that show you dominating your industry!). Taking into account your expansion (or lack of it), you can then set absolute targets.

All that said, there are plenty of good reasons to set targets that go beyond the calculated budget. More aspirational goals can be better for driving innovation and inspiring your people and your customers. Consider a goal to power your business with 100 percent renewable energy a challenge—and one that can reduce costs, reduce risk, build brand value, and increase resilience.

Moving on to other areas, let's quickly assess what a science-based target might look like. To be more accurate, perhaps we should call it "reality-based," since the science is not always clear for every issue.

A reality-based target for water should start from a place of "water neutrality." But that may overstate the need in some locations. You should look at each major watershed in which you operate before setting an enterprise-wide neutrality goal. As I mentioned in chapter 6, you can find tools to help, such as the World Resources Institute's Aqueduct tool for "measuring and mapping water risk." Companies can use these projections to set goals for their facilities. But there's a large caveat here: setting your own water goal in a region does very little if other major users, from industry to agriculture to municipalities, don't work off the same playbook. So you really need to set goals as a region and collaborate.

A reality-based goal on toxics or chemicals is really challenging. This is a minefield, but some substances require a zero goal, such as mercury, lead, and now high global warming gases like HFCs. For other chemicals it depends on the science of harm to people and the environment, but also on the nonscientific reality of public perception and customer demand. Going back to the idea of de facto regulation in chapter 11, when a company like Walmart says it wants to greatly reduce or eliminate the use of 10 chemicals in consumer products, think about what that means for the companies creating those products: doesn't "zero" now become the best goal for those chemicals?

There will always be large debates about toxics, but I have observed that when we hear concerns about some substance and its effects on human or ecosystem health, those worries rarely go away. The early science may suggest we limit the intake of a particular substance, such as lead, mercury, and now BPA and phthalates. Later science moves toward an outright ban, like the one the US government is now considering on trans fats. So I suggest that getting ahead of regulations and customer demand by setting very aggressive goals on chemicals of concern can create competitive advantage.

An issue like waste is not entirely science-based, but in a world of tightening resources and interest in a circular economy, logic dictates that zero-waste-to-landfill goals are logical and reality-based.

For the sourcing of natural resources like forest products or fish, there are science-based standards for sustainable harvesting.

So a science-based goal might be something like 100 percent procurement of products that are certified.

Moving onto the social agenda, we're clearly on less solid scientific ground. But health and wellness lends itself to some quantifiable basis. And many of the big food companies have set targets for reducing salt, sugar, and saturated fat based on recommended daily allowances and nutrition guidance from both government and academic studies.

Continuing on the social agenda, paying people a living wage could be based on data and the "science" of how much money people need to live in different regions. But safety goals like zero workplace fatalities are just morally right.

So, in conclusion, here are some solid examples of reality-based goals that companies have set publicly, in addition to the stories and examples in chapter 6. (You can find the following targets, and thousands of other goals, at www.pivotgoals.com.)

- Reduce GHG emissions intensity by 50 percent (of 2008 emissions) by 2013 (Samsung). This goes even further than the 6 percent per year target.

- Reduce absolute emissions by 25 percent by 2015 (General Electric), or 35 percent by 2020 (Wells Fargo).

- Reduce annual CO_2 emissions by 100 million tons for products and services by 2025 (Hitachi). In its reports, Hitachi specifically mentions the IPCC numbers and scientific basis for its target.

- Become a zero carbon business by 2050 (Tesco).

- Reduce "well-to-wheel" CO_2 emissions for new vehicles by 90 percent by 2050 (Nissan).

- Use only renewable energy (Apple, Walmart, P&G, Unilever, BMW—these are all open-ended goals).

- Replenish 100 percent of water used by 2020 (Coca-Cola).

- Remove BPA in linings of canned goods in all corporate brand items (Kroger).

- Eliminate landfill waste (many companies), or "completely close the loop for all resources and bring product life-cycle waste down to zero" (an open-ended goal set by Honda).

- Source 100 percent of the top 20 wild-caught species from fisheries that are MSC-certified or engaged in the WWF fishery improvement project by 2015 (Kroger).

- Ensure that 100 percent of children's products (sales value) meet the Nestlé Nutritional Foundation sodium criterion (Nestlé).

- Update living wage levels annually and adjust associate salaries that are below those levels (Novartis).

The bottom line here is that we can no longer set goals for environmental and social performance either from the bottom up (what our organizations think they can accomplish) or purely by comparing our targets to those of our peers. How you're doing in relation to the competition on carbon or water is not really the point on these crucial issues. We need, as much as possible, outside scientific standards for the goals we set.

NOTES

INTRODUCTION

1. See Gandel, Stephen, "How Con Ed Turned New York City's Lights Back On," *Fortune CNNMoney*, November 12, 2012, for an overview of what ConEd went through that week and afterward, including the estimate of $550 million in expense. The market cap did drop by $2 billion, then recovered over months. But by the end of 2013, the value of the company was back down to its poststorm numbers.

2. "Hurricane Sandy's Rising Costs," editorial, *New York Times*, November 27, 2012.

3. The science on this point is obviously very tricky. Most data now suggests strongly that climate change increases the odds of extreme weather. Jim Hansen of the National Aeronautic and Space Administration uses the metaphor of loaded dice. Putting more moisture in the air, for example, makes each roll of the storm dice more likely to yield something larger and more dangerous. Others have likened it to someone who always speeds or texts while driving and thereby increases the likelihood of an accident. The models on the question of whether climate change drives extreme weather are getting more specific, though. In 2013, the National Oceanic and Atmospheric Administration released a set of studies on 2012 weather, concluding that "high temperatures, such as those experienced in the U.S. in 2012, are now likely to occur four times as frequently due to human-induced climate change." The organization was unwilling to tie climate change directly to Hurricane Sandy specifically, but it said that a Sandy-like surge is twice as likely as it was 60 years ago and that "ongoing natural and human-induced forcing of sea level ensures that Sandy-level inundation events will occur more frequently in the future." See Kenneth Chang, "Research Cites Role of Warming in Extremes," *New York Times*, September 5, 2013.

4. Manny Fernandez, "Drought Takes Its Toll on a Texas Business and a Town," *New York Times*, February 27, 2013.

5. Kate Galbraith, "Getting Serious about a Texas-Size Drought," *New York Times*, April 6, 2013; Aman Batheja and Kate Galbraith, "Urging Government Action on Water, Roads and Power in Texas," *New York Times*, May 16, 2013.

6. Vikas Bajaj, "Fatal Fire in Bangladesh Highlights the Dangers Facing Garment Workers," *New York Times*, November 25, 2012; Associated Press, "Bangladesh Ends Search for Collapse Victims; Final Toll 1,127," *USA Today*, May 13, 2013.

7. Steven Greenhouse and Jim Yardley, "Global Retailers Join Safety Plan for Bangladesh," *New York Times*, May 13, 2013. In this situation, the US firms lagged the EU retailers. Some said it was about concerns over liability, which may be worse in the United States. The big US retailers did create their own group later, in August 2013. See Mike Hower, "Walmart, Gap Detail Bangladeshi Worker Safety Coalition Plan," *Sustainable Brands*, August 23, 2013, http://tinyurl.com/o5k8xrg.

8. Mehmet Oz, "The Dangerous Sopranos Diet: Why Wise Guys Need to Watch Their Weight," *Time* magazine, July 8, 2013.

9. Damian Carrington, "Australia Adds New Colour to Temperature Maps As Heat Soars," "Damian Carrington's Environment Blog," *Guardian*, January 8, 2013, http://tinyurl.com/b9ulchf.

10. For storm strength, Alan Boyle, "Typhoon Haiyan Pushed the Limit, but Bigger Storms Are Coming," NBC News, November 11, 2013, http://tinyurl.com/kzqduk5; for Category 6 proposal, Stéphane Foucart, "Scientists Call for the Addition of a Step in the Classification of Cyclones," *Le Monde*, November 11, 2013, via Google Translate, http://tinyurl.com/m78vcg4.

11. Matt Sledge, "Hurricane Sandy Shows We Need to Prepare for Climate Change, Cuomo and Bloomberg Say," *Huffington Post*, October 30, 2012, http://tinyurl.com/8q8u7n7.

12. Dan Akerson, interview by Geoff Colvin, "Transcript: GM CEO Daniel Akerson at Brainstorm Green," *Fortune CNNMoney*, April 30, 2013, http://tinyurl.com/k4oh6wt.

13. Nick Mangione, "Mother Nature and Her Pal Sandy Beat Us Up, Took All Our Lunch Money," *msnNOW.com*, June 14, 2013, http://tinyurl.com/mpgh4gx.

14. Tim Hume, "Report: Climate Change May Pose Threat to Economic Growth," *CNN.com*, October 30, 2013, http://tinyurl.com/jw9fqkb.

15. "Cotton Prices at All-Time High; Luxury Bedding Retailer, Elegant Linens, Encourages Consumers to Educate Themselves, Discern Quality Egyptian Cotton from Imitators," *PRWeb.com*, June 4, 2011, http://tinyurl.com/m9khdtm.

16. For Coca-Cola number, see Reuters, "Commodity Costs May Affect Fourth Quarter for Coke," *New York Times*, October 18, 2011; and for Tyson number, see Ken Perkins, "Sizing Up the Drought's Impact on Tyson Foods," *Morningstar*, November 14, 2012, http://tinyurl.com/l26gs4n.

17. For figures on the investment in the clean economy, see Ron Pernick, Clint Wilder, and Trevor Winnie, "Clean Energy Trends 2013," The Clean Edge, Inc., March 2013, http://tinyurl.com/kb7lucv, chart, p. 3, which shows $248 billion in 2012.

18. John Kotter, "Accelerate!" *Harvard Business Review*, November 2012.

19. Nassim Taleb, *Antifragile: Things That Gain from Disorder* (New York: Random House, 2012).

20. George Carlin, "George Carlin on the Environment (HQ)," video, YouTube, 7:39, posted by "candidskeptic," uploaded April 22, 2009, www.youtube.com/watch?v=EjmtSkl53h4.

21. Erin Brodwin, "Sans Protective Measures, Flooding Damage Could Cost the World $1 Trillion by 2050," *Scientific American*, August 21, 2013, http://tinyurl.com/k23378p. See also a chilling article on the sinking (sorry) prospects for cities like Miami: Jeff Goodell, "Goodbye, Miami," *Rolling Stone*, June 20, 2013.

22. Richard Branson, quoted in "The Situation," Carbon War Room website, accessed October 3, 2013, http://tinyurl.com/khpbetg.

PART I

1. Richard S. Tedlow, "The Education of Andy Grove," *Fortune*, December 12, 2005.

CHAPTER ONE

1. Michael Grunwald, "Sandy Ends the Silence," *Time* magazine, November 7, 2012.

2. Ken Caldeira, "How Far Can Climate Change Go? How Far Can We Push the Planet?" *Scientific American*, August 27, 2012, http://tinyurl.com/m5cev79.

3. "Confronting Climate Change in the U.S. Midwest," *Union of Concerned Scientists* (July 2009): 5.

4. Caldeira, "How Far Can Climate Change Go?"

5. Beth Gardiner, "We're All Climate-Change Idiots," *New York Times*, July 21, 2012.

6. Rodolfo Dirzo et al., *Scientific Consensus on Maintaining Humanity's Life Support Systems in the 21st Century: Information for Policy Makers*, introduction (Stanford, CA: Stanford University, May 21, 2013), iii.

7. Bill McKibben, "Global Warming's Terrifying New Math: Three Simple Numbers That Add Up to Global Catastrophe—and That Make Clear Who the Enemy Is," *Rolling Stone*, July 19, 2012.

8. Eric Beinhocker et al., "The Carbon Productivity Challenge: Curbing Climate Change and Sustaining Economic Growth" (McKinsey Global Institute, July 2008). These statistics are reported in the report summary available online, see http://tinyurl.com/meokzhh.

9. PwC, "Too Late for Two Degrees? Low Carbon Economy Index 2012," PricewaterhouseCoopers, November 2012, http://tinyurl.com/c3ua5d4.

10. Justin Gillis, "Climate Panel Cites Near Certainty on Warming," *New York Times*, August 19, 2013.

11. For an understanding of the IPCC numbers from a fairly non-scientist perspective, see T. F. Stocker, D. Qin, et al., "Summary for Policymakers," in *Climate Change 2013: The Physical Science Basis. Contribution of Working Group I to the Fifth Assessment Report of the Intergovernmental Panel on Climate Change* (Cambridge University Press, Cambridge, United Kingdom and New York, NY, USA), IPCC, 2013. A number as specific as McKibben's 565 gigatons of carbon dioxide ($GtCO_2$) comes in part from picking a particular level of probability of going past the 2-degree mark. His numbers came from Carbon Tracker analysis based on earlier IPCC reports, since the latest numbers came out a year after he wrote the article. The IPCC report cited here said the following about carbon budget: "Limiting the warming caused by anthropogenic CO_2 emissions alone with a probability of >33%, >50%, and >66% to less than 2°C since the period 1861–1880, will require cumulative CO_2 emissions from all anthropogenic sources to stay between 0 and about 1570 GtC (5760 $GtCO_2$), 0 and about 1210 GtC (4440 $GtCO_2$), and 0 and about 1000 GtC (3670 $GtCO_2$) since that period, respectively … An amount of 515 [445 to 585] GtC (1890 [1630 to 2150] $GtCO_2$), was already emitted by 2011." (Interpolation in the original.) So if we want a two-thirds chance of holding to 2 degrees, we have about 1000 GtC less 515 GtC, or 485 GtC left by 2100. But comparing that number to McKibben's gets tricky for a few reasons: (1) The IPCC numbers are most often cited in terms of carbon (even though some of their reports show CO_2 as well), while others like Carbon Tracker and PwC do the calculation based on CO_2 (for the chemists out there, CO_2 is 3.67 times as heavy as carbon alone); (2) the IPCC generally calculates the budget left until 2100, while the McKibben article used numbers for how much we have left to emit before 2050; (3) I believe McKibben was using scenarios from Carbon Tracker based on an 80 percent chance of holding the line, not 66 percent. So, all of that said, I rely on the detailed analyses of some colleagues, including the "Low Carbon Economy" report from PwC, which leads me back to the pace of change we need in carbon intensity, or 6 percent per year.

12. International Energy Agency, *World Energy Outlook 2012*, executive summary International Energy Agency, 2012, 3, http://tinyurl.com/d49a55v.

13. John Fullerton, "The Big Choice," "Capital Institute: The Future of Finance," July 19, 2011, http://tinyurl.com/kv4u6zn.

14. "The 3% Solution," World Wildlife Organization, 2013, http://worldwildlife.org/projects/the-3-solution.

15. "Extreme Weather Events Drive Climate Change up Boardroom Agenda in 2012," Carbon Disclosure Project, November, 2012, http://tinyurl.com/klk4pcu.

16. "Global 500 Climate Change Report 2013," CDP, September 15, 2013. The vast majority of the world's largest companies now respond to the CDP questionnaire.

17. Global investment of $250 billion from Ron Pernick, Clint Wilder, and Trevor Winnie, "Clean Energy Trends 2013," The Clean Edge, Inc., March, 2013, http://tinyurl.com/kb7lucv. Saudi Arabia data from Wael Mahdi and Marc Roca, "Saudi Arabia Plans $109 Billion Boost for Solar Power," *Bloomberg*, May 11, 2012. South Korea data from Jonathan Hopfner, "In South Korea, Going for the Green," *New York Times*, November 10, 2010. Chinese data from Sustainable Business News, "China Invests $372B to Cut Pollution, Energy Use," August 27, 2012, *GreenBiz*, http://tinyurl.com/n8elyhg. Japan data from "$628 Bln Green Energy Market Central to Japan Growth Strategy," *CleanBiz. Asia*, July 12, 2012.

18. "German Solar Power Plants Produce 50% of the Nation's Electric Energy on Saturday," *Wall Street Journal Market Watch*, May 26, 2012; Anders Lorenzen, "Breaking: Denmark Records Highest Ever Wind Power Output," *A Greener Life, A Greener World*, March 17, 2013, http://tinyurl.com/bulyx26; Chris Meehan, "Almost 50% of all New US Energy in 2012 Was Renewable," *SolarReviews*, August 23, 2013, http://tinyurl.com/mbemeb6; "Renewables 2013: Global Status Report," Renewable Energy Policy Network for the 21st Century, 2013; Chen Yang, "Wind Power Now No. 3 Energy Resource," *People's Daily*, January 28, 2013, http://tinyurl.com/agxa98m.

19. "Growth of Global Solar and Wind Energy Continues to Outpace Other Technologies," Worldwatch Institute, July 30, 2013, http://tinyurl.com/les34n7.

20. Robert Strohmeyer, "The 7 Worst Tech Predictions of All Time," *TechHive*, December 31, 2008, http://tinyurl.com/kpt2ybc.

CHAPTER TWO

1. Jeremy Grantham, "Time to Wake Up: Days of Abundant Resources and Falling Prices Are Over Forever," *The Oil Drum*, April 29, 2011, www.theoildrum.com/node/7853, exhibit 3.

2. For trading partner information see, Tayyab Safdar, "China's Growing Influence in Africa," *Express Tribune*, August 29, 2012, http://tinyurl.com/lnajwde. For Smithfield acquisition, Michael J. DeLaMerced and David Barboza, "Needing Pork, China Is to Buy a U.S. Supplier," *New York Times*, May 30, 2013, and also "Smithfield Foods Closes Sale to China's Shuanghui," *Associated Press*, September 27, 2013.

3. For size of middle class, Helen H. Wang, "Half a Billion Opportunities for U.S. Businesses," *Forbes*, November 30, 2012, http://tinyurl.com/bu2h5n5. For record online sales, ShanShan Wang and Eric Pfanner, "China's One-Day Shopping Spree Sets Record in Online Sales," *New York Times*, November 12, 2013.

4. Fraser Thompson (McKinsey Global Institute), e-mail correspondence with author, August 8, 2013.

5. Grantham, "Time to Wake Up," exhibit 4.

6. "CEO Concerns about Energy and Resource Costs at Highest Level for Three Years," PricewaterhouseCoopers UK press release, December 10, 2012.

7. Joe Romm, "Jeremy Grantham Must-Read, 'Time to Wake Up: Days of Abundant Resources and Falling Prices Are Over Forever,'" *Climate Progress*, May 2, 2011, http://tinyurl.com/m4q29va.

8. U.S. Department of the Interior, US Geological Survey, "The World's Water," accessed November 13, 2013, http://tinyurl.com/ycszcob.

9. "Water in 2050," Growing Blue, accessed November 16, 2013, http://growingblue.com/water-in-2050/. See also, "Sustaining Growth via Water Productivity: 2030/2050 Scenarios," Veolia Water and International Food Policy Research Institute, accessed November 16, 2013, http://tinyurl.com/lh5wbzs.

10. Andrew Winston and Will Sarni, "Is Water the Next Carbon?," *Harvard Business Review Blog Network*, January 3, 2011.

11. Royal Dutch Shell PLC, "Addressing the Energy-Water-Food Challenge," accessed November 13, 2013, http://tinyurl.com/mdcb5y4.

12. Energy wasted is calculated from US Energy Information Data presented by John Tozzi and David Yanofsky, "U.S. Energy: Where It's from, Where It Goes, and What's Wasted," *Bloomberg*, July 7, 2011, http://tinyurl.com/6hvljzp; for food waste; "UN: $750B in Global Food Waste per Year," *Aljazeera America*, September 11, 2013, http://tinyurl.com/on5m78v. For the remaining statistics in figure 2-2 see the following: for 40% US corn in biofuel, Mariola Kopcinski from FMC Corp. (presented at the Wharton IGEL Conference on the Nexus, Philadelphia, Pennsylvania, March 21, 2013); for 16% of US energy, Shelly K. Schwartz, "Food for Thought: How Energy Is Squandered in Food Industry," *USA Today*, May 1, 2011, http://tinyurl.com/mgxa9cv; for 13% of electricity, "The Water Energy Connection," National Environmental Energy Week,

http://www.eeweek.org/water_and_energy_wise/connection; for 70% of water, "Water Uses," Aquastat, *Food and Agriculture Organization of the United Nations*, accessed November 16, 2013, http://tinyurl.com/krlf8x9; for 16 gallons of water, "How Big Is Your Water Footprint?," *Technicians for Sustainability, LLC*, accessed November 16, 2013, http://tinyurl.com/lggddyk.

13. Andrew Zolli and Anne Marie Healy, *Resilience: Why Things Bounce Back* (New York: Simon & Schuster, 2012), 2.

14. Ariel Schwartz, "Whoops, Humans Officially Blew the Planet's Budget This Week," *Fast Company*, August 22, 2013, http://tinyurl.com/kv34o5d; "Earth Overshoot Day," FootPrint Network, last updated August 20, 2013, http://tinyurl.com/kwwkezx.

15. "Global Agenda Survey 2012," World Economic Forum, 2012, http://tinyurl.com/axz9r67; and "World Economic Forum Global Risks 2013," *World Economic Forum*, 2013, http://tinyurl.com/mr3fvt5.

CHAPTER THREE

1. Bill Pennington and Karen Crouse, "Attention, Second-Guessers: Golf Takes Calls (and Texts)," *New York Times*, April 13, 2013. See also Michael Bamberger, "The Story behind Tiger's Ruling at the Masters: How One Man Called in a Penalty and Saved Woods from Disqualification," Golf.com, May 1, 2013.

2. See, for example, these three Change.org petitions: Paul Kalinka, "Dunkin Donuts: Stop Using Styrofoam Cups and Switch to a More Eco-Friendly Solution," accessed October 30, 2013, http://tinyurl.com/cl85v84; Park School Paper Club, "Universal Pictures: Let the Lorax Speak for the Trees!" January 2012, http://tinyurl.com/l67umkq; Mr. Land's "Kids Who Care" from Sun Valley School, "Crayola, Make Your Mark! Set Up a Marker Recycling Program," June 2013, http://tinyurl.com/8fjhsa8.

3. Julie Bosman, "Chevy Tries a Write-Your-Own-Ad Approach, and the Potshots Fly," *New York Times*, April 4, 2006.

4. Walmart, "Walmart Announces Plan to Raise Inspection Standards and Provide Full Transparency on Safety Conditions at All Factories in Its Bangladesh Supply Chain," press release, May 14, 2013, http://tinyurl.com/bdpz76f.

5. Todd Woody, "I.B.M. Suppliers Must Track Environmental Data," *New York Times Green Blog*, April 14, 2010. See also Andrew Winston, "IBM's Green Supply Chain," *HBR Blog Network*, July 19, 2010.

6. Jonathan Klein, "Why People Really Buy Hybrids," Topline Strategy Group, 2007, http://tinyurl.com/6szjnpf.

7. Dara O'Rourke (Good Guide), speaking at Sustainable Brands 2010, Monterey, CA, June 7, 2010.

8. For every minute statistic on websites, "May 2013 Web Server Study," Netcraft.com, http://tinyurl.com/kgp2c9c; for app downloads, "Visibility for Your Apps," Android website, accessed November 11, 2013, http://tinyurl.com/l4wy4t9; for Facebook likes and comments, "The Power of Facebook Advertising," Facebook website, accessed November 11, 2013, http://tinyurl.com/mdwh8hn; for Facebook habits of 18 to 34 year olds, Cara Pring, "100 Social Media Statistics for 2012," *The Social Skinny*, January 11, 2012, http://tinyurl.com/6maw6jd; for YouTube uploads, YouTube, "Statistics," accessed November 11, 2013, http://tinyurl.com/capjhx8; for tweets, Hayley Tsukayama, "Twitter Turns 7: Users Send Over 400 Million Tweets per Day," *Washington Post*, March 21, 2013, http://tinyurl.com/kx6ch6b; and for texts, Wayne Balta (IBM), speech at World Environmental Center Gold Medal Gala, Washington D.C., May 9, 2013.

9. Rebecca Smith, "Utilities Try to Learn from Smart Meters," *Wall Street Journal*, September 22, 2013.

10. Balta, speech at World Environment Center Gold Medal Gala.

11. Bart King and Mike Hower, "AT&T, Carbon War Room Say 'Internet of Things' Can Cut Emissions by 19%," *Sustainable Brands*, February 27, 2013, http://tinyurl.com/mjm3jfw.

12. HP ad, *Washington Post*, April 9, 2013; Saleem Van Groenou, e-mail correspondence with author, August 22, 2013; Chris Librie, e-mail correspondence with author, August 22, 2013.

13. We also need the right kinds of metrics and data to support a real pivot. At the microeconomic level, we should take a hard look at whether corporate quarterly earnings are really a good measure of value. At the macro level, consider GDP, which we use as a measure of a country's economic health. It's a remarkably squishy number—in the summer of 2013, the Bureau of Economic Analysis added $560 billion to the US GDP by redefining some things (it included "intellectual property products"). And GDP is actually a poor representation of how we're doing since all activity raises the number—cancer increases GDP, as does an oil spill. Numerous thought leaders, from Nobel Prize–winning economist Joseph Stiglitz to the tiny country of Bhutan, have been working on the problem and looking for a better measure of well-being. Bhutan developed its own "gross national happiness" measure, which sounds kooky, but makes a lot more sense the more you learn about it.

14. Robin Wauters, "A Clone Scales: 9Flats, 'Europe's Airbnb', Grows from 100K to 250K Beds in Four Months," *The Next* Web, November 29, 2012, http://tinyurl.com/cbrucq7; Airbnb, "About Us," Airbnb website, accessed October 30, 2013, www.airbnb.com/about/about-us.

15. Robin Chase, quoted in Channtal Fleischfresser, "Can the Sharing Economy Help Slow Down Climate Change?" *Smart Planet Blog*, May 2013, http://tinyurl.com/oygs7rt.

16. Kurt Wagner, "Who's Getting Crowded Out of Crowdfunding?" *Fortune*, March 14, 2013, http://tinyurl.com/dyso43u; Lanford Beard, "'Veronica Mars': Kickstarter Campaign Closes with $5.7 Million," *Entertainment Weekly*, April 14, 2013, http://tinyurl.com/m337tco.

17. Andy Ruben (Yerdle), interview with author, March 15, 2013.

18. See Dava Sobel's fantastic book *Longitude: The True Story of a Lone Genius Who Solved the Greatest Scientific Problem of His Time* (New York: Walker, 1995).

19. Mike Addison, "P&G Connect and Develop: An Innovation Strategy That Is Here to Stay," Inside P&G website, accessed October 30, 2013, http://tinyurl.com/mb2c4c5.

20. Osvald M. Bjelland and Robert Chapman Wood, "An Inside View of IBM's 'Innovation Jam,'" *Harvard Business Review*, October 1, 2008, http://tinyurl.com/pm6zxys.

CHAPTER FOUR

1. Dan Bartlett, speech at Walmart's Global Sustainability Milestone Meeting, September 12, 2013, http://tinyurl.com/m9mbvhk.

2. Ray said this many times, and was quoted even more. For more of his wisdom, see his wonderful TED talk: "Ray Anderson: The Business Logic of Sustainability," TED, February 2009, www.ted.com/talks/ray_anderson_on_the_business_logic_of_sustainability.html. As the founder of Interface, Ray had firm ground to stand on since he was, as green guru Hunter Lovins told me (via e-mail on May 24, 2013), "one of the first to *prove* the business value." Interface's "Mission Zero" vision (zero waste, zero impact) was one of the first pivots by a sizable business. Lovins pointed out that the numbers speak for themselves: "Bad stuff, like waste and use of nonrenewable materials, went down (CO_2 by 41 percent) and good stuff, sales and profits, went up."

3. "Alcoa Releases 2011 Sustainability," Alcoa press release, May 9, 2012, http://tinyurl.com/mor6ofe; and "Integrating Sustainability into Business Strategies," Alcoa, accessed November 11, 2013, http://tinyurl.com/m4gpcun.

4. "We can't solve problems … " Albert Einstein cited in David Mielach, "5 Business Tips from Albert Einstein," *BusinessNewsDaily*, April 18, 2012, http://tinyurl.com/maovcej.

5. Nestlé data, titled "Nestle_environmental_performance_indicators_2012.xls" provided to author by Hilary Parsons and Pascal Gréverath (Nestlé), via e-mail October 31, 2013. See also similar calculations at Nestlé, "Nestlé in Society: Creating Shared Value and Meeting Our Commitments," Nestlé, March 2013, 38, accessed November 11, 2013, http://tinyurl.com/kf62usv.

6. Unilever, "Unilever Sustainable Living Plan," November 2010, p. 3, http://tinyurl.com/k9aprho.

7. Mike Duke, speech at Walmart quarterly milestone meeting, Bentonville, AR, April 15, 2013.

8. See also Tim Jackson, *Prosperity without Growth: Economics for a Finite Planet* (New York: Routledge, 2011). Jackson questions the whole idea of growth as a goal, even with decoupling slowing down material use.

9. For P&G, Shelley DuBois, "P&G's Bob McDonald Is Going Green for the Long Haul," *CNNMoney*, April 30, 2013, http://tinyurl.com/m2p7wzq; for GM, General Motors, "Waste Reduction," accessed November 11, 2013, http://tinyurl.com/l5syzcf; for Dupont, Wendy Koch, "Companies Try to Recycle All Waste, Send Nothing to Landfill," *USA Today*, January 29, 2012, http://tinyurl.com/cndww5e; and for Waste Management, "Renewable Energy," accessed November 11, 2013, http://tinyurl.com/lnptmwc.

10. Hewlett Packard, "HP 2011 Global Citizenship Report," 35, http://tinyurl.com/mx8tpd3.

11. John Elkington, *The Zeronauts: Breaking the Sustainability Barrier* (New York: Routledge, 2012).

12. Jonathan Porritt, *Capitalism As If the World Mattered* (Sterling, VA: Earthscan, 2005), 10.

13. "Towards the Circular Economy: Economic and Business Rationale for an Accelerated Transition: Executive Summary," Ellen MacArthur Foundation, 2012, http://tinyurl.com/me4xt6p. McKinsey's work on the value of a circular economy was in conjunction with the Dame Ellen MacArthur Foundation, working also with Cisco, B&Q, BT, National Grid, and Renault.

14. For Patagonia, Mike Hower, "Patagonia Launches New Program to Upcycle Flip-Flops," *Sustainable Brands*, August 2, 2013, http://tinyurl.com/l2y2wph; for Puma, Marlene Ringel and Baljinder Miles, "PUMA Introduces C2C-Certified, Recyclable Track Jacket, Backpack as Part of InCycle Collection," *Sustainable Brands*, February 12, 2013, http://tinyurl.com/koxwchr.

15. Gina-Marie Cheeseman, "Nike's New Shanghai Store Is Made from 100 Percent Trash," TriplePundit, August 28, 2013, http://tinyurl.com/qgy5wy7.

16. Rob Hayward et al., "The UN Global Compact-Accenture CEO Study on Sustainability 2013," Accenture, September 2013, 34, http://tinyurl.com/owbjghy.

17. Nassim Taleb, *Antifragile: Things That Gain from Disorder* (New York: Random House, 2012), 351.

18. For my own inspiration, I think of the story of William Kamkwamba, a young man born in a small village in Malawi. At 14 years old—yes, an age when

I was focused mainly on video arcades—William built a working wind turbine from some appliances, trees, bicycle parts, and scrapyard materials. Genius like this doesn't sit idle, so his story got out. A book about his exploits, a TED talk, and a *Daily Show* visit, were all part of a 10-year path that included studying at Cambridge, Johannesburg, and Dartmouth. If we're looking for the Steve Jobs for a new century, William gets my vote.

19. I am by no means the first to point out chinks in the capitalist armor. A large body of impressive literature has made the case for business leading the charge to a healthier, more equitable, and sustainable form of commerce. Some of the better entrants in this discussion include Paul Hawken, *The Ecology of Commerce: A Declaration of Sustainability* (New York: Collins Business, 2005); Paul Hawken, Amory Lovins, and Hunter Lovins, *Natural Capitalism: Creating the Next Industrial Revolution* (Boston: Little, Brown and Co., 1999); David C. Korten, *When Corporations Rule the World* (West Hartford, CT: Kumarian Press, 1995); Stuart Hart, *Capitalism at the Crossroads: The Unlimited Business Opportunities in Solving the World's Most Difficult Problems* (Upper Saddle River, NJ: Wharton School, 2005); Jonathan Porritt, *Capitalism As If the World Matters* (Sterling, VA: Earthscan, 2005); Naomi Klein, *The Shock Doctrine: The Rise of Disaster Capitalism* (New York: Metropolitan Books/Henry Holt, 2007); James Gustave Speth, *The Bridge at the End of the World: Capitalism, the Environment, and Crossing from Crisis to Sustainability* (New Haven: Yale University Press, 2008); Umair Haque, *The New Capitalist Manifesto: Building a Disruptively Better Business* (Boston: Harvard Business Press, 2011); and the ongoing work of economists, thought leaders, or documentarians such as Joel Bakan, Marjorie Kelly, Michael Moore, Robert Reich, Joseph Stiglitz, Allen White, and many more.

20. Hawken, Lovins, and Lovins, *Natural Capitalism*, 263.

21. Umair Haque, *The New Capitalist Manifesto: Building a Disruptively Better Business* (Boston: Harvard Business Review Press, 2012), xv.

22. Rebecca Henderson, e-mail correspondence with author, October 2, 2013.

23. Alfred Rappaport, *Saving Capitalism from Short-Termism: How to Build Long-Term Value and Take Back Our Financial Future* (New York: McGraw Hill, 2011), ix.

24. See the seminal work by Donella Meadows, *Thinking in Systems: A Primer* (White River Junction, VT: Chelsea Green, 2008).

25. Robert Gifford, a social scientist from University of Victoria in British Columbia, has listed thirty of what he calls, "dragons of inaction," psychological barriers that we need to slay to tackle climate change. See Paramaguru, Kharunya, "The Battle over Global Warming Is All in Your Head," *Time*, August 19, 2013.

26. Cass R. Sunstein, "People Don't Fear Climate Change Enough," *Bloomberg*, August 27, 2013, http://tinyurl.com/mq8x592. Or consider our inability to understand the so-called "Black Swan" extremes (the world is not a normal curve). As economist Gernot Wagner points out, you will never see a ten-foot woman, so you can't easily picture outliers in other settings where extremes can be orders of magnitude larger than expected (like storms and droughts). We have trouble seeing how skewed reality is from the idea of a normal curve and preparing for those extremes.

27. Andrew C. Revkin, "Stuck on Coal, and Stuck for Words in a High-Tech World," *New York Times*, December 4, 2007. Revkin has described people's inability to worry about issues like climate change because "daily struggles swamp even life-threatening long-term risks."

28. A fun thought experiment by physicist Tom Murphy offers an example of how exponential growth leads to absurd numbers. Murphy calculated what would happen if global energy use grew at 3 percent per year, as it has for a few hundred years. In another four hundred years, he says, we'd need the equivalent of *all* of the sun's energy that hits the earth. At some point—and a lot sooner than centuries from now—the growth rates clearly have to slow and we have to find new ways of operating.

29. Hayward et al., "UN Global Compact-Accenture CEO Study on Sustainability 2013," 34.

CHAPTER FIVE

1. Jennifer Reingold, "Can Procter & Gamble CEO Bob McDonald Hang On?," *Fortune* magazine, February 25, 2013.

2. John R. Graham, Campbell R. Harvey, and Shiva Rajgopal, "The Economic Implications of Corporate Financial Reporting," *Journal of Accounting and Economics* 40 (December 2005), 3–73.

3. Tom Falk (Kimberly-Clark Corporation), interview with author, May 5, 2013.

4. John Bogle, *The Clash of the Cultures: Investment vs. Speculation* (New York: Wiley, August 2012).

5. For the myth of 11 seconds, Barry Ritholtz, "No, the Average Stock Holding Period Is Not 11 Seconds," *Business Insider*, October 28, 2010, http://tinyurl.com/mdtayyo. For high-speed trading making up 50 percent of total market volume, Bogle, *Clash of the Cultures*, 3. For Polman quotation, Kamal Ahmed, "Davos 2011: Unilever's Paul Polman Believes We Need to Think Long Term," *The Telegraph*, January 15, 2011, http://tinyurl.com/5wt4nt6. For 7-year

holding period, Alfred Rappaport, *Saving Capitalism from Short-Termism: How to Build Long-Term Value and Take Back Our Financial Future* (New York: McGraw Hill, July 2011), 75.

6. Ken Favaro et al., "CEO Succession 2000–2009: A Decade of Convergence and Compression," *Strategy+Business* magazine, Summer 2010.

7. Rappaport, *Saving Capitalism from Short-Termism*, xvii and 48.

8. For Associated Press Twitter hacking, "AP Twitter Account Hacked, 'Explosions at White House' Tweet Crashes DOW," RT.com, April 23, 2013, http://tinyurl.com/kque8dl. For "flash crash," Wikipedia contributors, "2010 Flash Crash," *Wikipedia, The Free Encyclopedia*, accessed November 4, 2013, http://tinyurl.com/3wtk9o7.

9. Rappaport, *Saving Capitalism from Short-Termism*, ix.

10. Marc Gunther, "Waste Management's New Direction," *Fortune*, December 6, 2010, http://tinyurl.com/ldsyh6e.

11. For Exxon Mobil, Clifford Krauss, "Oil Industry Hums as Higher Prices Bolster Quarterly Profits at Exxon and Shell," *New York Times*, October 28, 2011. For Apple, John Paczkowski, "Apple Shares Down 11 Percent on Fourth-Most-Profitable Quarter Posted by Any Company Ever," *All Things D*, January 24, 2013, http://tinyurl.com/kl5z7wt.

12. Jie He and Xuan Tian, "The Dark Side of Analyst Coverage: The Case of Innovation," *Journal of Financial Economics*, February 5, 2013, http://ssrn.com/abstract=1959125.

13. Claire Cain Miller and Nick Bilton, "Google's Lab of Wildest Dreams," *New York Times*, November 14, 2011.

14. Adam Lashinsky, "Inside Apple," *Fortune* magazine, May 23, 2011.

15. Josie Ensor, "Unilever's Polman Hits Out at City's Short Term Culture," *The Telegraph*, July 5, 2011, http://tinyurl.com/3emwn4f.

16. For "rat race", Deborah Zabarenko, "Unilever Swaps Earnings Rat Race for Sustainability," *Reuters*, November 2, 2012, http://tinyurl.com/mnbnh5v; for "sell their grandmother," Ahmed, "Davos 2011: Unilever's Paul Polman Believes We Need to Think Long Term."

17. For cash flow quotation, Ahmed, "Davos 2011." For doing the right things quotation, Paul Polman, interview with Adi Ignatius, "Unilever's CEO on Making Responsible Business Work," *Harvard Business Review Blog Network*, May 17, 2012, http://tinyurl.com/lmc3hj6.

18. Paulette Frank (Johnson & Johnson), e-mail correspondence with author, July 23, 2013 and August 7, 2013.

19. Erika Karp, speech at NIRI/FEI Sustainability Summit, New York City, April, 9, 2013.

20. Eva Zlotnicka (UBS), interview with author, April 4, 2013.

21. Kevin Anton (Alcoa), e-mail correspondence with author, June 26, 2013.

22. Greg Sebasky (Philips), interview with author, March 29, 2013.

23. Peter Graf (SAP), e-mail correspondence with author, May 14, 2013.

24. Mindy Lubber (Ceres), speech at Kimberly Clark Sustainability Advisory Board Meeting, Roswell, GA, March 27, 2013.

25. Jay Coen Gilbert (B Lab), interview with author, December 12, 2012.

26. Susan Mac Cormac (Morrison & Foerster), interview with author, January 8, 2013.

27. Lyell Clarke (The Clarke Group), interview with author, April 13, 2013.

28. Tom Falk (Kimberly-Clark Corporation), interview with author, May 20, 2013.

29. A.G. Lafley (Proctor & Gamble), "The Customer Is the Boss," Big Think video, 1:59pm, March 20, 2013, http://tinyurl.com/kafe6u5.

30. Johnson & Johnson, "Our Credo," accessed November 5, 2013, http://tinyurl.com/lh3bzfr.

31. Francesco Guerrera, "Welch Condemns Share Price Focus," *Financial Times*, March 12, 2009. See also Steve Denning, "The Dumbest Idea in the World: Maximizing Shareholder Value," *Forbes*, November 28, 2011, http://tinyurl.com/7f9tput.

CHAPTER SIX

1. Tim Wallington (Ford), interview with author, May 23, 2012. See also "Ford's Science Based CO_2 Targets," Ford Motor Company, accessed November 6, 2013, http://tinyurl.com/ka5vtar.

2. Tim Wallington (Ford), interview with author, May 23, 2012.

3. Alan Mulally (Ford), speaking at Fortune Brainstorm Green conference, Laguna Niguel, CA, April 16, 2012. Transcript available at http://tinyurl.com/7asrluv.

4. John Viera (Ford), interview with author, July 6, 2010.

5. "Blueprint for Sustainability: The Future at Work," Ford Motor Company, accessed November 6, 2013, http://tinyurl.com/n5puc6v.

6. Kevin Moss (BT), interview with author, February 28, 2013. See also "Better Future Report 2013," BT, accessed November 6, 2013, http://tinyurl.com/qhk2p73.

7. Kevin Moss (BT), interview with author, February 28, 2013.

8. For Dell, "Dell 2020 Legacy of Good Plan," accessed November 16, 2013, http://tinyurl.com/mmhsahg. For Disney and Rio Tinto, Sissel Waage, "Why Sustainability Aspiration Leads to Innovation," *GreenBiz*, February 25, 2013,

http://tinyurl.com/mergtuq. For LG, Bart King, "LG Electronics to Cut US Emissions in Half by 2020," *SustainableBrands*, November 29, 2011, http://tinyurl.com/mogfupw. For Mars, "Sustainable in a Generation," Mars, Incorporated, accessed November 6, 2013, http://tinyurl.com/qytrvxe. For 100 percent renewable energy goals, see www.pivotgoals.com and "IKEA Plans for 100% Clean Energy by 2020," CleanTechnica, October 23, 2012, http://tinyurl.com/kwmsxr3. For Unilever, "Unilever Sustainable Living Plan," November 2010, p. 3, http://tinyurl.com/k9aprho. For Toshiba, "Corporate Social Responsibility Report, 2012," Toshiba Group, August 2012, p. 22, 35–40, http://tinyurl.com/lj32owv.

9. "Thinking Forward: 2012 EMC Sustainability Report," EMC Corporation, p. 23, accessed November 7, 2013, http://tinyurl.com/lho6vs5.

10. "About CSO," Center for Sustainable Organizations, accessed November 7, 2013, http://tinyurl.com/lkhgedv.

11. Bill Baue, "Embracing Science to Bridge the Sustainability Gap," TheGuardian.com, April 23, 2012, http://tinyurl.com/kq997p4.

12. Richard Dunne (Diageo), interview with author, November 28, 2012.

13. Joseph Romm, "The United States Needs a Tougher Greenhouse Gas Emissions Reduction Target for 2020," Center for American Progress website, January 13, 2009, http://tinyurl.com/l5r9u62. This number is usually suggested as the target for industrialized countries, with the developing world needing to cut less. The 2013/2014 IPCC report is still being issued as of this writing, but the goals will most certainly get tighter, not looser.

14. "Thinking Forward: 2012 EMC Sustainability Report," p. 46.

15. "Carbon Action," Carbon Disclosure Project website, accessed November 7, 2013, http://tinyurl.com/n3we7f6.

16. "Setting a Target for Corporate Greenhouse Gas Reduction," AutoDesk Inc., accessed November 7, 2013, http://tinyurl.com/kvoryp4.

17. "World Energy Outlook 2012," International Energy Agency, November 2012, p. 2, http://tinyurl.com/d49a55v.

18. "Carbon Action," Carbon Disclosure Project.

19. Rob Hayward et al., "The UN Global Compact-Accenture CEO Study on Sustainability 2013," Accenture, September 2013, 31, http://tinyurl.com/owbjghy.

CHAPTER SEVEN

1. "If I had an hour to solve a problem …" Albert Einstein cited in "Why Innovators Should Never Listen to Albert Einstein," posted by "mhargrave," February 12, 2012, blog.hbs.edu/hbsinov8/?p=1238.

2. See "UPS Sustainability Report Hits 'A+' Mark for Transparency," UPS press release, July 31, 2012, http://tinyurl.com/mtks4tw. This is the only story I've used in all three of my books, but in my talks, I hear from readers that this story was one of the most memorable, so it's worth revisiting again.

3. Martin Wright, "Indian Businesses Are Reveling in 'Unreasonable Goals,'" *Green Futures Magazine*, February 20, 2013.

4. Leon Kaye, "Adidas Rolls Out Waterless 'DryDye' T-Shirt," *TriplePundit*, August 9, 2012, http://tinyurl.com/mt2nwss.

5. Hannah Jones (Nike), interview with author, April 2, 2013.

6. "Scott Naturals Pioneers "Green Done Right,'" Kimberly-Clark Corp. press release, April 22, 2013, http://tinyurl.com/lzhn5ks.

7. "PUMA Clever Little Bag," IDSA, June 8, 2011, www.idsa.org/puma-clever-little-bag.

8. Marco Iszlaji and Peggy Ward (Kimberly-Clark), e-mail correspondence with author, May 1, 2013.

9. Glenn Paufler (Hewlett Packard), interview with author, May 13, 2013.

10. Jim Collins and Morten Hansen, *Great by Choice: Uncertainty, Chaos, and Luck: Why Some Thrive Despite Them All* (New York: HarperCollins, 2011), 61.

11. Mike Hower, "P&G's New Plastic Mold Process Could Save $1 Billion Annually," *Sustainable Brands*, accessed November 18, 2013, http://tinyurl.com/mbdwder.

12. Eric Bellman, "Indian Firms Shift Focus to the Poor," *Wall Street Journal*, October 21, 2009; Vijay Govindarajan, *Reverse Innovation: Create Far from Home, Win Everywhere* (Boston: Harvard Business Press, 2012).

13. Beth Comstock (GE), conversation with author, July 8, 2011.

14. Hannah Jones (hjones_nike), "As I said at #FortuneGreen: system change or go home: example of how we seek 2 make it happen: #LAUNCH2020 http://is.gd/XByQki," April 30, 2013, 10:39 am. Tweet.

15. Richard Bergfors (Max Hamburgers), conversation with author, November 29, 2011. See also Andrew Winston, "A Swedish Burger Chain Says 'Minimize Me,'" *Harvard Business Review Blog Network*, June 30, 2011, blogs.hbr.org/2011/06/a-swedish-burger-chain-says-mi/.

16. Annie Longsworth (alongsworth), "S Wicker @ups We look at brown delivery fleet as a rolling laboratory—experimenting with every technology you can imagine. #fortunegreen," April 30, 2013, 1:22 pm. Tweet.

17. Valerie Casey, speech at Clarke Environmental AI Summit, Chicago, IL, February 7, 2012.

18. Peter Sims, *Little Bets: How Breakthrough Ideas Emerge from Small Discoveries* (New York: Free Press, 2011); Collins, *Great by Choice*, 78–82.

19. For Intuit, Mark Schar (Intuit), speech at Brandworks University, Madison, WI, May 25, 2006, cited by Ben McConnell, Zmetro.com, www.zmetro.com/archives/005442.php; and for failure bow, Beth Kanter, "Go Ahead, Take a Failure Bow," *Harvard Business Review Blog Network*, April 17, 2013, blogs.hbr.org/2013/04/go-ahead-take-a-failure-bow/.

20. Wobi, "Ed Catmull: Innovation Lessons from Pixar," accessed July 14, 2013, http://tinyurl.com/ld8bq4h.

CHAPTER EIGHT

1. James K. Harter et al., "Q12 Meta-Analysis: The Relationship between Engagement at Work and Organizational Outcomes," *Gallup*, August 2009, http://tinyurl.com/lslhoto.

2. SAP, "Combined Management Report: Employees and Social Investment," accessed November 18, 2013, http://tinyurl.com/cn7oav4.

3. Tony Schwartz, "New Research: How Employee Engagement Hits the Bottom Line," *Harvard Business Review Blog Network*, November 8, 2012, blogs.hbr.org/2012/11/creating-sustainable-employee/.

4. Michael Porter, "Restoring Pride in Capitalism," video, *WOBI*, 2:48, filmed October 2012, www.wobi.com/wbftv/michael-porter-restoring-pride-capitalism.

5. Mary Gorham, e-mail correspondence with author, May 21, 2013.

6. Andrew Savitz, *Talent, Transformation and the Triple Bottom Line Talent: How Companies Can Leverage Human Resources to Achieve Sustainable Growth* (San Francisco: Jossey-Bass, 2013), Kindle edition, location 4791.

7. Ibid, location 4832. Savitz is drawing on the well-known model that Edgar Schein laid out with three levels of organizational culture: "artifacts" (what Savitz calls "what we do"), espoused values (Savitz's "what we say"), and assumptions (Savitz's "what we believe"). For more on Schein's work, see Edgar Schein, last modified November 10, 2013, en.wikipedia.org/wiki/Edgar_Schein.

8. Alfred Rappaport, *Saving Capitalism from Short-Termism: How to Build Long-Term Value and Take Back Our Financial Future* (New York: McGraw-Hill, 2011).

9. Chuck Fowler (Fairmount Minerals), interview with author, March 12, 2013.

10. Jeff Rice (Walmart), interviews with author, September 7, 2012 and April 2, 2013.

11. Eddie Makuch, "Angry Birds Hits 1 Billion Downloads," *GameSpot*, May 9, 2012, http://tinyurl.com/k9uuakd.

12. "GE and Exopack Conduct 'Ecomagination Treasure Hunt,'" *Environmental Leader*, September 23, 2011, http://tinyurl.com/lgaev26.

13. Susan Hunt Stevens (Practically Green), interview with author, March 1, 2013.

14. Gwen Migita (Caesar's), interview with author, April 2, 2013.

15. Gary Loveman, "How a Sustainability Scorecard Is Creating Value," *GreenBiz*, November 11, 2013, http://tinyurl.com/m8zx7mn.

16. Doug McMillon (Walmart), e-mail correspondence with author, March 24, 2013.

17. Jim Collins, *Good to Great: Why Some Companies Make the Leap—and Others Don't* (New York: HarperBusiness, 2001).

18. Hannah Jones (Nike), interview with author, April 2, 2013.

19. Lyell Clarke (Clarke), interview with author, April 2, 2013.

20. Andrew Winston, "Five Ways to Use Green Data to Make Money," *Harvard Business Review*, November 19, 2009, http://tinyurl.com/l3s5533.

21. Gwen Migita (Caesar's), interview with author, April 2, 2013.

22. Grant Ricketts, "Big Data: The Ultimate Sustainability Job Aid at U.S. Postal Service," *Sustainable Brands*, August 23, 2013, http://tinyurl.com/mod2z6f.

23. Andy Savitz (Sustainable Business Strategies), e-mail correspondence with author, May 28, 2013.

24. "LinkedIn's Most InDemand Employers," LinkedIn, accessed October 6, 2013, http://talent.linkedin.com/indemand/. As of autumn 2013, the top 20 are Google, Apple, Unilever, P&G, Microsoft, Facebook, Amazon, PepsiCo, Shell, McKinsey, Nestlé, Johnson & Johnson, BP, GE, Nike, Pfizer, Disney, Coca-Cola, Chevron, and L'Oréal.

CHAPTER NINE

1. Suhas Apte (Kimberly-Clark), interview with author, March 26, 2013; and Mark Buthman (Kimberly-Clark), e-mail correspondence with author, May 24, 2013.

2. John Wanamaker (attributed). See en.wikipedia.org/wiki/John_Wanamaker.

3. Mark McElroy, "Move Over Eco-Efficiency, Here Comes Eco-Immunity—Part Two," *SustainableBrands*, September 17, 2013, http://tinyurl.com/mvb9wp2.

4. "Half of Multinationals to Choose Suppliers Based on CO_2 Emissions," *Environmental Leader*, September 26, 2011, http://tinyurl.com/3hzz9qc; and Edgar Blanco and Ken Cottrill, "Engaging with Suppliers to Meet Supply Chain Sustainability Goals," MITA Global Scale Network white paper, Summer 2012, http://tinyurl.com/mmvt5g7.

5. "Energy Use and Alternative Energy," Johnson & Johnson, accessed November 8, 2013, http://tinyurl.com/ltvpooa.

6. John Matthews (Diversey), speaking at Sustainability Innovators Working Group meeting, New York, September 23, 2011. See also John Davies, "Diversey's Portfolio Approach Toward Sustainability ROI," *GreenBiz*, March 7, 2011, http://tinyurl.com/ky6gp9n.

7. Auden Schendler, "Rotten Fruit: Why 'Picking Low-Hanging Fruit' Hurts Efficiency and How to Fix the Problem," *edc* magazine, November 5, 2012.

8. For 3M, Daniel C. Esty and Andrew S. Winston, *Green to Gold: How Smart Companies Use Environmental Strategy to Innovate, Create Value, and Build Competitive Advantage* (New Haven: Yale University Press, 2006), 212. For food and beverage company, anonymous interview with author, March 28, 2013.

9. Esty and Winston, *Green to Gold*, 212. See also Kristen Korosec, "IKEA Pursues Energy Independence by 2020," *SmartPlanet*, October 23, 2012, http://tinyurl.com/ntsn47z.

10. Alex Perera and Samantha Putt del Pino, "AkzoNobel and Alcoa Link Sustainability to Capital Projects," *GreenBiz*, March 21, 2013, http://tinyurl.com/n8aauc7.

11. Fred Bedore (Walmart), speaking at GreenBiz Forum 2012, New York, January 24, 2012. See also Andrew Winston, "Walmart Broadens ROI for Green Power," *Harvard Business Review Blog Network*, February 7, 2012, blogs.hbr.org/2012/02/walmart-broadens-roi-for-green/.

12. Dan Hesse (Sprint Nextel), speaking at Fortune Brainstorm Green, Laguna Niguel, CA, April 17, 2012.

13. Robert Bernard, "Microsoft Signing Long-Term Deal to Buy Wind Energy in Texas," *Microsoft Green Blog*, November 4, 2013, http://tinyurl.com/lp85nc6.

14. Beth Stevens (Disney), interview with author, March 7, 2013 and e-mail correspondence with author, May 22, 2013.

15. Stevens, e-mail correspondence with author, May 22, 2013.

16. Rob Bernard (Microsoft), interview with author, March 16, 2012. See also Andrew Winston, "Microsoft Taxes Itself," *Harvard Business Review Blog Network*, May 8, 2012, blogs.hbr.org/winston/2012/05/microsoft-taxes-itself.html.

17. T.J. Dicaprio (Microsoft), interview with author, March 25, 2013.

18. Roberta Barbieri (Diageo), interview with author, November 28, 2012.

19. Rob Hayward et al., "The UN Global Compact-Accenture CEO Study on Sustainability 2013," Accenture, September 2013, http://tinyurl.com/owbjghy.

20. Tom Falk (Kimberly-Clark), interview with author, May 20, 2013.

21. Charles Ewald (New Island Capital), interview with author, San Francisco, January 8, 2013.

CHAPTER TEN

1. See Garrett Hardin, "The Tragedy of the Commons," *Science* 162 (1968): 1243–1248.

2. Joel Makower, "Who Are the Leaders in Natural Capitalism?" *GreenBiz*, September 9, 2013, http://tinyurl.com/pl9hhnk.

3. Sissel Waage and Corinna Kester, "Private Sector Uptake of Ecosystem Services Concepts and Frameworks: The Current State of Play," BSR, March 2013, http://tinyurl.com/lp9z3l3, mentions work from companies such as AEP, AkzoNobel, Coca-Cola, Dow, Disney, Hitachi, Holcim, Puma, Rio Tinto, and Shell.

4. Mark Tercek, *Nature's Fortune: How Business and Society Thrive by Investing in Nature* (New York: Basic Books, 2013), xviii and 20–21.

5. For $33 trillion annual value provided by nature, Robert Costanza et al., "The Value of the World's Ecosystem Services and Natural Capital," *Nature*, May 15, 1997, http://tinyurl.com/atlmao. For $7 trillion annual damage to natural capital, Joel Makower, "Assessing Businesses' $7.3 Trillion Annual Cost to Natural Capital," *GreenBiz*, April 15, 2013, http://tinyurl.com/k4xknq7.

6. Tercek, *Nature's Fortune*, 4.

7. "Dow and The Nature Conservancy Announce Collaboration to Value Nature," Dow Chemical Company press release, January 24, 2011, http://tinyurl.com/pbto7oc.

8. Michelle Lapinski (The Nature Conservancy), interview and e-mail correspondence with author, June 23, 2013.

9. Mark Weick (Dow), speaking at Sustainable Brands Metrics Conference, Philadelphia, PA, September 27, 2012.

10. Michelle Lapinski (The Nature Conservancy), interview and e-mail correspondence with author, June 23, 2013.

11. Jochen Zeitz (Puma, B Team), interview with author, May 3 and May 7, 2013. See also "PUMA's Environmental Profit and Loss Account for the Year Ended 31 December 2010," PUMA, November 16, 2011, http://tinyurl.com/6v3dctw.

12. Alexander Perera et al., "Aligning Profit and Environmental Sustainability: Stories from Industry," World Resources Institute working paper, February 2013, http://tinyurl.com/o8xe63d.

13. Mark Weick (Dow), interview with author, April 8, 2013.

14. Neil Hawkins (Dow), interview with author, April 8, 2013.

15. Jochen Zeitz (Puma, B Team), interview with author, May 8, 2013.

16. Craig Hanson et al., "The Corporate Ecosystem Services Review," World Resources Institute, February 2012, http://tinyurl.com/7ybylyo.

17. Kate Dillon Levin (Code REDD), interview with author, August 16, 2013. See also "What Is REDD+?" REDD-net, accessed October 30, 2013, http://tinyurl.com/mdk6fbd.

CHAPTER ELEVEN

1. Suzanne Goldberg, "Top US Companies Shelling Out to Block Action on Climate Change," *The Guardian*, May 30, 2012, http://tinyurl.com/lf6nune.

2. Paul Polman, "Business Leaders Must Take on Challenge at Doha," *The Guardian*, November 23, 2012, http://tinyurl.com/lcsha93.

3. Gernot Wagner (EDF), interview with author, November 29, 2012.

4. For Mathur quotation, Elisabeth Rosenthal, "Carbon Taxes Make Ireland Even Greener," *New York Times*, December 28, 2012. For carbon "fee," N. Gregory Mankiw, "A Carbon Tax That America Could Live With," *New York Times*, August 31, 2013, http://tinyurl.com/kdp8scq.

5. Congress of the United States, Congressional Budget Office, *Effects of a Carbon Tax on the Economy and the Environment*, May 2013, 1, http://tinyurl.com/l8qbh98.

6. "Data: CO_2 Emissions: Metric Tons per Capita," The World Bank, accessed November 13, 2013, http://tinyurl.com/24wtm9u.

7. For Ireland, Rosenthal, "Carbon Taxes Make Ireland Even Greener"; and for China, "China to Introduce Carbon Tax: Official," Xinhua News Agency, February 19, 2013, http://tinyurl.com/bavluxk.

8. "George P. Shultz: A Cold Warrior on a Warming Planet," *Bulletin of the Atomic Scientists* (January/February 2013), http://bos.sagepub.com/content/69/1/1.full.

9. For IMF estimate, Reuters, "Study Challenges Fuel Subsidies," *New York Times*, March 28, 2013. For 1 trillion in profits, Daniel J. Weiss and Susan Lyon, "Powering an Oil Reform Agenda," Center for American Progress, June 2, 2010, http://tinyurl.com/mfjtebm and author's calculations. Oil profits for the big five have continued to run at well over $100 billion per year.

10. Jigar Shah, interview with author, May 29, 2013.

11. Gernot Wagner (EDF), interview with author, May 23, 2013.

12. Polman, "Business Leaders Must Take on Challenge at Doha."

13. Ehren Goossens, "Google-Backed Offshore Wind Line to Start in New Jersey," *Bloomberg*, January 15, 2013, http://tinyurl.com/k2l6bsc.

14. Norm Augustine et al., "A Business Plan for America's Energy Future," American Energy Innovation Council, 2010, 4, http://tinyurl.com/losv5cb.

15. Jeffrey Sachs, "On the Economy, Think Long-Term," *New York Times*, April 1, 2013.

16. Ibid.

17. Greg Sebasky (Philips), interview with author, March 29, 2013.

18. For quotation, "Champions of the Earth—2011 Laureate," United Nations Environment Programme, accessed November 12, 2013, www.unep.org/champions/laureates/2011/yue.asp. For thermostat, Keith Bradsher, "Chinese Tycoon Focuses on Green Construction," *New York Times*, December 8, 2010.

19. "Policy Support for Renewable Energy Continues to Grow and Evolve," Worldwatch Institute, Washington, DC, August 22, 2013, http://tinyurl.com/n8wcbex.

20. For quotation, Cal Dooley (American Chemistry Council), speaking at Koppers Annual SAG meeting, Bedford Springs, PA, March 10, 2013. For Walmart, Jonathan Bardelline, "Walmart Seeks to Clear Toxics from Its Shelves," *GreenBiz*, September 12, 2013, www.greenbiz.com/news/2013/09/12/walmart-seeks-clear-toxics-its-shelves.

21. Heather Clancy, "HP Steps Up to Ask Suppliers to Slash Emissions," *GreenBiz*, October 3, 2013, www.greenbiz.com/blog/2013/10/03/hp-asks-supply-chain-cut-emissions-20-percent-2020.

22. Herve Gindre (3M), speech at 3M Sustainability Event for Employees, Minneapolis/St.Paul, MN, April 18, 2012.

23. For wind tax credit, Zach Colman, "Starbucks, Ben & Jerry's Join Lobby Push for Wind Credit," *The Hill* (blog), September 18, 2012, http://tinyurl.com/kzugzr3. For eBay, Mindy Lubber, "eBay and Republican Lawmaker Score Clean Energy Win in Utah," Forbes.com, March 22, 2012, http://tinyurl.com/7ya9dmc.

24. Hannah Jones (Nike), interview with author, April 2, 2013.

25. "The 2°C Challenge Communique," University of Cambridge Programme for Sustainability Leadership, 2011, 2, accessed November 12, 2013, http://tinyurl.com/ll5lf2f.

26. Hannah Jones (Nike), interview with author, April 2, 2013.

27. Rob Hayward et al., "The UN Global Compact-Accenture CEO Study on Sustainability 2013," Accenture, September 2013, 45, http://tinyurl.com/owbjghy.

28. Hannah Jones (Nike), interview with author, April 2, 2013.

29. For Coca-Cola, Jeff Seabright (Coca-Cola), interview with author, March 29, 2013. For Apple, David Fahrenthold, "Apple Leaves U.S. Chamber Over Its Climate Position," *Washington Post*, October 6, 2009, http://tinyurl.com/lhy8nty.

For Nike, Kate Galbraith, "Nike Quits Board of U.S. Chamber," *New York Times*, October 1, 2009.

30. Rebecca Henderson, speech at "Beyond Sustainability: The Road to Regenerative Capitalism," Capital Institute Symposium, New York, June 20, 2013.

CHAPTER TWELVE

1. Eric Lowitt, *The Collaboration Economy: How to Meet Business, Social, and Environmental Needs and Gain Competitive Advantage* (San Francisco: Jossey-Bass, 2013), Kindle edition, location 362.

2. Kara Hurst (TSC), interview with author, April 26, 2013.

3. Geoff Colvin et al., "50 Greatest Business Rivalries of All Time," *Fortune*, March 21, 2013, http://tinyurl.com/p4h2c53.

4. Paula Tejon Carbajal, "Natural Refrigerants: The Solution," Greenpeace International website, http://tinyurl.com/p2weu9k.

5. Jeff Seabright (Coca-Cola), interview with author, March 29, 2013.

6. For car company efforts on fuel cells, see Bart King, "Daimler, Ford, Renault-Nissan to Co-Develop Fuel Cell Vehicles," *Sustainable Brands*, January 30, 2013, http://tinyurl.com/leyb9ln. For hotel carbon footprint work, see "Hilton, Marriott, Hotel Giants Get in Bed to Count Carbon," *GreenBiz*, June 12, 2013, http://tinyurl.com/mbo8kkr. For UPS and USPS, see Jennifer Inez Ward, "UPS and USPS Teamed Up to Create a New Industry Standard," *GreenBiz*, January 9, 2013, http://tinyurl.com/bjpoz6c.

7. Hannah Jones (Nike), interview with author, April 2, 2013.

8. Martin Medina, "Waste Pickers in Developing Countries: Challenges and Opportunities," WorldBank.org website, accessed November 16, 2013, http://tinyurl.com/nz5rnoc. See also, "Waste Pickers," WIEGO website, accessed November 16, 2013, http://tinyurl.com/p9pd6mx. The World Bank study dates back to 1988 (see Bartone, C, "The Value in Wastes," *Decade Watch*), but a more recent study calculates that 1.5 million people work as waste pickers in India alone. See Chaturvedi, Bharati, "Mainstreaming Waste Pickers and the Informal Recycling Sector in the Municipal Solid Waste," *Handling and Management Rules 2000, A Discussion Paper.*

9. Paulette Frank (Johnson & Johnson), interview with author, May 28, 2013.

10. Michael E. Porter and Mark R. Kramer, "Creating Shared Value," *Harvard Business Review*, January 2011. For more on Jed Emerson's Blended Value concept, see http://www.blendedvalue.org/framework/. For Bulcke's quote, see "CEO Interview,"

video, Nestlé website, 2:18, http://www.nestle.com/csv. Nestlé is seeking to create value for shareholders and the rest of society by addressing issues of nutrition, water, and rural development. At the concrete level, this undertaking translates into everything from reducing salt, sugar, and fat in products, to increasing consumption of whole grains, to working with farmers, to helping develop rural areas.

11. David Cooperrider and Michelle McQuaid, "The Positive Arc of Systemic Strengths," *Journal of Corporate Citizenship*, May 2013, pp. 3–4.

12. Lyell Clarke (Clarke), interview with author, April 2, 2013.

13. "Business Partnership Hub," United Nations Global Compact website, accessed November 16, 2013, www.businesspartnershiphub.org.

14. Sally Uren (Forum for the Future), interview with author, April 8, 2013.

15. "Nike, NASA, State Department and USAID Aim to Revolutionize Sustainable Materials," Nike Inc. website, April 25, 2013, http://tinyurl.com/mpugaaj.

16. Ibid.

CHAPTER THIRTEEN

1. "Nissan LEAF: Polar Bear," YouTube video, 1:02. Posted by "NissanMalaysia," http://www.youtube.com/watch?v=VdYWSsUarOg.

2. Rebecca Sizelove, "Nearly Half of Adults Are More Inclined to Buy Eco-Friendly Products, and Four in Ten Would Pay More for Them," Ipsos, April 19, 2012, http://tinyurl.com/nejvuhu; "6 Ways to Make Brand Sustainability Resonate with Customers," *Fast Company*, accessed October 30, 2013, http://tinyurl.com/kzs9dwg.

3. HBS Environment (HBSBEI), "Making green products for green people is totally pointless; we need to make them for everyone else." April 30, 2013, 6:52 pm. Tweet.

4. Daniel C. Esty and Andrew S. Winston, *Green to Gold: How Smart Companies Use Environmental Strategy to Innovate, Create Value, and Build Competitive Advantage* (New Haven: Yale University Press, 2006).

5. "Patagonia's New VC Fund to Invest in Trailblazing Green Firms," *GreenBiz*, May 9, 2013, http://tinyurl.com/kxrouvx.

6. Kingfisher PLC, "Our Strategy—Creating the Leader: Purpose," accessed November 16, 2013, http://tinyurl.com/otr2yzv.

7. Patagonia Inc., "Don't Buy This Jacket," Patagonia website, accessed November 16, 2013, http://tinyurl.com/82vt8ke.

8. Rick Ridgeway (Patagonia), e-mail correspondence with author, June 7, 2013.

9. Jennifer Elks, "Patagonia Launches 'Responsible Economy' Campaign," *Sustainable Brands*, October 1, 2013, http://tinyurl.com/ov7jz3u; Patagonia: "Responsible

Economy: You Are Part of It," Patagonia website, accessed October 30, 2013, http://tinyurl.com/24d4vnh.

10. Adam Elman (Marks & Spencer), interview with author, January 31, 2013.

11. Mike Barry (Marks & Spencer), e-mail correspondence with author, May 22, 2013.

12. KoAnn Skrzyniarz (Sustainable Brands), e-mail correspondence with author, April 7, 2013.

13. Jonathan Atwood (Unilever), speech at World Environment Center Colloquium, Washington, DC, May 10, 2013.

14. Kees Kruythoff (Unilever), speech at World Environment Center Colloquium, Washington, DC, May 10, 2013.

15. "AXE Showerpooling—Save Water ... Together," video, YouTube, 1:00, posted by "AXE," uploaded September 13, 2012, http://tinyurl.com/8hggevv.

16. Paul Polman (Unilever), speech at World Environment Center Gold Medal Dinner, Washington, DC, May 9, 2013.

17. Kruythoff, speech at World Environment Center Colloquium.

18. Bob McDonald (P&G), speech at Fortune Brainstorm Green, Laguna Niguel, CA, April 30, 2013. Transcript available at http://tinyurl.com/lp5ctqe.

19. Bart King, "Ikea to Sell Only LEDs by 2016," *Sustainable Brands*, October 2, 2012, http://tinyurl.com/p7bzwcr.

20. Elane Stock (Kimberly-Clark), interview with author, April 26, 2013.

21. World Economic Forum, "More With Less: Scaling Sustainable Consumption and Resource Efficiency," January 2012, 2, http://tinyurl.com/nvgqkc4.

22. Lysanne Currie, "If You Don't Do Good, It Will Be Harder to Do Well," *Director*, June 2012, http://tinyurl.com/nlff36h.

CHAPTER FOURTEEN

1. Resilience in business is an idea that's been floating around for at least three decades since a report to the Pentagon titled "Brittle Power" (by Lovins and Lovins) laid out the serious risks of a modern, hyperconnected energy system. Along with its close cousin, robustness, resilience is hot now.

2. Andrew Freedman, "New York Launches $19.5 Billion Climate Resiliency Plan," *Climate Central*, June 11, 2013, http://tinyurl.com/mstabu2; NYC Special Initiative for Rebuilding and Resiliency, "Read the Report," City of New York website with links to "A Stronger, More Resilient New York" report, accessed October 30, 2013, http://tinyurl.com/n2xre5p.

3. Nassim Nicholas Taleb, *Antifragile: Things That Gain from Disorder* (New York: Random House, 2012), 69. Emphasis in original.

4. Ibid., 44.

5. For 1,000 factories, Thomas Fuller, "Thailand Flooding Cripples Hard-Drive Suppliers," *New York Times*, November 7, 2011. For Hitachi and Western Digital, Rade Musulin et al., "2011 Thailand Floods Event Recap Report," Aon Benfield Analytics report, March 2012, http://tinyurl.com/krg7rdm.

6. Bill Visnic, "Tide Still Rising on Woes from Thailand Floods," Edmunds .com, November 14, 2011, http://tinyurl.com/muhjc8o. See also Musulin et al., "2011 Thailand Flood Event Recap Report."

7. "Risk Ready: New Approaches to Environmental and Social Change," PricewaterhouseCoopers white paper, November 2012, accessed November 18, 2013, http://tinyurl.com/kcte7nr.

8. Taleb, *Antifragile*, 45.

9. Ibid.

10. Ibid, 141–142.

11. Thomas Kaplan, "State Tells Investors That Climate Change May Hurt Its Finances," *New York Times*, March 27, 2013.

12. For Valero, "Operational Integrity for Oil and Gas," 26, SAP website, accessed November 18, 2013, http://tinyurl.com/mptmr9u. For Dow water, "New Technology Saves Dow Plant One Billion Gallons of Water – and $4 Million," Dow Chemical Company and Nalco Company press release, January 28, 2010, http://tinyurl.com/mtoq68h.

13. Sturle Hauge Simonsen, "The Nine Planetary Boundaries," Stockholm Resilience Center website, accessed November 18, 2013, http://tinyurl.com/9s6d2m5.

14. Lindsay Bragg, "R. James Woolsey: Our Energy Future," *The Digital Universe* (Brigham Young University), November 6, 2011, http://tinyurl.com/owpajuo.

15. For "threat multiplier," "The Climate and National Security," *New York Times* editorial, August 18, 2009. For all other data, Elisabeth Rosenthal, "U.S. Military Orders Less Dependence on Fossil Fuels," *New York Times*, October 5, 2010.

16. Leslie Dach (Walmart), speech at Global Sustainability Milestone Meeting, Bentonville, AK, April 15, 2013.

17. Taleb, *Antifragile*, 160.

APPENDIX A

1. "HP 2011 Global Citizenship Report," Hewlett Packard website, p. 9, accessed November 18, 2013, http://tinyurl.com/lgtlgm7.

2. For Philips, Bart King and Mike Hower, "Green Products Account for Roughly Half of Philips' 2012 Revenue," *Sustainable Brands*, March 1, 2013, http://tinyurl.com/lwwj6k2. For Toshiba, "Toshiba Environmental Report: 2012," 4, http://tinyurl.com/l5uphr7. For P&G, "60 Years of Sustainability Progress," P&G website, accessed November 18, 2013, http://tinyurl.com/krfclen. For GE, "'We Are Only Getting Started': GE's Ecomagination Tops $100 Billion in Revenues," GE website, June 28, 2012, http://tinyurl.com/k3dg9rc; and Renee Schoof, "Investors See Climate Opportunity to Make Money, Create Jobs," McClatchy DC website, January 12, 2012, http://tinyurl.com/mln8foj.

3. "HP 2011 Global Citizenship Report," 10.

4. Bob McDonald (Procter & Gamble), speech at Fortune Brainstorm Green, Laguna Niguel, CA, April 30, 2013. Transcript available at http://tinyurl.com/lp5ctqe.

5. For Unilever, "Unilever Factories and Logistics Reduce CO2 by 1 Million Tonnes," Unilever PLC press release, April 15, 2013, http://tinyurl.com/kc7oeg7. For Dow, Mark Weick (Dow), e-mail correspondence with author, April 9, 2013. For Walmart, Adrian Gonzalez, "How Walmart Improved Fleet Efficiency by 69 Percent," *Logistics Viewpoints*, April 25, 2012, http://tinyurl.com/l2vqbre.

6. Kevin Anton (Alcoa), e-mail correspondence with author, June 26, 2013.

7. Hunter Lovins (Natural Capitalism Solutions), e-mail correspondence with author, May 29, 2013.

8. Thibault Worth, "PNC Bank Pushing Efficiency Toward Zero," *GreenBiz*, April 16, 2013, http://tinyurl.com/m7nth7r.

9. Daniel C. Esty and Andrew S. Winston, *Green to Gold: How Smart Companies Use Environmental Strategy to Innovate, Create Value, and Build Competitive Advantage* (New Haven: Yale University Press, 2006), 97.

10. Andrew Winston, "A New Tool for Understanding Sustainability Drivers," *HBR Blog Network*, July 13, 2010, http://blogs.hbr.org/2010/07/a-new-tool-for-understanding-s/.

INDEX

ACKNOWLEDGMENTS

A book is a labor of love . . . and of favors. A large number of people gave generously of their time to help make this book possible. I have been lucky enough to beg, borrow, and steal the insights of a large number of dedicated people doing some of the hardest work in the business world—driving change. So let me first recognize the people who work mainly within the organizations that I featured. These people shared their challenges and victories on the path to the Big Pivot.

Thank you Kevin Anton, Suhas Apte, Jonathan Atwood, Wayne Balta, Roberta Barbieri, Mike Barry, Tim Bent, Rob Bernard, Eric Bruner, Mark Buthman, Lyell Clarke, Jay Coen Gilbert, Beth Comstock, Jim Crilly, Leslie Dach, TJ DiCaprio, Cal Dooley, Richard Dunne, Adam Elman, Charles Ewald, Tom Falk, Chuck Fowler, Paulette Frank, John Fullerton, Kathy Gerwig, Kohl Gill, John Ginder, Hervé Gindre, Mary Gorham, Peter Graf, Jim Hartzfeld, Rebecca Henderson, Del Hudson, Kara Hurst, Hannah Jones, David Jones, Erika Karp, Jason Kibbey, Riva Krut, Kees Kruythoff-Tielenius, Michelle Lapinski, Kate Dillon Levin, Chris Librie, Eric Lowitt, Mindy Lubber, Suz Mac Cormac, Dick Marklein, Doug McMillon, Gwen Migita, Keith Miller, Kevin Moss, Brenda Nelson, Dara O'Rourke, Glenn Paufler, Asheen Phansey, Jeff Rice, Rick Ridgeway, Andy Ruben, Auden Schendler, Jeff Seabright, Greg Sebasky, Andrew Shapiro, Susan Hunt Stevens, Beth Stevens, Elane Stock, Mark Tercek, Sally Uren, John Viera, Gernot Wagner, Tim Wallington,

Peggy Ward, Chris Wellise, Scott Wicker, Sandy Winkler, Kathrin Winkler, Jochen Zeitz, and Eva Zlotnicka.

A second group of colleagues helped my research in a variety of ways, by connecting me with the right people or by providing specific analyses, charts, and research that helped me make the case for the Big Pivot. Thank you Matt Banks, Bob Brand, Jamie Butterworth, Michael Chui, Alix Dunn, Rhys Gerholdt, Jonathan Grant, Pascal Gréverath, Marco Iszlaji, Krzysztof Kwiatkowski, Anita Larsen, Devon Long-Lytle, Lit Ping Low, Hilary Parsons, Tara Raddohl, Julie Reiter, Rachel Rosenblatt, Leah Sailovic, Amy Shanler, Jessica Sobel, Kerry Strapazon, Fraser Thompson, and Marni Tomljanovic.

A few colleagues went above and beyond, reading early excerpts of the book and providing invaluable critiques and support. Thank you to Neil Hawkins and Mark Weick for pulling together an impromptu focus group at Dow to provide very useful push-back on how I was positioning the book. Andy Savitz provided a sounding board at a critical juncture for one chapter I was struggling to get right. KoAnn Skrzyniarz, keeping a streak going of reading my books before everyone else, helped me identify some areas for improvement. My father, Jan Winston, an accomplished business executive and lifelong inspiration for me, once again read the whole book and gave me a practical businessperson's perspective. And to Jeff Gowdy and Hunter Lovins, I can't thank you enough for the absurd amount of time you spent reading and commenting on the full draft. The book is much richer for your help.

I've been working in the strange Venn diagram that is business and environmental/social issues for well over a decade now. Over the years, I've relied on thought leadership from many who came before me and a good number who came after me. I got into the field because of some of these great thinkers, and I have been privileged to get to know many of them since. My work would not be possible without the following group of idea generators: The late, great Ray Anderson, Janine Benyus, Sir Richard Branson, Valerie Casey, Marian Chertow, Aimee Christensen, Jim Collins, David Cooperrider, John Elkington, Dan Esty, Gil Friend, Al Gore, Jeremy Grantham, Marc Gunther, Stuart Hart, Umair Haque, Paul Hawken, Jeffrey Hollender, Chris Laszlo, Anthony Leiserowitz, Amory Lovins, Joel Makower, Michael Mann, the late Donella Meadows, Bill McDonough, Bill McKibben, Malini Mehra, Jacquie Ottman, Paul Polman, Sir Jonathan Porritt, Michael Porter, Jeffrey Sachs, Edgar Schein, Dov Seidman, Peter Senge, Jigar Shah, Peter Sims, Joseph Stiglitz, Pavan Sukhdev, Bob Willard, and Jim Woolsey.

With another group of thought leaders, I leveraged specific parts of their work. Thanks to Mark Campanale, Luke Sussams, and the whole team at Carbon Tracker whose groundbreaking analysis underpins the "climate math" that Bill McKibben has made famous. Bill Baue and Mark McElroy helped me understand the world of context-based metrics, which is core to setting science-based goals. Alfred Rappaport's book *Saving Capitalism from Short-Termism* provided deep insight for the first, overarching pivot strategy. The closing strategy chapter on building resilient enterprises relies in part on the book *Resilience* by Andrew Zolli and Ann Marie Healy and more heavily on *Antifragile,* a wonderful book from the guru of uncertainty, Nassim Nicholas Taleb. Taleb's work has deeply impacted my thinking about systems and reality. I've learned that even though the future is uncertain, we can always expect the unexpected.

I'd also like to thank some groups of people I work with more regularly. My business runs smoothly due to a diligent "back office": Gretchen Plender, my assistant Dina Satriale, and Gail Winston (my mother and top-notch bookkeeper, who will finally be laying down her green eyeshades for a well-deserved retirement). Thank you also to both Michelina Docimo, my ongoing research assistant, and Ryan Meinke for providing critical research support.

An important element of my work—both for research and for developing the story line I'm trying to convey—is the speaking I do at corporate leadership meetings and industry events. I could not succeed at this part of my "evangelism" mission without the help of my agents, the team at Ode Management, including Leanne Christie, Jay Kemp, Tanja Markovic, and Julie Winterbottom. Thank you for helping me get my ideas out to audiences around the world.

As part of the consulting side of Winston Eco-Strategies, I work in partnership with PricewaterhouseCoopers (PwC). I spend a good deal of time kicking around ideas and debating the finer points of how companies can manage mega challenges with my colleagues at PwC. So I'd like to thank a subset of the team (there are many more than I can list) for their thought partnership: George Favaloro, Amy Longsworth, Clinton Maloney, Kathy Nieland, Malcolm Preston, Don Reed, and Jason Theros.

To the team at Harvard Business Review Press, I thank you for your broad and deepknowledge of what makes a compelling business book and your concerted efforts to get it into as many hands as possible. My editor, Jeff Kehoe, saw the potential in the pivot story and helped sharpen the argument. Thanks also to Gretchen Gavett, Gardiner Morse, Erica Truxler, and Ania Wieckowski, the extended edit team I've worked with on the book, my HBR blog, and other projects; they make my work better. The business, production, and marketing teams at the Press have been incredibly supportive and excited about *The Big Pivot*. Thank you to publisher Sarah McConville, Press editorial director Tim Sullivan, and the team: Sally Ashworth, Erin Brown, Mary Dolan, Giulio Lavini, Nina Nocciolino, Jon Shipley, and Jennifer Waring.

Finally, to my family . . . it's hard to convey how much inspiration I draw from you. My wife Christine has been there from the very beginning of this strange journey I call my career. From graduate degrees to years of research, writing, and building my business—sometimes while bringing in limited income—Christine supported us financially and spiritually. As an experienced businessperson, she's also acted as a tough editor and sounding board. Oh, and she takes the lead on child rearing while I run my business, speaking and consulting in places nowhere near home. My two boys, Joshua and Jacob, provide constant motivation to do what little I can to make the world a better place.

Thank you *all* for your support and help along the way.

ABOUT THE AUTHOR

Andrew Winston is a globally recognized expert on how companies can navigate and profit from the world's biggest environmental and social challenges. His first book, *Green to Gold*, sold over 100,000 copies in seven languages and was an instant classic, offering a plan for businesses to create value from environmental strategy. *Inc.* magazine included *Green to Gold* on its all-time list of 30 books that every manager should own.

As founder of Winston Eco-Strategies, Winston has advised some of the world's leading companies, including Bank of America, Bayer, Boeing, Bridgestone, Johnson & Johnson, and Pepsi. He serves on sustainability advisory boards for the Kimberly-Clark Corporation, Hewlett-Packard (HP), and Unilever, and he acts as a Sustainability Advisor to PwC.

Winston is also a highly respected and dynamic speaker, reaching audiences of thousands with an entertaining message of practical optimism: the world's challenges are great, but business has the tools, resources, and creativity to create a sustainable world. He has spoken all over the world—in Europe, Russia, Brazil, the Middle East, and China—bringing his ideas to leadership meetings of the top executives of *Fortune* 500 companies, large industry conferences, and high-profile business events like the World Innovation Forum.

Winston has written three business strategy books—*Green to Gold*, *Green Recovery*, and now *The Big Pivot*. He is a regular blogger and contributor to *Harvard Business Review* online, the Guardian Sustainable Business, the *Huffington Post*, and his own popular blog at www.andrewwinston.com. He has been quoted or appeared in major media such as the *Wall Street Journal, Time, BusinessWeek,* the *New York Times,* and CNBC.

Winston's work is based on significant business experience and education. His earlier career included advising companies on corporate strategy while at the Boston Consulting Group and management positions in strategy and marketing at Time Warner and MTV. He received his BA in Economics from Princeton, an MBA from Columbia, and a Masters of Environmental Management from Yale.